THE JUDAISM THE RABBIS
TAKE FOR GRANTED

SOUTH FLORIDA STUDIES IN THE HISTORY OF JUDAISM

Edited by
Jacob Neusner
William Scott Green, James Strange
Darrell J. Fasching, Sara Mandell

Number 102
THE JUDAISM THE RABBIS
TAKE FOR GRANTED

by
Jacob Neusner

THE JUDAISM THE RABBIS
TAKE FOR GRANTED

by

Jacob Neusner

Scholars Press
Atlanta, Georgia

THE JUDAISM THE RABBIS
TAKE FOR GRANTED

Publication of this book was made possible by a grant from the Tisch Family Foundation, New York City. The University of South Florida acknowledges with thanks this important support for its scholarly projects.

Library of Congress Cataloging in Publication Data
Neusner, Jacob, 1932-
    The Judaism the rabbis take for granted / by Jacob Neusner
        p.   cm. — (South Florida studies in the history of Judaism ;
    102)
    Includes index.
    ISBN 1-55540-954-7
    1. Judaism—Essence, genius, nature. 2. Rabbinical literature—
History and criticism. 3. Judaism—History—Talmudic period,
10-425. I. Title. II. Series
BM565.N482 1994
296.1—dc20   93-49771
                                              CIP

Printed in the United States of America
on acid-free paper

Table of Contents

Preface

All we know concerning the Judaism that the rabbis take for granted in a long sequence of basic writings concerns diverse documents' specific propositions and the presuppositions they yield, the premises of various writings. These need not be found internally contradictory, but they also do not coalesce into a coherent systemic statement. The sources at hand do not validate the conception of an encompassing Judaism that underpins everything every document states and that reaches expression, in one detail or another, in one document or another. This book yields a negative result, but one with important, positive consequences. On the basis of the evidence in hand, we cannot describe the "Judaism" that the rabbis of the Judaism of the Dual Torah took for granted.

When we examine the premises and presuppositions of sages' writings, we find shards and fragments of this and that, not a complete and coherent Judaism; and, moreover, propositions in the form of premises or presuppositions do not circulate from document to document at all. Some form the foundations of one document or a set of documents, others prove critical elsewhere. Few presuppositions play an active, provocative role in the formation of writings in all canonical documents treated here, that is, everything except for the two Talmuds. Generalizing on the cases we are given, whether of law or of exegesis, we produce generalizations that remain particular to their documents or to the genre of their documents. So if there was a Judaism that formed the ground of thought and speculation for sages, we do not have much evidence of its character or contents.

Accordingly, this book produces only negative findings, opening an entirely fresh range of problems for inquiry. For reasons I shall specify at the end, the next step must be the definition of Rabbinic Judaism through the description of not all the documents in sequence – a type of work I have pursued for nearly twenty-five years – but rather one piece of writing, specifically, the document that that Judaism selected for itself as its definitive and authoritative statement. That is, of course, the Talmud of Babylonia. This book closes off work that has proceeded in a fairly straight and connected path from 1972 onward.

To define the Judaism yielded by the canon of the Dual Torah, I long ago determined that the focus for analysis must be its documents, the writings that Rabbinic Judaism valued and preserved. No religion can be described on any basis other than the concrete evidence that gives expression to that religion; there is no "reconstructing" what we do not have in fact but can supposedly imagine in theory. Having conducted sustained analysis of these books, severally and then jointly, one by one and then sequentially, I now realize that if I want to understand Rabbinic Judaism, only one document counts; all the rest assume subordinate positions in relationship to that one writing. In the last of these analytical and comparative works, *Judaism States its Theology: The Talmudic Re-Presentation* (Atlanta, 1993: Scholars Press for South Florida Studies in the History of Judaism), I reached the conclusion, on quite different grounds, that all formulation of the Judaism of the Dual Torah, its premises, presuppositions, and theology, was laid out by our sages in the Bavli and only there. In simple terms, if we want to define Judaism in its formative statement, it is in that place alone. But how defining that Judaism is to be carried forward in dialogue with that document demands consideration in its own terms, not in the setting of comparison and contrast among documents, on the one side, or of the inquiry into the premises and presuppositions of documents, on the other. That accounts for my plan to proceed with *Making Connections and Drawing Conclusions. An Academic Commentary to the Talmud of Babylonia* (Frankfurt, Berne, and New York, from 1994: Verlag Peter Lang). I expect this work to be protracted, contemplating a decade of labor on a kind of Talmud commentary that has never been attempted.

In this book, therefore, I reach the end of many years of study of the usefulness of the concept, "Judaism." Turning away from completed work to an inquiry that has too long now awaited me, here I conclude that just as that conception, upon close examination, defies all rational inquiry, so the concomitant conception, "Rabbinic Judaism," proves equally elusory. And since that outcome is manifestly unsatisfactory – reason dictates that we must be able to define that about which we are talking – as I just explained, I have had to conclude that the method I have pursued for a quarter of a century is wrong – interesting, productive, but wrong. At issue is the notion that we may define a single religion, or a single religious system out of a given family of kindred religious systems, with special reference to "its" beliefs and practices, and that we may therefore speak of the Judaic conception of one thing or another by reference to the documents conceived to attest, here there and everywhere, to one or another detail of that main structure, that Judaism. Hence if we know one thing, we know much else, about that Judaism. If we know from one document that that Judaism takes a position on one matter, we also know – as a matter of hypothesis – that that one matter fits together with many other matters to comprise a single religion, Judaism.

I have argued, and in Chapter One continue to argue, that the conception of "Judaism," a single religion, with a linear, incremental, unitary history, bears no relationship whatsoever to the character of the evidence that is adduced in behalf of the demonstration of such a Judaism. But in Chapter Two I explain why the shank of this book leads us to wonder whether we may speak any more confidently of "Rabbinic Judaism" than we may of "Judaism." These familiar propositions come to refinement and improvement in these pages. But at the same time I reach an unanticipated conclusion.

What comes to an end here is a subset of the conception of a single, unitary, incremental, harmonic Rabbinic Judaism. That is to say, because of the results set forth here, I find myself forced to conclude that just as we have little basis in documentary evidence for imagining a single Judaism characteristic of all Judaic faithful, so we have just as slight basis in documentary evidence to suppose there was a single, cogent Rabbinic Judaism. I do not think the documents of "our sages of blessed memory" permit us to define a coherent, cogent Judaism that is taken for granted by all writings and expressed in some specific detail in each. When we read the documents one by one or in small groups, we find little basis for imputing to them all the status of components of the canon of a single coherent religious system. That, sum and substance, is the report I set forth in this book.

This is a free-standing inquiry, but one that completes prior research and raises a new set of questions. The origins of the project are set forth in Chapter One, and the program of the project is explained in detail in Chapter Two. Here it suffices to state the simple facts that account for this book in its monographic context. In a five-volume catalogue, published in seven parts, *The Judaism behind the Texts* (details given below), I have set forth a systematic account of what I conceive to be the premises and presuppositions of the principal documents of the canon of the Judaism of the Dual Torah of antiquity. In those exercises, I examined the writings one by one, listing the givens that I believe form the foundations of the contents of each of the books. Here I examine the results of that survey as a whole. But to what do these premises add up? Specifically, I want to know whether, when we take all together and all at once the givens of the various documents, we can describe a complete religious system, or at least the main outlines thereof.

In this final component of the study, I point to a profound flaw in the conception that documents tell us about more than themselves, and I define a research problem that seems to me worth a measure of attention in time to come. The already published volumes of this research report is as follows:

The Judaism behind the Texts. The Generative Premises of Rabbinic Literature. I. *The Mishnah.* A. *The Division of Agriculture* (Atlanta, 1993: Scholars Press for South Florida Studies in the History of Judaism).

The Judaism behind the Texts. The Generative Premises of Rabbinic Literature. I. *The Mishnah.* B. *The Divisions of Appointed Times, Women, and Damages (through Sanhedrin)* (Atlanta, 1993: Scholars Press for South Florida Studies in the History of Judaism).

The Judaism behind the Texts. The Generative Premises of Rabbinic Literature. I. *The Mishnah.* C. *The Divisions of Damages (from Makkot), Holy Things and Purities* (Atlanta, 1993: Scholars Press for South Florida Studies in the History of Judaism).

The Judaism behind the Texts. The Generative Premises of Rabbinic Literature. II. *The Tosefta, Tractate Abot, and the Earlier Midrash Compilations: Sifra, Sifré to Numbers, and Sifré to Deuteronomy* (Atlanta, 1993: Scholars Press for South Florida Studies in the History of Judaism).

The Judaism behind the Texts. The Generative Premises of Rabbinic Literature. III. *The Later Midrash Compilations: Genesis Rabbah, Leviticus Rabbah and Pesiqta deRab Kahana* (Atlanta, 1994: Scholars Press for South Florida Studies in the History of Judaism).

The Judaism behind the Texts. The Generative Premises of Rabbinic Literature. IV. *The Latest Midrash Compilations: Song of Songs Rabbah, Ruth Rabbah, Esther Rabbah I, and Lamentations Rabbati. And The Fathers According to Rabbi Nathan* (Atlanta, 1994: Scholars Press for South Florida Studies in the History of Judaism).

The Judaism behind the Texts. The Generative Premises of Rabbinic Literature. V. *The Talmuds of the Land of Israel and Babylonia* (Atlanta, 1994: Scholars Press for South Florida Studies in the History of Judaism).

No work of mine can omit reference to the exceptionally favorable circumstances in which I conduct my research as Distinguished Research Professor in the Florida State University System at the University of South Florida. I wrote this book as part of my labor of research scholarship, expressed through both publication and teaching at the University of South Florida, which has afforded me an ideal situation in which to conduct a scholarly life. I express my thanks for not only the advantage of a Distinguished Research Professorship in the Florida State University System, which for a scholar must be the best job in the world, but also of a substantial research expense fund, ample research time, and some stimulating and cordial colleagues. In the prior chapters of my career, I never knew a university that prized professors' scholarship and publication and treated with respect those professors who actively and methodically pursue research.

The University of South Florida, among all ten universities that comprise the Florida State University System as a whole, exemplifies the high standards of professionalism that prevail in publicly sponsored higher education in the USA and provides the model that privately sponsored universities would do well to emulate. Here there are rules, achievement counts, and presidents, provosts, and deans honor and respect the University's principal mission: scholarship, scholarship alone – both in the classroom and in publication. Here at last I find integrity, governing in the lives of people true to their vocation and their mission.

As it happens, I enjoy the remarkable benefits of yet another splendid locus for sustained research. I wrote this book in my term as Visiting Research Professor at Åbo Akademi Forskningsinstitut and in association with my colleagues at Åbo Akademi's Theologisk Fakultetet. My dual position as Research Professor and also Theological Faculty member brought me into contact with a variety of Finnish professors and students, and I found not only a warm welcome but also much stimulating conversation in that intellectual community. I express thanks to the Åbo Akademi Forskningsinstitut for a generous research stipend for April through August, 1993, and for providing comfortable living and working conditions; and, among many valued Finnish friends, both Suomi and Swedish speaking, to my host and friend, Professor Karl-Johan Illman, for inviting me and making the visit memorable and happy.

Since I used the opportunity to improve my Swedish, I express my appreciation, also, to many patient Finns, both Finnish and Swedish speaking, who formed a language laboratory without walls for my continuing education in one of their languages. It was certainly one of the most interesting summer terms I can remember.

JACOB NEUSNER

Visiting Research Professor
ÅBO AKADEMI FORSKNINGSINSTITUT
SF 20700 Åbo, Finland
and
Distinguished Research Professor of Religious Studies
UNIVERSITY OF SOUTH FLORIDA
Tampa, FL 33620-5550 USA

Introduction

At issue in this book is whether and how, beyond the evidence of what an authorship has given us in so many words in its particular piece of writing, we may describe what that authorship knew, tacitly had in mind, implicitly took for granted, and otherwise affirmed as its larger and sustaining "Judaism." What is not only tacit but encompassing, taken for granted but generative? That formulation of matters rests on the premise that each document derives from an intellectual context, and to begin with is to be read in that context and interpreted, at the outset, as a statement of a larger setting. Specific problems for solution are identified by general principles of conviction; a realm of sentiment, emotion, and conception forms the matrix for thought. And when we can identify the wherewithal of reflection and feeling, we may define that which sustains specific propositions, of which the discrete documents are made up.

So if we know what a given document's writers formulate as their statement, we may investigate, with some small measure of thought, what they took for granted in proposing problems for solution, propositions for demonstration, attitudes for concrete realization in law, theology, or exegesis of the Torah. If we know what they said, the "what else" we know is what they had in mind in so stating. Then such constructs such as -*isms* and -*ities* formulate into well-crafted compositions that "what else" we assume we know on the strength of the premises and presuppositions of the data that we know to begin with. In these few sentences the problem of this book is set forth.

Here, however, examining a continuous series of writings that all together are taken to form the canon of the Judaism of the Dual Torah in its formative age, I call into question the notion of not only the possibility of defining a single Judaism, but the plausibility even of speaking of Judaisms. I point out that, the closer we come to sources singled out as deriving from a particular Judaic system, the more profoundly we delve into their foundations, the further we seem to find ourselves from that coherent systematic statement, that well-crafted, encompassing, proportionate, harmonious -*ism*, that Judaism, that we take for granted must hold together the diverse sources even of that one distinct Judaism. Just as we have no fully-formulated Judaism, everywhere attested in each datum we classify as Judaic, so we come to the conclusion that there also is no fully formulated Judaic system of a particular order, percent, Rabbinic Judaism, that is supposed to be everywhere attested in each document we classify as Rabbinic. All we have are the evidences, one by one by one.

And that observation leads to the question at hand. If in advance I did not know that the community of Judaism treats the writings before us (among others) as a canon, would the traits of thought exhibited by the documents have told me that the writings at hand are related? In this study, these "traits of documents" are the most profound and pervasive: premises and presuppositions. I cannot think of a more penetrating test of the proposition that the documents form a unity and are continuous with one another. The inquiry is inductive, concerns intrinsic traits of not form or proposition but premise, and therefore pursues at the deepest layers of intellect, conviction, attitude, and even emotion the matter of connection between document and document.

We are justified in asking what holds these documents together, not on the surface but at their depths. Since from antiquity this Judaism has treated all of these writings as a single, seamless Torah, the one whole Torah revealed by God to Moses, our rabbi, at Mount Sinai, the received hermeneutic naturally does the same. All of the writings are read in light of all others, and words and phrases are treated as autonomous units of tradition, rather than as components of particular writings, percent, paragraphs – units of discourse – and books – composite units of sustained and cogent thought. The issue of connection therefore is legitimate to the data. But the issue of continuity is a still more profound and urgent one, and it is that issue that the present project is formulated to address.

What I really want to find out here is not only the answer to the question, if I know this, what else do I know? It is also, what are the things that all of the documents that make up the writings accorded the status of the Oral Torah know and share? When I ask about the Judaism behind the texts, I mean to find out what convictions unite diverse writings and form of them all a single statement, a cogent religious system? Every document stands on its own; each is autonomous. Many documents furthermore establish points of contact or intersection; they are connected. But, as a matter of fact, the Judaism of the Dual Torah maintains that every writing is continuous with all other writings, forming a whole, a statement of comprehensive integrity. If that is so, then at the premises or presuppositions of writings I ought to be able to identify what is continuous, from one writing to another, and what unites them all at their deepest layers of conviction, attitude, or sentiment.

One statement of the contrary view, that we may impute to data premises or presuppositions that they do not contain or express explicitly or even tacitly, in the theory that all of the data derive from a single system, an *-ism*, in this case "Judaism," derives from Dr. Hyam Maccoby in his critique of my *Judaism: The Evidence of the Mishnah:*

> Neusner does not answer the point...that the liturgy being presupposed by the Mishnah, is surely relevant to the Mishnah's exegesis. Nor does he answer the charge that he ignores the aggadic material within the Mishnah itself, percent, Abot; or explain why the copious aggadic material found in roughly contemporaneous works should be regarded as irrelevant.[1]

What is important in Maccoby's statement is the premise that if we know something, we know much else about that thing; if we know – to turn to the case in hand – that the Mishnah is a document of "Judaism," then we impute to the Mishnah a variety of other convictions, attitudes, beliefs, theological principles, such as accrue to any datum of that same Judaism. Therefore the exegesis of a given document must respond to everything else we know about the setting or context in which that document is located.

Hence the question, if I know this, what else do I know? is answered, if I know that a document belongs to "Judaism," then what else I know is that all of the other convictions and principles of that same Judaism, deriving from other documents or sources, play a role in the exegesis of that document. He provides an excellent example of the kind of thinking that emerges when we "ism-ize" a religion, that is, when we treat a religion as something that encompasses all of the sources classified as belonging to that religion but that transcends and imposes its character upon each one of them.   But I think his question correct and urgent: If we know this, what else, really, do we know? If, I maintain, it is not an entire *-ism*, still, we do gain access, through what people say, to what they are thinking, what they take for granted, what forms the premise and presuppose of their argument and proposition – an entire realm of facts not articulated but still anticipated.

Where I part company from Dr. Maccoby is at the notion of an *-ism*. In my sustained reply to the mode of thought and analysis represented by Maccoby's comment, I showed that the assumption of an *-ism* finds no

---

[1]Writing in the symposium, "The Mishnah: Methods of Interpretation," *Midstream*, October, 1986, p. 41.

justification in the sources of Rabbinic Judaism. This book forms the final stage in that demonstration. But until now, I did not then draw the obvious conclusion that my own findings had compelled me to reach. That is, while I denied there was a single Judaism at all, still I took for granted that the sources on which I concentrated, those attributed to "our sages of blessed memory," bearing in common the names of masters and disciples assumed to form a single chain of tradition that worked itself out over many centuries, assuredly formed a single Judaism. So – until now, I have taken for granted – while there was no one Judaism, there still were Judaisms. And among the Judaisms, one that certainly is well documented as a coherent system is Rabbinic Judaism, or, to invoke its definitive myth in search of an appropriate name for it, the Judaism of the Dual Torah. I took that view for granted despite my own findings, that, in studies of the documentary unfolding of one major idea after another, many conceptions dominant in the final statements of Rabbinic Judaism play no material role whatsoever in the system of the Mishnah, or, for that matter, of Tosefta and Abot.

I have known that fact for more than a decade, but I drew every conclusion but the obvious one until now. But when, for the purpose of this study, I examined the results of the five volume catalogue of *The Judaism behind the Texts* with the present volume in mind, matters did not emerge as I had anticipated. I could find no reason based on evidence at the foundations of the writing – as distinct from formal traits, such as the inclusion of shared forms and the names of the same authorities – to think so. To the contrary, I had already found enormous and decisive evidence to refute any notion of a single, cogent, coherent, linear, harmonious. incremental Rabbinic Judaism. The same data that argued against a single unitary Judaism called into question the notion of a single unitary Rabbinic Judaism. I had found the evidence, but I had not appreciated its meaning. I was ready to impute a single Judaic system to authors of a sequence of documents, even though as I examined the "unfolding" of principles or conceptions from document to document, I persistently found cogency among groups of writing, but nothing coherent in the depths of conception, as distinct from form, from beginning to end.

A single case suffices to make the point. No one who has looked for the conception of "the Oral Torah" in the Mishnah or in the documents that succeeded it, for the next two hundred years, will understand why Maccoby is so certain that the category of Oral Torah, or the myth of the Dual Torah, applies at all. I did look for that conception in my *The Foundations of Judaism. Method, Teleology, Doctrine* (Philadelphia, 1983-5: Fortress Press). I-III. III. *Torah: From Scroll to Symbol in Formative Judaism.* Second printing: Atlanta, 1988: Scholars Press for Brown Judaic

Studies. I found it here, but not there, in some places, not everywhere. For the mythic category of "Oral Torah" makes its appearance, so far as I can discern, only with the Yerushalmi and not in any document closed prior to that time, although a notion of a revelation over and above Scripture – not called "Oral Torah" to be sure – comes to expression in Abot. Implicitly, moreover, certain sayings of the Mishnah itself, percent, concerning rulings of the Torah and rulings of sages, may contain the notion of a secondary tradition, beyond revelation. But that tradition is not called "the Oral Torah," and I was disappointed to find that even in the Yerushalmi the mythic statement of the matter, so far as I can see, is lacking. It is only in the Bavli, percent, in the famous story of Hillel and Shammai and the convert at b. Shab. 30b-31a, that the matter is fully explicit. Yet, having reached that finding, I continued to speak of "the Judaism of the Dual Torah," even though the bulk of the sources that, along with everyone else, I assigned to the Dual Torah knew nothing of the myth of the Dual Torah, or of that myth in its fully articulated formulation. So, for a long time, I have missed the point of my own systematic inquiry.

Not only so, but one commentator on my debate with Dr. Maccoby and his colleague, Professor E.P. Sanders, picked out the issue with a more certain eye than I had. Commenting on this debate, William Scott Green says, Sanders "reads rabbinic texts by peering through them for the ideas (presumably ones Jews or rabbis believed) that lie beneath them." This runs parallel to Maccoby's criticism of my "ignoring" a variety of conceptions I do not find in the Mishnah. Sanders, in Green's judgment, introduces a distinct premise:

> For Sanders, the religion of Mishnah lies unspoken beneath its surface; for Neusner it is manifest in Mishnah's own language and preoccupations.[2]

That formulation, stressing my emphasis upon analyzing the traits of language and form – rhetoric, logic, topic – refers precisely to what I have insisted upon doing, and the words, "manifest in Mishnah's own language and preoccupations," of course show a close reading of my systematic description of not only the Mishnah, but the Tosefta, the Midrash compilations, and the two Talmuds. In fact I have carried on the same analytical project for every important document of the Judaism of the Dual Torah produced in antiquity.

Indeed, I had described the systemic statement of each document in turn, its topical program, its propositional intent, the relationship

---

[2]William Scott Green in his Introduction, *Approaches to Ancient Judaism* (Chicago, 1980: Scholars Press for Brown Judaic Studies) II, p. xxi.

between its message and its media of rhetoric and logic of coherent discourse. So I knew full well that the religion of each document is manifest in its own language and preoccupations. And yet, in that observation Green more perceptively grasped what I had done than did I. I insisted that a document says what it says, right on the surface; that the analysis of a document takes place within the document's own limits; and that we cannot impute to a document ideas it does not contain. But I still took for granted – never even articulating my preconception – that we may demonstrate out of analysis of evidence the existence of a Judaic system of cogency and coherence, Rabbinic Judaism, that animated all the writings and formed the matrix in which each was to be read. The same reason that had led me to dismiss the notion of "Judaism" ought to have forced me to question my deepest premise. Here I do just that.

When, in *The Judaism behind the Texts*, I took up the problem of defining premises and presuppositions, I did not set out to pursue the problem that the results of the completed work have defined for me. I wanted to know what conceptions lay before the writers of the Rabbinic documents; it never occurred to me that I should find compelling an inquiry into whether any such conceptions travel from document to document, the inquiry that defines the work of this book. I was responding to challenges set forth in a different context, and to place this book into its proper position, I have to spell out the context in which this inquiry originally began. It was to respond to what struck me as important questions that I asked about the premises and presuppositions of documents.

Specifically, because I concurred with Maccoby and Sanders that documents contain presuppositions and premises, I undertook *The Judaism behind the Texts*. I differed only on how these were to be catalogued and interpreted. I denied the view of Maccoby and Sanders, that we can read everything only in light of everything else, fore and aft. I insisted that we read each item first of all on its own, a document as an autonomous and cogent and utterly rational, syllogistic statement, a unit of discourse as a complete and whole composition, entire unto itself, taking account, to be sure, of how, in the larger context imposed from without, meanings change(d). Then I planned to review the premises of documents the right way, meaning, document by document. I assumed that I should be able at that point to respond to Sanders's challenge and to describe the Judaism behind the texts that he postulated in his language, "to press behind..." the contents to find out the Judaism that is taken for granted. But, having done so, I grasp the outcome of that reading, which calls into question the basis on which we join document to document and treat the whole as formations and formulations of an *-ism*.

For it is not enough to posit such premises; we have in detail to identify just what they were. And when we do and further investigate how one premise relates to some other, as we shall in this book, we are left to wonder whether we know that "what else," that "Judaism of the rabbis," that we have assumed these premises would outline for us. For we now ask, are there premises and presupposes that engage thought throughout the documents? Or are the documents discrete episodes in a sustained procession of thought that requires description upon some basis other than a documentary one? The exercise in the further definition of the Judaism of the Dual Torah then encompasses not only what its principal documents make articulate but also what they mean to imply, on the one end, and how what they presuppose coheres (if it does), on the other. Since many of the answers to those questions are either obvious or trivial or beg the question, we have to refine matters with a further critical consideration. It is this: Among the presuppositions, the critical one is, which ones matter? And how can we account for the emergence of the system as a whole out of the presuppositions demonstrably present at the foundations of systemic documents?

What Rabbinic documents tell us that bears consequence for the definition of their Judaism in particular – not merely what was likely to be common to all Judaism, percent, a sacred calendar, a record of generations' encounter with God and the like – then requires specification. But as we turn to the deeper, implicit affirmations of documents and ask what they know that stands behind what they say, as I show in the shank of this book, we find ourselves unable to move from document to document, or from a set of kindred documents to a different set of kindred ones. A close reading of both law and lore, *halakhah* and *aggadah*, yields no glimpse at a vast structure of implicit conceptions. When, following Sanders's prescription, we do "press behind the contents of the Mishnah and attempt to discover what the contents of the Mishnah presuppose," we find the answer to that question only – not the key to a broad and encompassing Judaism contained, also, within those presuppositions.

I had supposed that we should see that all of them would circulate hither and yon through the law and the theology of the various documents. But, as this book will show, that is not the case. We cannot in fact find out how they coalesce, so we do not understand the Judaic system of the Dual Torah – law and theology alike – that comes to concrete expression in the Rabbinic writings. To clarify the issues treated here, let us consider, in succession, the issue of "Judaism" and then that of "Rabbinic Judaism." Having done so, in Chapters One and Two, we move in the shank of the book to a survey of the findings of *Judaism behind the Texts,* and in the concluding chapter draw the proper conclusions from that survey. It remains to note that I have omitted from consideration the two Talmuds, because the second of the two, the Bavli, does fully and authoritatively state Judaism, not the Judaism that the rabbis take for granted, but Judaism: the entire Torah, Oral and Written, in a single coherent statement. Since that is the case, there is no reason in the world to ask about what the rabbis take for granted in a document in which they reveal everything and fully expose their premises and presuppositions, in character and consequence alike.

Let me conclude this introduction by pointing to what awaits me in a labor I anticipate will require many years of patient work. It is that that fact once more places into perspective my *Making Connections and Drawing Conclusions. An Academic Commentary to the Talmud of Babylonia,* the natural next step beyond this book. Since I can find no traits characteristic of the entire set of documents – none of form, none of substance, beyond some platitudes that pertain to every writing of pretty much every Judaism – I am left to investigate not the canon but the authoritative document that took the place of all prior writings: the book that itself defined the canonical ideas and laws, theology and norms, of Judaism.

1

The Question of "Judaism"

The conception of "Judaism," or "Christianity," or "Buddhism," serves the purpose of holding together in a coherent philosophically harmonious and proportionate construction diverse and otherwise inchoate facts, for example, writings, artifacts of material culture, myths and rites, all of them, without distinction as to provenience or origin, deemed to contribute to an account of one and the same systematic composition, an *-ity* or an *-ism*; and, further, all of them – beliefs, rites, attitudes and actions alike – are assumed to animate each. So when we speak of a religion as a whole, not simply a body of texts – documents or archaeological findings or contemporary social scientific description – of a particular group of people who confess a single set of beliefs, we take for granted that beyond the social facts there is a system of thought that can be defined in a systematic way.

That assumption serves to clarify and organize otherwise chaotic facts. The reason is that, assuming all facts pertain to one whole and cogent construction of ideas, one thing, we form an account, frequently framed in terms of propositional beliefs, of that one thing, assumed to encompass everything in its classification and, I stress, also to infuse each item of its class. That is what happens when we define a religion, in the present instance, Judaism. We then define a religion not only in terms of its social order – the way of life, worldview, and theory of the social entity of people who believe certain things and consequently form a community that does things in one way, rather than some other – but in terms of its abstract system of belief and behavior. This we view out of all context, imputing the presence of this *-ism* at all points at which any of its characteristic data turn up.

Having formed such a definition, we therefore take for granted that a datum that falls into the classification of that systematic statement or that *-ism* bears within itself not only its own facts but a large body of other facts imputed to the datum by reason of the character of the classification that encompasses it. When we speak of "Judaism," for example, we take for granted that beyond a given datum we define as "Judaic" lies an entire structure, one that imparts context and meaning to each of its data in turn and that both encompasses transcends them all. On that basis, we may speak of Judaism: the Judaic view of this, that, and the other thing, and so, too, with Buddhism, Hinduism, Christianity and a variety of other -*isms* and -*ities*. When, therefore, in the study of religion, we invoke the conception of an -*ism* that transcends its own data and organizes them, much is at stake. Precisely what we study when we study religion comes under discussion.

The issue of definition – the question of "Judaism" writ large – flows far beyond the narrower limits of defining a religion or religious tradition. A fundamental question of learning is, if I know a given datum, what else do I know by reason of knowing that datum? What does a given fact carry in its wake, beyond itself but implicit within itself? Applied to religion, that mode of thinking maintains that if I may classify a datum as "Judaic" or "Christian" or "Buddhist," I know much more about that datum by reason of the classification into which said datum falls than merely that the datum tells me. Indeed, I know much, much more. Treating a religion in such a way requires that we form a large composite of facts, treated as coherent and mutually supportive, with the result that, if a given fact is deemed present, then all other facts are assumed represented as well; what I know about everything, I know about one thing, and what I know about one thing applies to all. The mode of thought that seeks to form large-scale ideas, encompassing data and infusing them with meaning and providing them with a context, aids in sorting out the complexities of the specific facts, the data, that in fact define all that we actually do know.

The result is to define a religion, for example, an -*ism* or an -*ity* such as Judaism or Christianity, as a body of beliefs and practices that are broadly present where anyone such belief or practice is present. A standard way of thinking about a religion or religious tradition is to form of details that occur in a variety of evidences of said religion a composite, deemed to stand for the whole. All details are then held to exhibit the basic character of the whole. If, therefore, we find a datum, within this theory, we impute to that datum the traits of the whole; whatever characterizes any component held to fall into the classification of that religion then is imputed to all other components, and each component, whatever its character, is held to contain within itself the traits of the religion overall.

Thinking in such a way, then, we view a religion as we would a philosophical system, in which each element of thought fits together with all other elements to comprise the whole. It then follows, as I said, that if we know that a given datum belongs to a given religion, then the presence of that datum carries in its wake a great many other facts that we impute to the circumstance in which that datum makes its appearance. We therefore take for granted that we may define a religion, since if we have a given set of data, we may specify what else we know by reason of the presence of said data.

In the case of Judaism, it is now generally understood, such a premise serves rather poorly. The reason is that important bodies of data contradict the character or implications of other bodies of data, with the result that, if one body of data is present, we cannot suppose that other bodies of data are accurately represented as present too. To give one example, synagogue archaeology yields a corpus of symbols that we do not find in literary evidence for antiquity; digging up synagogues does not then prepare us for what we find in documents, and the documents of the same time and place do not prepare us for what we find in the dirt. So the "what else" in these instances yields, "nothing else" – at least, not that. A synagogue in the ground does not bear in its wake evidence that the kind of Judaic practices and beliefs represented by documents characterized the worldview, way of life, and theory of the social entity that they formed, of the Jews who built that synagogue; the concept of an -*ism*, a Judaism, then falls away, because it requires that we join contradictory data and form a harmonization of opposites. Anyone who has studied the histories of Christianities, even merely the Reformation, will find these observations unexceptionable.

The generality of learning no longer takes seriously the proposition that there is now, or ever has been, a single Judaism that defines the norm by which all allegations about what Judaism teaches or imagines are measured. Books on Judaism in the formative age that posit a single, normative Judaism, dismissing as heretical or sectarian evidences that do not conform to the law or theology or that official Judaism no longer gain a serious hearing. Outside of the Jewish institutions with their imposition of theology or ideology on academic learning, textbooks that purport to describe such a single unitary, incremental, official Judaism rarely are adopted; dissertations on such a foundation rarely are written and their authors seldom find positions; and, in all, the fabrication of "normative Judaism" or "Orthodox Judaism," for late antiquity nowadays meets with not so much incredulity as indifference. Efforts to respond to the multiplicity of Judaisms take the place of a single Judaism, and, whether these appeal to the lowest common denominator or allege what was essential to all Judaisms, they respond to the new episteme: not Judaism but Judaisms.

In the study of ancient Judaism, "Judaism" has nearly everywhere given way to "Judaisms," a brief way of stating a complex category. For antiquity, we can find no single Judaism practiced everywhere. We have diverse bodies of writings, which scarcely acknowledge anything in common beyond Scripture. We identify various social groups through archaeological evidence, so asking about the interplay of religion and the social order, and then discover that correlating archaeological and literary evidence presents enormous difficulties for those who wish to harmonize everything into a single Judaism. The conception of a unitary, continuous, incremental "Jewish law," with a beginning, a middle, and a conclusion (for example, in the Talmud of Babylonia) scarcely correlates with the consequences of not only archaeological challenge to some of the laws of documents, but literary evidence, for example, from Elephantine and from Qumran, harmonized only with difficulty with law found in later documents.

Analytical questions addressed to diverse documents produce diverse and contradictory answers. If we ask any of the bodies of writing deemed to coalesce, apocalyptic, Rabbinic, Christians who identify themselves as Israel, that found in the Dead Sea library, Philo's, Josephus's, not to mention Jewish writing in Greek and Aramaic, the diverse translations of Scripture being only one, if enormous, body of evidence – if we ask the same question to all of these writings, each will give a well-formed answer that stands entirely on its own and contradicts all the others. Whether we ask about God, or Torah, or Israel, to identify the three generative categories of any Judaic religious system (standing for the system's ethos, ethics, and ethnos), what we find is everything and its opposite. Indeed, the real question now demanding attention, as I shall explain, has shifted. If Rabbinic Judaism constitutes a single, coherent Judaism, as is presently broadly taken as fact, then can we find a set of premises that animate all of its canonical writings, and, if so, where and how are we to locate them? The analytical program has now come to a problem of inductive synthesis. In Chapter Two I explain what is at stake. It suffices here to signal what is coming.

The upshot is simple. The issue, how do we define Judaism, is now settled: we do not. We define Judaisms, and the first step in the work of definition requires identifying the particular Judaic community that stands behind a given set of writings or that values and lives by those writings. All analytical work in the academy proceeds from that premise, and books on Judaism that posit a single, unitary, incremental Judaism, deriving from Sinai through written and oral tradition, command slight attention these days. In that context, books that claim to define essential Judaism or common denominator Judaism simply ratify the change that has taken place; in the sectarian world, people did not find urgent the problem that such books propose to solve. Consequently, we find ourselves asking theological questions concerning the coherence of discrete truths, but we propose to answer those questions out of not doctrine but, for literary study, hermeneutics. Precisely where the Jewish sponsored centers of learning alleged to locate their greatest strengths – exegesis of texts, philology, even text criticism – the academy has now to carry its venture. For we cannot abdicate the most grave intellectual responsibility of all: the reading of the texts in the new, and sole right way.

It follows that all Judaic systems – accounts of the way of life and worldview of a social entity that calls itself an "Israel" – share in common a vast corpus of ideas and institutions, practices and convictions. That is because, for nearly the entire history of Judaic religious systems – there never having been a single, linear, incremental, unitary and harmonious Judaism to produce a single history – all Judaisms have appealed to the same Scriptures. These are the Pentateuch in particular, but, more generally, the Hebrew Scriptures of ancient Israel, a.k.a., "the Old Testament." True, verses of Scripture critical for one Judaism do not take an important position in the systemic statement of some other. One simple criterion for differentiating one Judaism from some other simply lists the verses of Scripture commonly cited by the one in comparison with a counterpart corpus of verses cited by the other. Few verses will appear on both lists, and none will enjoy equal prominence on both. But in the nature of things, Judaic systems that appeal to the Pentateuch will share in common a huge corpus of revealed laws, for example, concerning time (the calendar, the Sabbath); concerning home and family (food and incest taboos), and the like.

Any account of the Judaism that system builders take for granted will share with accounts of all other Judaisms a sizable corpus of religious truths: beliefs and practices. That is so whether we deal with "our sages of blessed memory," who stand behind the Rabbinic canon treated here, or the authors of the documents collected in the library at Qumran or those who collected and valued those documents, or that other body of heirs of ancient Israel that produced the New Testament, or the people who wrote and valued the apocalyptic writings that stand for a Judaic system as well. We may concede, to give three obvious examples, none permitted sons to marry their father's wives; none permitted eating pork; all practiced circumcision – and so forth. If by Judaism, then, we mean merely the corpus of shared practices among religious affines, that minimalist definition omits nearly all the traits that make the several Judaic systems distinctive and that impart to each its particular character.[1]

But accounts of that corpus of beliefs and practices common to all Judaic systems or Judaisms prove implausible. What renders such a common-denominator Judaism implausible is simple. We cannot understand any particular system by appeal to that Judaism in general that supposedly nourishes them all. The common denominator not only obscures difference – what defines one system apart from some other – but it also makes it impossible to explain difference, the presence of diverse Judaic systems or Judaisms. That is for three reasons.

First, listing what characterizes all Judaic systems affords no means of answering the simple question, with so much in common, why do the diverse systems differ, as they do, on if not nearly everything, then, on everything that counts? And yet a striking characteristic of the Judaic writings that survive from ancient times is their profound sectarianism. Each system carefully differentiates itself from everybody else, either the rest of "Israel," or the rest of humanity, treating even other Jews as no longer "Israel." The documents of a given Judaic group cohere and also ignore all other Judaic writings, just as the Mishnah's writers dismiss as simply nonexistent all Judaic writings between the Mishnah and Scripture. Even more, every document not only speaks for its writers' viewpoint; it also identifies its writers' opposition, whether the opposition find a place within the fold or beyond.

That nearly all of the evidence at hand is sectarian – and reaches us because of that fact – is readily exemplified. Anyone who has read even a few lines of the Dead Sea library knows that, in addition to the children of light, children of darkness flourish; "our sages of blessed memory" leave us no doubt that within Israel were many who did not share their views. Even the Mishnah, so bland and ecumenical in its laconic, irenic voice, is explicit in fundamental laws that the observant Israelite must take account of the presence of the unobservant one, and the points of difference are systematic, explicit, and encompassing. The Gospels carefully sort out responses to the person of Jesus, telling us who is saved and who is not saved. While many have proposed a common denominator among Judaisms, none has shown how these various Judaisms in fact coalesce into a single Judaism. The reason is that

---

[1]Later in this book I shall ask whether, in the end, the concept of "Judaism" serves in any way at all, and that is in the context of only a single Judaism. In Chapter Six I revert to the matter of "what else," namely, if I know that there was such a thing as "this Judaism," then what else do I know on that account? And my answer is, the same arguments amassed here against "Judaism" call into question the conception of "Rabbinic Judaism," too.

defining the common denominator among Judaisms explains everything but the main thing: the differences among Judaisms, and why they mattered. And that is not only because the sources speak only for distinct groups. It is, as I shall suggest in the concluding chapter, because the very category, "Judaism," is an invention, imposed upon sources, not a native category of those sources, nor, yet, a category that corresponds to those native to the sources.

Second, it is the simple, and now broadly acknowledged, fact that the evidence of diverse Judaic systems – whether the evidence of the Dead Sea scrolls or of Rabbinic Judaism, whether that collected by R.H. Charles as "the apocrypha and pseudepigrapha of the Old Testament" or the writings of the earliest Christians – not only cannot be harmonized into a single encompassing Judaism, but also cannot be juxtaposed to yield a coherent system encompassing all systems. Efforts to do just that all have failed, even while accomplishing the theological, not religious-historical, goals of their authors. The reason is self-evident. Each system exhibits its own generative problematic; each defines its own recurrent points of tension; what troubles one system scarcely receives attention in some other. Just as, for the study of the beginnings of Christianity, no one troubles with harmonies of the Gospels any more, so in the study of Judaic systems from the completion of the Pentateuch in ca. 450 B.C.E. to the conclusion of the Talmud of Babylonia in ca. 600 C.E., defining a single Judaism proves a progressively less productive exercise.

True, we may point to points in common, as I just said, belief in one God, affirmation of the Torah as God's revelation to Moses at Sinai, circumcision, the Sabbath, dietary laws, incest taboos, and other laws of the Torah, and the like. But if all that we know about a Judaism is that a given group believed in the Sabbath, one God, and the Torah, we cannot then account for the structure and system of that group's Judaism. We cannot explain anything that that Judaic system deems definitive of itself, we can only catalogue the things that that system, among all systems, regards as self-evident and systemically inert.

Let me make this point more concrete. We only can identify facts that that system takes over from Scripture. But what it has taken over from Scripture involves a principle of selection that leads to other choices not made by other groups. And it is that principle of selection that defines that Judaism, as we move from all of its choices backward to the rationality of its choices, that is, the definition of the systemic rationality that characterizes that system's Judaism. Along these same lines, we cannot describe any system at its points of tension and resolution simply by appealing to data that all systems have in common. If we do so, we simply leave out too much of any one system's choices reasonably to claim to deal with any system in its own terms.

It follows, third, that when we catalogue traits common to all Judaisms, we find ourselves unable to describe, analyze, and interpret any one of those Judaisms; the facts that all have in common for the reasons now spelled out prove inert; they do not generate important issues. They do not precipitate ongoing exercises of exegesis of received texts, myths, or practices. They do not tell us how the system works or why it matters to those who constitute its community. Indeed, no important question of systemic analysis of a Judaism demands as its answer an appeal to what this system has in common with other Judaisms. And for the same reason no Judaic system or Judaism fits easily into the context of a common, encompassing Judaism.

In fact, for considerations now amply listed, the postulate of a single Judaism that is prior to and forms the foundations of all Judaisms and is shared among them all impedes the study of each Judaism. That postulate – the fabricated "Judaism behind all Judaisms" – diverts our attention from the critical question, which is how to characterize a given system. Knowing what systems have in common helps us not at all in explaining what makes one system both cogent within itself and different from all others. But that, in my view, forms the task of learning, and it moreover contradicts the deepest bias of every body of sources. Such a lowest-common-denominator Judaism turns out to be the invention of scholars, not the expression of the sources of any Judaism or of all the Judaisms put together.

The reason is very specific and concrete. It is that very Judaic system that has yielded documents we are able to examine[2] identifies itself as much by differentiating itself from others as by defining itself in its own terms. In one way or another, all Judaic systems the writings of which we have in hand point to the existence of other Judaisms, besides themselves, and each is explicit on the character of its claim. That the earliest Christians, seeing themselves as part of Israel, explicitly pointed to differences between themselves and the rest of Israel, is well known. But our sages of blessed memory say no less when they issue their single most fundamental definition of their "Israel," in the language that leaves unmistakable evidence of a partisan and sectarian claim:

Mishnah-tractate Sanhedrin 10:1

A.   All Israelites have a share in the world to come,

---

[2] I omit reference in this context to the Judaic system that evidently animated the selections of symbols used in synagogues in the second through the seventh centuries. I have discussed this problem in its own terms in *Symbol and Theology in Early Judaism* (Minneapolis, 1991: Fortress Press).

B. as it is said, "Your people also shall be all righteous, they shall inherit the land forever; the branch of my planting, the work of my hands, that I may be glorified" (Isa. 60:21).

C. And these are the ones who have no portion in the world to come:

D. (1) He who says, the resurrection of the dead is a teaching which does not derive from the Torah, (2) and the Torah does not come from Heaven; and (3) an Epicurean.

E. R. Aqiba says, "Also: He who reads in heretical books, and he who whispers over a wound and says, 'I will put none of the diseases upon you which I have put on the Egyptians, for I am the Lord who heals you' (Ex. 15 :26)."

F. Abba Saul says, "Also: He who pronounces the Divine Name as it is spelled out."

At the very stunning and decisive declaration of the universality of the status of Israel among Israelites – the claim on the share in the world to come – we find the particularization of excluded parties. Surely the most ecumenical Judaic system of antiquity, that of the Mishnah, which formulated the ambition of defining the life of the entire world of the Jews and contained legislation for a common government and social order (and no other Judaic system of antiquity thought in such broad terms as these), shows the state of affairs in general. Judaisms take for granted the opposite of a common Judaism; each Judaic system, addressing its Israel, accorded recognition to all other Judaisms by excluding them from its Israel; and no Judaic system knew an Israel other than its own, which accounts for the enormous problem solved by Paul in Romans 9-11.

The case at hand shows the deeply sectarian character of the most encompassing Judaic system known to us, for these are not minor exclusions: denying resurrection as a doctrine of the Torah, denying that God gave the Torah, some other false philosophy. The statement should be read not to point to the sociology of the Jews of some given time or place but the theology of the system builders who speak through the document. And from their perspective, they are prepared explicitly to claim that theirs is the right Torah, and others' Torahs are wrong. That fact explains why I said that the premise of a common Judaism stands in the way of the accurate characterization of any one Judaic system, all the more so of all of them all together. Here we have a fine example of what I mean.

The concept that a datum may be both important and systemically inert now may be explained in a very simple way. We take for granted that all Judaisms believed in one God, the Sabbath, and the Torah. If, however, we opened the Mishnah commencing with the premise that that document, like those of all other Judaisms, affirmed the unity of God, the holiness of the Sabbath, and the rite of circumcision –

convictions that the framers of the document obviously sustained – we still cannot account for what is before us. What I mean is readily seen in the answer to a specific question: knowing the priority of monotheism, the Sabbath, and circumcision, should we have predicted the basis on which those same writers would have differentiated themselves from others, also "Israel," whom they wished to exclude from a share in the world to come? I do not see how we should ever have known that at stake in this Judaism's definition would be the matters of the origin in the Torah of the belief in the resurrection of the dead, let alone the heavenly origin of the Torah itself!

The very fundamental self-definition contained in the passage at hand will wholly have eluded our grasp, had we proposed to characterize the system by reference to its commonalities with other systems. Knowing that this group, like all others, believed in one God, the Sabbath, and circumcision, we should know nothing that this group thought important about itself. Seeing all Judaisms as part of a single Judaism leads us to account for everything but the main thing, which is, what defined and characterized each of the various Judaisms, viewed on their own. There never was, in real, social terms, that single Judaism, there were only the infinite and diverse Judaic systems, as various social entities gave expression to their way of life, worldview, and theory of the social entity that they formed. Only if we take for granted that "all Israel" formed "a people, one people," are we compelled to take seriously a social entity so vast as would sustain the category, Judaism – a single Judaism, one Judaism, for a single people, one people. If we ask, where did this single Judaism flourish, which supposedly encompassed and held together all Judaisms, and if we wonder, where were its synagogues, and how did its adherents negotiate the differences between and among themselves, the full complexity of the problem of "Judaism" emerges. There is no evidence that permits us to locate where and when this single Judaism flourished, any more than evidence of a material or literary character allows us to treat the Jews as "a people, one people," except in relationship to those outer limits that told people who was, if not legitimately part of holy Israel, at least, a Jew, and who was not.

Indeed, I defy scholarship to walk the limns of that encompassing territory. In fact, all literary evidence that defines a group as Israel – that is to say, all literary evidence that has survived – also explains why others who claim to form "Israel" or "an Israel" do not in fact do so. That is what I mean when I dismiss components of a lowest-common-denominator Judaism as valid but systemically inert, characteristic everywhere but important nowhere. Any definition comprising these elements in particular will therefore describe a Judaism that existed everywhere but made a difference nowhere.

Accordingly, I can find no more obvious or simple case to illustrate the claim that knowing what all Judaisms have in common tells us everything but the main thing, which is, why all each of the Judaisms made the choices that it made. Every Judaism offered its way of life, worldview, and definition of "Israel." All of them stood for people who claimed to be "Israel" or who claimed to possess the Torah or who claimed to constitute God's people; each therefore formulated a doctrine of both itself and the other – the other Israelite, the gentile other. And if we cannot explain how people knew the difference between themselves and outsiders, other Israelites and gentiles alike, we also cannot describe, analyze, or interpret the system at hand.

That is what I mean when I insist, knowing the commonalities among Judaic systems tells us everything but the main thing, which is, why the systems took the shape that they did, laid emphasis upon the particular things that mattered to them, and formed the judgments that they did concerning all the rest of the Jews as well as the gentiles. For the work of the exegesis of documents and myths, practices and institutional forms alike requires that we account for the character of those documents, myths, practices, and institutions. If we propose to define (even as a matter of theory) a "Judaism" that stands behind said documents, myths, practices, and institutions, then the measure of our success will be that we can explain the character of the documents and worldly formulations of that Judaism: conduct an exegesis of the exegesis of the Torah contained therein.

This we cannot do when we point to how one Judaism is like other Judaisms. The reason, I stress, is not that the various Judaisms did not coalesce, or did not intersect at important points, or did not concur on many basic convictions. They manifestly did. The reason is that where they concur, it is on matters that prove inert, and where they differ, it is on issues of definitive conviction. The Judaisms prove sufficiently alike so that they can be meaningfully differentiated. Our task is to account for the differences, and points of commonality legitimate the effort to do so. That is to say, we have now to find out whether, having abandoned "Judaism," we may preserve the notion of "Judaisms," one by one if not all together and all at once. The remainder of this book presents an honest answer to that difficult question.

So to conclude, Judaism itself has long since formed a useful category in the study of this religion or family of religions. A philosophical construction, meant to refer to a religion as a whole and specifically to define the normative conceptions that all together constitute that cogent -*ism*, that concept here emerges as still less useful than to this point I had been prepared to concede. In Chapter Two I shall spell out why, and in Chapters Three through Five, lay out the evidence that proves the point. Chapter Six then draws the conclusions compelled by that survey and points to what is now to be done toward the definition of "Judaism." The first step, clearly, will be to explain what it is that we mean to define when we define "Judaism."

2

The *Particular* Judaism the Rabbis Take for Granted

...One must press behind the contents of the Mishnah and attempt
to discover what the contents of the Mishnah presuppose....
E.P. Sanders[1]

While, for reasons spelled out in Chapter One, we dismiss the notion
that we can define one Judaism out of the many that antiquity lays before
us. But until now I have taken for granted that there certainly was one
cogent Rabbinic Judaism, with a coherent corpus of myths, symbols, and
rites, and deriving from a linear, unitary history, such as I have outlined
in a variety of works, most notably, *The Transformation of Judaism. From
Philosophy to Religion.*[2] That history struck me as incremental and
harmonious; that impression guided me through more than a quarter-
century of systematic work. But now, having addressed a question about
considerations of premise and presupposition and asked how the
Rabbinic writings reveal what their authors take for granted, I have to
call into doubt what I had taken for my generative principle. It is that the
writers of the Rabbinic documents take little for granted, and nothing for
granted that matters very deeply in the formation of any one of those
documents. What that fact, substantiated and spelled out in Chapters
Three through Five, the shank of the book, means, then, is simple. We do
not now know very much about that Judaism that the rabbis took for
granted, because the documents that comprise their canon for late
antiquity provide only very limited access to the general conceptions that
underlie the specific writings in hand.

---

[1]E.P. Sanders, "Puzzling Out Rabbinism," in William Scott Green, ed., *Approaches
to Ancient Judaism*, 1980, 2:73
[2]Champaign, 1992: University of Illinois Press.

Before proceeding, let me offer a brief definition of what I mean by premises and presuppositions. To produce a piece of writing requires meeting a variety of prior conditions. Writers must know the rules that govern communication with their readers, what is expected, what is off limits; they must have a theory of what their readers already know, and what their readers will want in their writing to find out. Laws of rhetoric govern how writers frame their ideas; laws of logic dictate how they will formulate ideas that can be communicated and understood and be found persuasive. In any given community of writers and readers, therefore, readers and writers join together in affirming the givens of effective communication of thought: formation, formulation, transmission.

Not only do rules of communicable thought and expression govern, but a shared corpus of facts and authoritative principles will inform readers what writers take for granted, and define for writers the possibilities of thought: about what may one speculate, and what propositions must one refrain from entertaining. These truisms scarcely require amplification, let alone instantiation. But they set the stage for the problem of this book, which is to spell out what I think "our sages of blessed memory," the rabbis responsible for the documents of the canon of the Judaism of the Dual Torah from the Mishnah through the Talmud of Babylonia, roughly the first six centuries of the Common Era, took for granted.

For a long time, then, I have assumed that, while we cannot define a single Judaism characteristic of all ancient Judaists (Jews who practice a religion they call Judaism), we certainly may speak of a single, coherent Rabbinic Judaism. That is, I understood as a matter of premise that all of the Rabbinic documents hold together in a single corpus, one that is not only coherent because of its organization as exegeses of received writings (Scripture, the Mishnah), but also cogent in its principal points of belief. But now I find that that is not the case; there is no positive evidence, deriving from the documents examined here, that sustains the conception of a single cogent Rabbinic Judaism. We have little reason based on internal evidence to explain why a given document finds its place in the canon of that Judaism as it had reached definition at the end of ancient times.

What I want to know here is whether the canonical documents of the Judaism of the Dual Torah point to a shared corpus of attitudes or convictions, and whether behind what the documents say, in all its specificity, lie principles that in all their generality come to whole, systemic expression in the here and now of the law, theology, or exegesis of the Torah that the canonical writings set forth. Is there such an encompassing system, a Judaism, emerging from, or underpinning, the givens of the documents read one by one and all together? If, in light of what I have said in Chapter One, we cannot define a Judaism that both characterizes all Judaic writings and also accounts for the distinctive traits of each, then can we at least define the Judaism of the rabbis, that is, the sages who produced and valued the documents of Rabbinic Judaism? The answer must come to us in the givens of the rabbis' writings. Then once we identify the premises and presuppositions of those documents, have we moved a step closer to the definition of that Judaism that all of those documents take for granted and, in one way or another, bring to expression? To address these closely-related questions, we commence with the issue of hermeneutics.

To begin with, let us reexamine the hermeneutics that a quest for the Judaism behind the text presupposes. In fact, the same hermeneutics that serves for the great conception ("Judaism") serves for the small one ("a Judaism," "one Judaism" among many, such as "Rabbinic Judaism") as well. Its principal parts are readily delineated. The conception of one unitary, linear, incremental "Judaism" reaches its critical force with the claim that there is a "Judaism out there," beyond any one document of any particular Judaism, to which in some way or other all documents of all Judaisms in various ways and proportions are supposed to attest. And that Judaism out there, prior to, encompassing all documents, each with its "Judaism in here," imposes its judgment upon our reading of every sentence, every paragraph, every book. A reading in terms of a single Judaism of a single document therefore is improper.

In accord with this hermeneutics, as my discussion in Chapter One explains, all documents have to be read in light of all other documents; all Judaisms in light of all other Judaisms; none sustains a distinctive reading of its own literature, and no document of a single Judaism may be read on its own either. A hermeneutics serving one explains all the others. This view may be framed in the phrase, "Judaism behind the texts," which is to say, we have to read the various documents to find evidence of the nurturing, sheltering Judaic system that transcends them all and encompasses each one equally well. To discover that Judaism, we have to identify the premises and presuppositions of documents and their contents, for when we find out what the documents take for granted, we are led into the documentary matrix, which is to say, that Judaism that comes prior to any particular Judaic system, that Judaism to which all Judaisms subscribe.

Now, it is self-evident, the conception of a single Judaism beyond all Judaic texts, nurturing and sheltering each, cannot be distinguished in principle from the notion of a particular Judaism's joining all of its systemic documents. If we have as a unitary composition not Judaism but (at least) one particular Judaism, for example, "Rabbinic Judaism," then we may reasonably ask about the Judaism that the rabbis took for granted: where and how we may identify its components, and, particularly, its intellectual elements (stories, principles, attitudes and the like). The difference between the hermeneutics of a single encompassing Judaism, to which I raised objections in Chapter One, and that of a particular Judaism or Judaic system lies not in theory. It is whether or not, in practice, we can demonstrate that a particular Judaic system can be shown to speak at the deepest layers of all of its documents.

If we are able to identify, at the level of premises or presuppositions of various canonical writings, a set of ideas that persist throughout, that define the generative problematics of various specific documents or at least explain how the diverse problematics cohere, then we may say that the hermeneutics of a uniform Judaism does dictate the reading of individual documents. It will not be the hermeneutics of Judaism, one and uniform throughout all evidences, of course, but only that of a Judaism. But we shall have defined, at least, what we may call "a Judaism's Judaism." That somewhat odd formulation means to refer to the ideas that come prior, and that hold together and impart cogency to an entire corpus of documents that we maintain belong together as the canon of a particular Judaism. Then we shall have defined how diverse writings are to be read in a uniform way, showing what is taken for granted everywhere. Having "pressed behind" a set of documents and uncovered the presuppositions in play in each, we shall have shown that all of the writings point to a single system, and we shall have found it possible on the strength of documentary evidence that transcends any particular writer to define that system, that Judaism. That is the task before us: to try to do what defining a Judaism out of its documentary evidence requires.

This theoretical statement brings us to the issues investigated in the five volumes in seven parts of *Judaism behind the Texts*. In asking about not the Judaism beyond, but the Judaism behind, the texts, what I want to know is how the various writings hold together. Can we identify a set of premises that animate all writers, presuppositions that guide every compilation's compositions' authors and compositors' framers? If we can, then we shall have found what makes that Judaism into a single coherent religious system. If we cannot, then we shall have to ask a fresh set of descriptive questions concerning the theology of that religious system – a different set from those that guide the present work. Let me state with heavy emphasis what in that work I wanted to find out: at stake is not only the Mishnah and its premises (presumably bringing us back into circles of first-century thinkers) but the presuppositions of numerous representative documents of Rabbinic Judaism throughout its formative period. The second question vastly outweighs the one that animates interest in premises and presuppositions: Is there a Judaism that infuses all texts and forms of each part of a coherent whole? At issue in the quest for presuppositions is not the Judaism that lies beyond the texts (which the texts by definition cannot tell us and indeed do not pretend to tell us), but the Judaism that holds together all of the texts and forms the substrate of conviction and conscience in each one.

What makes the task plausible to begin with? I need not fall back to the defense that, anyhow, everybody assumes these documents all come from "the rabbis," and perhaps more documents than I have analyzed too. What everybody assumes still have to be demonstrated through appeal to concrete, material evidence. The reason that to begin with, I assume that writings that flow from the Mishnah, as Mishnah-exegesis, and from Scripture, as Scripture-exegesis under the auspices of "our sages of blessed memory" belong in a single canon is simple. It is that that body of writings in formal traits, which are intrinsic to the writing and not merely imposed by printers or copyists, is continuous, formed as it is as commentaries on the Written Torah or the Mishnah. The same names run from document to document. The period in which the writings are assumed to have taken shape for formal and substantive reasons also is continuous.[3] As to the Midrash-compilations, these not only flow from Scripture in an unbroken stream, but cite the names of the same authorities throughout. So the palpable traits of the writings certainly validate the inquiry into how, at their foundations, they rest upon bedrock that is common to them all. So I begin with the theory that the Judaism of the Dual Torah, viewed in its formative canon, is single and whole, and the premises and presuppositions of any of its writings should cohere.

That having been said, it is necessary to spell out what it means to investigate the premises and presuppositions of the documents of a given Judaism, in our case, Rabbinic Judaism. By systemic premises and presuppositions I refer to what is active and not inert in a given system. We recall the stress I placed on what is systemically definitive as against what is merely present, for example, resurrection of the dead derives from the Torah, the Torah comes from heaven, as against circumcision,

---

[3]And of course not to be truncated at its very starting point, with the Mishnah, as Sanders's formulation, cited at the head of this chapter, proposes. For the Mishnah presents only the first among a long sequence of problems for analysis, and cutting that writing off from its continuators and successors, in both Midrash compilations and Talmuds, represents a gross error, one commonplace, to be sure, among Christian scholars of Judaism, for whom, as in Sanders's case, Judaism ends in the first century or early second and ceases beyond that point to require study at all.

monotheism, or the Sabbath and prayer, for instance.[4] I mean by that qualification to exclude conceptions that do not lead us into the systemic center of a given Judaism but only define its superficial, indicative traits. To make this point, we must remember the distinction between what is necessary for the classification of a system and what is sufficient for the description, analysis, and interpretation of that same system. Necessary to any Judaic system will be traits that, as a matter of a priori definition, we impute to all systems: monotheism, affirmation of the Torah of Moses, practice of circumcision, and the various other universal traits we noted in Chapter One. These traits are necessary for a system to find its place among Judaisms. But they do not suffice to tell us how a specific Judaism conducts its exegesis of the givens of all Judaisms (if we wish to take that route) or formulates its definition of the things that matter within its own way of life, worldview, and theory of the social entity realized in by the society of its devotees, its Israel.

Let me make concrete this distinction between the necessary, which is banal, and the sufficient, which defines what is at stake. A very long list of platitudes and banalities can readily be constructed and every item on the list can be shown to be present throughout the documents under study here; but those platitudes and banalities make no contribution to the shaping of our documents and the formulation of their system. Therefore, having proven that the sun rises in the east, from those systemically inert givens, we should know no more about matters than we did beforehand. True, to those in search of "Judaism," as distinct from the diverse Judaic systems to which our evidence attests, that finding – God is one, God gave the Torah, Israel is God's chosen people, and the like – bears enormous consequence. But that God is one in no way accounts for the system's specific qualities and concerns, any more than does the fact that the laws of gravity operate. The concrete illustration given in Chapter One serves to fill out this argument, which lies at the foundations of our consideration of documentary premises here.

What makes a Judaic system important is what marks that system as entire and imparts to that system its integrity. That is what makes one system different from other systems and also what holds that system together. When we know how to define a system's rationality, the

---

[4]And yet even that distinction bears qualification. For, after all, what is a systemic given in one statement turns out to be a systemic point of tension in another, circumcision being a fine example. For our sages of blessed memory, it is routine and part of the inert background of accepted facts; for the Israelites of earliest Christianity, it was anything but inert; explaining the systemic rationality must encompass not only what is active but also what is inert; modes of explanation have themselves to be reckoned with.

principle of its exegesis of the received materials, we then can explain the system in its own terms and context. That rationality will account for what the particular system makes of the heritage of what is necessary – monotheism, the Torah, Israel, circumcision, and much else – and transform what is required to mark the system as Judaic into what is distinctive to the system, as all things, whether shared with other Judaisms or particular to this Judaism, prove to be. As Chapter One has already argued, efforts to find that one Judaism that holds together all Judaisms yields suffocating banalities and useless platitudes: we do not understand anything in particular any better than we did before we had thought up such generalities. So by "generative premises" I mean the premises that counted: those that provoked the framers of a document's ideas to do their work, that made urgent the questions they address, that imparted self-evidence to the answers they set forth.

This brings us to the evidences that are sorted out in Chapters Three through Five. In my research report, I worked document by document and group by group. The analytical grid derived from the documents, [1] the Mishnah, then [2] The Tosefta, Tractate Abot, and the Earlier Midrash-compilations: Sifra, Sifré to Numbers, and Sifré to Deuteronomy; [3] The Later Midrash-compilations: Genesis Rabbah, Leviticus Rabbah and Pesiqta deRab Kahana; [4] The Latest Midrash-compilations: Song of Songs Rabbah, Ruth Rabbah, Esther Rabbah; [5] The Talmuds of the Land of Israel and Babylonia. Here I omit reference to the two Talmuds, since they present a special problem, for reasons specified in the conclusion. I therefore made possible the formulation of a documentary history of ideas, specifically, an account of how, over time, various premises or presupposes entered into, or surfaced within, the Judaism that these documents portrayed. That description at once was historical and anti-historical. It presupposed that the sequence of documents yielded a sequence of the representation of ideas, hence something akin to a history of ideas. But it also represented the anti-historical notion of this Judaism, whole and complete, surfacing in one detail here, in another detail there, without reference to the specificities of time and circumstance. It is this second, anti-historical approach that now comes to the fore.

In collecting those evidences, to begin with, I wanted to know simply, what premises underlie the various documents of Rabbinic Judaism. The survey set forth here calls into question the certainty with which Professor Sanders has raised his question – his assumption that there really is a corpus of presuppositions at all. The results cast doubt upon the confidence with which I accepted his question as an appropriate one. Like him, I wanted to know what the documents took for granted all together and all at once. But now, as we shall see, I find nothing that characterizes all writings and little that coheres from one writing to the next. If I want to know whether out of all of the documents of a single Judaism, we can identify shared premises or presuppositions that contribute to the definition of that single Judaism that supposedly is under study, I have created the opportunity to find out. "The Judaism the rabbis take for granted" then defines what is at stake, which is whether we may define such a Judaism that is prior to all the Rabbinic documents and characteristic of each one of them.

What I want to know here has nothing to do with the sequence of documents and the formation or appearance of ideas they contain as premises. What I want to know is how things look overall, at the end, in a literature that has come to formally coherent formulation and cogent, well-crafted conclusion: the Judaism of the Dual Torah at closure. The framing of the question in an other-than-historical mode is for a specific reason, one required, as will be self-evident, by the experiment at hand. I here want to know whether a single system really does form the foundations of all the documents, so I have to ignore the documentary sequence and, seeing everything all together and all at once, ask whether from beginning to end some one set of premises forms the underpinning of all the writings; and, if so, of what it might consist. For that purpose the structure's stresses flow through types of premises, rather than along documentary lines.

As I said in the Preface, I want to know whether out of all of the documents of a single Judaism, we can identify shared premises or presuppositions that contribute to the definition of the Judaism that is attested, in one chapter or another of its larger statement, in a given document. The answer will dictate whether or not we may speak of a Judaism that comprises all these writings, whether or not the canon of writings identified as authoritative forms more than a convention imposed by authority, whether or not the writings flow from a common system and serve, in one detail or another, to expose its basic structure. Now that we recognize the difficulty of postulating a single Judaism behind all known Judaisms, we move toward a more difficult question. Faced with a variety of documents universally, and I think validly, assigned to a single Judaic system and deemed evidence of that system's viewpoint – way of life, worldview, theory of the social order – are we able to identify the givens of the system as a whole as we work our way through the parts that constitute the canon? We take up the Judaism of the Dual Torah and its writings, and, having inspected them one by one and catalogued their premises, we proceed to this further question. It is in three parts.

[1] What premises animate the documents as a whole, viewed not one by one but as a group? Can we find evidence of a common theology, law, philosophy, and hermeneutics throughout?

[2] Do the premises we have identified play a role throughout the writings, so that we may speak of a Judaism that underlies all of the writings? Or do the premises appear particular to the documents that appear to rest on them?

[3] Once we catalogue the operative premises and governing presuppositions, are we able to put together a coherent Judaic system out of them? Do the givens of the documents, viewed all together, permit us to speak of a Judaic system at all? Or are they, too, fragmentary to allow us to compose of them a cogent and whole systemic statement?

Chapters Three through Five respond to the first question, Chapter Six to the second and third.

I have identified four major categories of premises. These are premises that may be classified as philosophical, theological, and legal. By "theological," Chapter Three, I mean, premises that pertain to, or derive from the revelation that is unique to holy Israel and is contained in Scripture; truths that apply only to Israel; allegations of a unique character, for example, laws of history that govern only for Israel; interventions by God into the world that affect only Israel. Theological premises appeal for validation to not the nature of things but the revealed Torah, and adequate proof derives from a proper reading of Scripture (or tradition). Appeal to the common traits of things will be set aside in favor of what is special to the case of Israel.

By "philosophical," in Chapter Four, I mean, premises that concern the natural world or the social world; premises that are subject to generalization; premises that derive from or apply to not revealed but observable truth; premises that affect not only holy Israel and its special case, but humanity in general and its universal condition. These are premises that may be treated as universally pertinent ("universalizable").

By "legal," in Chapter Five, I mean, presuppositions as to correct behavior, in accord with the law of the Torah (oral and written); norms of practical conduct; definitions of how things are to be done overall in Israel.

My method, within the scheme just now defined, is simple. I survey the results of the seven parts, in five volumes, of *Judaism behind the Texts* and identify what strike me as consequential premises, presuppositions bearing relevance at more than a few passages; recurrent points of tension; repeated points of emphasis. These I recapitulate among the four classifications among which I now propose to sort out premises and presuppositions, looking for two things.

First, I want to know where and how the various consequential premises lay themselves out, their documentary provenience, the extent to which they make an appearance in more than a single document. It is one thing to identify a presupposition, it is another to find out whether said presupposition proves particular to the document that invokes it or general to a variety of documents. Only presuppositions of the second type seem to me to demand attention in any account of the Judaism the rabbis took for granted.

Accordingly, in Chapter Six I ask whether the premises that we have identified transcend the documents in which they occur or turn out to form propositions, of a fundamental or to be sure, particular to the documents that contain them. Then I want to find out whether all together the presuppositions and premises form a set of coherent statements that we may in the end set forth as a Judaic system, an account of the ethos, ethics, and ethnos of a distinctive social entity. So I ask whether, if we concede that every item we have identified as a premise or presupposition in fact serves a very broad and encompassing systemic purpose, we can then define that Judaism behind the texts that we sought at the beginning of this work. For the alternative may well be, the premises prove particular to their documents and may not be asked to speak to a fully articulated Judaic system at all.

The program of the shank of the book is therefore clear. Seeing the premises all together, and classifying each within a standard system – law, theology, philosophy, and the like – I am led to formulate the problem, how, from the documents in hand, may we reconstruct the corpus of presuppositions and premises that lie behind those documents and define the Judaism that the documents take for granted? My inquiry moves from documents to the several premises that have now come to the surface, and what I wish to know is, how broadly do these premises characterize the documentary heritage of the Judaism of the Dual Torah? If the documents as a whole refer to the same few propositions, then we may rightly speak of a Judaism common to them all – the Judaism the rabbis take for granted. But if, as we shall see, the premises of the several documents prove particular to the writings in which they occur, then we have a result we cannot have anticipated at the outset, and one that precipitates a fresh range of questions for contemplation.

While the method of this book seems to me simple and routine, the stakes are high, and, clearly, the question at hand is fresh. A survey of prior inquiries into the same problem hardly takes much space. For I cannot point to any prior study of Rabbinic Judaism that has pursued the issue set forth here. Everyone has taken for granted either that all

Judaisms form one Judaism, or that the Rabbinic documents form one Judaism. No one has asked about the premises that underpin those documents or whether and how they coalesce to unit the specificities of one piece of writing with those of some other. True, we have a literature of definition of Judaism and of Rabbinic Judaism, and important works, produced by such scholars of standing as E.E. Urbach, Abraham J. Heschel, and Max Kadushin, through systematic study of the appropriate documents have defined Rabbinic Judaism. But Urbach, Heschel, and Kadushin share an interest in what the documents say, not what they take for granted. And, it seems to me clear, if we want to define the Judaism that the rabbis of the Dual Torah wished to put forth, we have to know not only what they said but also what they took for granted.

As is clear, the specific point of entry, the documentary one, is utterly without precedent in received scholarship. For, working within theological premises, Urbach and Heschel treated all documents as part of a single, undifferentiated Torah, citing statements in the names of various rabbis without regard to their documentary origin. The little-appreciated pioneer, Kadushin certainly recognized that documents have to be read one by one, not only all together and all at once but each in its own terms, and he did just that. But he made only very modest progress in documentary differentiation, and none at all in the reconstruction of the documents that have been differentiated.[5]

So I ask a question that has not received any attention until now, and I answer it in a simple and systematic manner, simply by sifting and resifting already well sifted evidence. There is no other way. The way forward now leads through three stages. First, we have to identify fundamental premises; second, we have to investigate the occurrence of these premises, document by document; third, we have to ask whether these premises comprise a system of some ample dimensions and coverage. Accepting the discipline of the documentary history of ideas, I

---

[5]He erred by ignoring his own results and presupposing the unity of language among differentiated documents, and that led him into a morass from which he never really was able to extricate himself. His end result, that words have different meanings depending on the context in which they are used, brought him to the cusp of the documentary hypothesis that I have worked out in my own way. But he did not then recognize the importance of the documentary imperative in the framing of writing, the priority of the document over its contents, which I have been able to show in a variety of demonstrations. My discussion of Kadushin's pioneering thought is in my *Symbol and Theology in Early Judaism* (Minneapolis, 1991: Fortress Press). Kadushin was a heroic figure, pursuing his scholarship under exceedingly difficult and disheartening conditions, and I do not think that, in his lifetime, he received the recognize that he deserved.

follow the order of documents, so allowing the Mishnah to define matters first of all, then the later documents to make their contributions in sequence.

3

Religious and Theological Premises

In this chapter, we take up the givens of religion and their reconstitution as theology: truths that our sages know by reason of the Torah's revelation of them. In the next we take up the presuppositions of philosophy, sages' thinking on matters accessible not through the Torah alone but through natural reasoning about this-worldly facts.

For the present purpose the distinction between religious and theological thinking is immaterial, but should be spelled out. By religious premises I mean those givens about God, God's covenanted relationship to Israel, and what God demands of Israel that come to expression, either tacitly or explicitly, in the concrete laws or exegesis of Scripture or formulations of virtue throughout the documents under study. When these matters of attitude, sentiment, emotion, conviction, conscience, or social theory take the form of a well-crafted formulation of an idea or attitude as a proposition for philosophical consideration, then a religious premise changes into a theological statement. For the purposes of this survey, the difference between religion and theology plays no role; what concerns us is not the form and uses of ideas but simply the contents, and whether these reach us in legal, mythic, or philosophical form makes slight difference. In the case of the rabbis' Judaism, God's self-manifestation takes place in the Torah, so theology is rigorous thought about religious truths deriving from the Torah.

I. The Mishnah

A. Intentionality

We begin with the single most critical theological conception of the law, corresponding to the matter of hierarchical classification, which defines the single most important philosophical conception of the law. The most profound conviction of our sages is that God's and Israel's attitudes and emotions are consubstantial, so that both respond in the same way to the same things; and that God not only loves and cares for Israel, but responds to Israel's attitudes, will, desires, and emotions, in a way that corresponds to the way in which Israel feels or wants or plans things to be. The issues of intentionality may be sorted out entirely in a philosophical framework, to be sure, but in this context, I regard intentionality as a theological, not at all a philosophical, category, because the ultimate effect of intentionality is to evoke a response from God to what one has thought, said, or done. Without heaven's ratification of a statement or a deed, or response to an unstated intent, a situation produces no consequence. Hence while for philosophy in this same time and place, the matter of intentionality proves critical, for instance invoking attitude or intent as an objective taxonomic indicator, as we shall see in Chapter Four, in the context of the documents of Judaism we deal with an issue deeply engaged in theology, expressed in law and in exegesis of Scripture equally well.

Intentionality forms both a theological and a philosophical category. It is theological in that God and the human being share traits of attitude and emotion. They want the same thing. For example, it is made clear in Mishnah-tractate Maaserot, man and God respond in the same way to the same events, since they share not only ownership of the Land but also viewpoint on the value of its produce. When the farmer wants the crop, so, too, does God. When the householder takes the view that the crop is worthwhile, God responds to the attitude of the farmer by forming the same opinion. It is philosophical in that most of the concrete issues concern not Israelite traits in particular, but abstract and general issues, subject to universal analysis, on the interplay of deed and intention and the effect upon what one has done and how one is judged therefor on what one has intended to do. That issue in its own terms is philosophical and is treated in the next chapter.

Let us now define the matter with greater precision. By "intentionality" we find a variety of closely related attitudes and convictions put forth. Under discussion is what a person wants to accomplish by a given deed, what one wants to say by a given formula, and other aspects of the attitude and desire of a person, viewed independent of what the person actually says or does and as a principal factor in assessing the weight and meaning of what he or she has said or done. Because intentionality is a primary consideration in governing the affect on heaven of what one has said or done on earth, I view the matter as a major chapter in the theology that the rabbis simply take for granted.

Intentionality forms a transaction between the Israelite and God. God responds to the Israelite's will or plan or intention. That especially pertains to what is made holy or consecrated. When, for instance, human beings voluntarily give up what is their right, God may respond through counterpart uncoerced grace. When people fast and otherwise refrain from pleasures, God is more likely to answer their prayers than otherwise. It is the Israelite who has the power to consecrate an object, by an intention to do so; God responds to that intention by regarding the object as holy and invoking the penalties of sacrilege to protect said object. The thought and act of the Israelite householder – the nonpriest – have the power to made the produce holy. He formulates the intention to consecrate produce; then he does the act of pronouncing the formula that orally designates a portion of the produce to be heave-offering; then he physically separates that portion from the rest of the batch.[1] No produce is intrinsically holy. That is shown by the fact that someone who has two batches of produce can designate from one of them the heave-offering required of both; liability of both batches to heave-offering is carried out, and that could not be the case if each batch contained a quantity of already-holy produce that had to be removed. If that were the case, what the householder did with one batch would have no effect upon a different batch (Peck, p. 3).

The religious dimension of intentionality is best illustrated to begin with in the cult in particular. The priest's intentionality in carrying out an act of sacrifice affects the validity of that act of sacrifice. If the priest expresses an improper intentionality, the rite is nullified, and that covers a variety of distinct phases of the rite:

2:3   A.   This is the general rule:
       B.   Whoever slaughters, or receives [the blood], or conveys [the blood], or sprinkles [the blood] [intending]
       C.   to eat something which is usually eaten [flesh], to burn something which is usually burned [entrails],
       D.   outside of its proper place [the court for Most Holy Things, Jerusalem for Lesser Holy Things] –
       E.   it is invalid [and the flesh may not be eaten]. And extirpation does not apply to it.
       F.   Supply: Whoever slaughters, or receives the blood, or conveys the blood, or sprinkles [the blood], intending to eat something which is usually eaten, to burn something which is usually burned
       G.   outside of its proper time –
       H.   it is refuse.
       I.   And they are liable on its account to extirpation [even if they eat the flesh within the time limit].
       J.   And [the foregoing rule applies] on condition that what renders the offering permissible [the blood, which permits the sacrificial portions to be burned on the altar and the flesh to be eaten by the

---

[1] Alan J. Avery-Peck, *The Priestly Gift in Mishnah. A Study of Tractate Terumot* (Chico, 1981: Scholars Press for Brown Judaic Studies) p. 3.

priest or owner, that is, the proper sprinkling or tossing of the blood] is offered in accord with its requirement.

So, too, the intentionality governing the status of a beast designated as a Holy Thing is that of the officiating priest and not the owner of the beast. Once the beast has been designated by the owner, then the condition of sanctification takes over, and further intentionality affecting the beast is that of the holy caste:

Mishnah-tractate Zebahim

4:6   A.   For the sake of six things is the animal-offering sacrificed: (1) for the sake of the animal-offering, (2) for the sake of the one who sacrifices it, (3) for the sake of the Lord, (4) for the sake of the altar fires, (5) for the sake of the odor, (6) for the sake of the pleasing smell.

B.   And as to the sin-offering and the guilt-offering, for the sake of the sin [expiated thereby].

C.   Said R. Yosé, "Even: One who was not [mindful] in his heart for the sake of one all of these [but slaughtered without specifying these things] – it is valid, for it is a condition imposed by the court, that intention follows only [the mind of] the one who carries out the act [not the owner; and the officiant does not specify the six things at all]."

Along these same lines, meal-offerings that have been designated as holy for a particular purpose remain holy even though they are shifted from one to another holy purpose. In the case of meal-offerings designated for some offerings, if the meal-offering that has been designated for some other purpose is utilized, by the priest's own intentionality, for that purpose, the offering is a valid one, but the owner must meet his obligation by providing another animal. Intentionality therefore is in two parts: sanctification or designation of the meal-offering as holy, and offering up of the meal-offering for a particular cultic purpose:

Mishnah-tractate Menahot

1:1   A.   All meal-offerings from which the handful was taken not for their own name are valid [for offering up, and, in the case of the residue, for the priests' eating].

B.   But they have not gone to their owner's credit in fulfillment of an obligation,

C.   except for the meal-offering of a sinner and the meal-offering of jealousy [of a suspected adulteress] [which, if improperly designated, are invalid].

D.   The meal-offering of a sinner and the meal-offering of a suspected adulteress (1) from which the handful was taken not for their own name, (2) [or which] one put into a utensil, and (3) conveyed and (4) offered up not for its own name,

E.   or for its own name and not for its own name,

F.   or not for its own name and for its own name,

G.   are invalid.

H. How so [in a case of doing one of the aforelisted actions] is it for its own name and not for its own name?
I. [If one did one action] (1) for the sake of the meal-offering of a sinner, and (2) [another action] for the sake of a freewill meal-offering.
J. Or [how do we define a case of doing one of the aforelisted actions] not for its own name and for its own name?
K. For the sake of (2) a freewill meal-offering, and for the sake of (1) the meal-offering of a sinner.

The priest's intentionality in carrying out an act of meal-offering affects the validity of that act. If the priest expresses an improper intentionality, the rite is nullified, and that covers a variety of distinct phases of the rite.

Everything is relative to intention, even the permissibility or forbidden status of an action. In assessing the permissibility of an action, we take account of motivation. An act that is forbidden by reason of one intention would be permitted if done with another intention. Actions by themselves have no intrinsic character, but are differentiated into forbidden or permitted categories by reason of the intention of the one who does them:

Mishnah-tractate Shabbat

2:5 A. He who puts out a lamp because he is afraid of gentiles, thugs, a bad spirit,
B. or if it is so that a sick person might sleep,
C. is exempt [from liability to punishment].
D. [If he did so], to spare the lamp, the oil, the wick,
E. he is liable.
F. And R. Yosé exempts [him from liability to punishment] in all instances except for [one who does so to spare] the wick,
G. because he [thereby] makes [it into] charcoal.

Along these same lines, one is liable for an action only if it is done deliberately, but not if it is done inadvertently:

Mishnah-tractate Shabbat

11:6 A. He who throws [an object] and realizes [remembers what he has done] after it leaves his hand,
B. [if] another person caught it,
C. [if] a dog caught it,
D. or [if] it burned up in a fire [intervening in its flight path]
E. he is exempt.
F. [If] he threw it intending to inflict a wound,
G. whether at a man or at a beast,
H. and realizes [what he has done] before it inflicted the wound,
I. he is exempt.
J. This is the general principle: All those who may be liable to sin-offerings in fact are not liable unless at the beginning and the end, their [sin] is done inadvertently.

K.   [But] if the beginning of their [sin] is inadvertent and the end is deliberate, [or] the beginning deliberate and the end inadvertent, they are exempt –

L.   unless at the beginning and at the end their [sin] is inadvertent.

Actions prove reliable indicators of intentionality. By one's action, he shows his intent; and if he intends to derive benefit from what another party has made, he has to bear his share of the costs; if by his action, he shows he does not care to derive benefit, then he does not have to share part of the costs of what the other has made:

Mishnah-tractate Baba Batra

1:3   A.   He who [se land] surrounds that of his fellow on three sides,

B.   and who made a fence on the first, second, and third sides –

C.   they do not require [the other party to share in the expense of building the walls].

D.   R. Yosé says, "If he built a fence on the fourth side, they assign to him [his share in the case of] all [three other fences]."

Intentionality further governs in a negative way. If one has acted in violation of his own will, he is not responsible for the consequences. An act that one has carried out without intent is null; a circumstance in which he finds himself by reason of constraint bears no consequence:

Mishnah-tractate Erubin

4:1   A.   He whom gentiles took forth [beyond the Sabbath limit],

B.   or an evil spirit,

C.   has only four cubits [in which to move about].

D.   [If] they brought him back, it is as if he never went out.

E.   [If] they carried him to another town,

F.   or put him into a cattle pen or a cattlefold,

G.   Rabban Gamaliel and R. Eleazar b. Azariah say, "He may walk about the entire area."

H.   R. Joshua and R. Aqiba say, "He has only four cubits [in which to move about]."

If one makes a mistake as to the facts, he is bound by his intention, based as it is on facts; or he is not bound by an intention formed on the basis of a misapprehension of the facts:

Mishnah-tractate Erubin

4:4   A.   "He who took up a resting place while on the road [on the eve of Sabbath at twilight, and there acquired the place where he would spend the Sabbath],

B.   "and [at dawn] got up and saw, and lo, he is near a town,

C.   "since it was not his intention [to enter that town],

D.   "he may not enter the town," the words of R. Meir.

E.   R. Judah says, "He may enter it."

F. Said R. Judah, "Such a case happened, and R. Tarfon entered a town which he had not previously intended [to make his Sabbath residence]."

We note a mixture of this-worldly and other-worldly contexts in which intentionality takes on a commandment position. The other-worldly matters involve the cult, the this-worldly ones, matters of law and social ethics. We cannot find surprising that the power of intentionality extends into the matter of the Sabbath. Actions permitted on the Sabbath may be carried out only for the purpose of the Sabbath, but may not be done in such a way as to provide for the week beyond; and only a person knows what that intentionality really is.

Mishnah-tractate Shabbat

16:2 A. They save food enough for three meals –
B. what is suitable for human beings for human beings, what is suitable for cattle for cattle.
C. How so?
D. [If] a fire broke out on the night of the Sabbath, they save food for three meals.
E. [If it broke out] in the morning, they save food for two meals.
F. [If it broke out] in the afternoon, [they save food for] one meal.
G. R. Yosé says, "Under all circumstances they save food for three meals."

We distinguish between what happens by accident and what is done with clear intent, imposing a different penalty in accord with circumstance:

Mishnah-tractate Makkot

2:2 A. He who throws a stone into the public domain and it committed homicide – lo, this one goes into exile.
B. R. Eliezer b. Jacob says, "If after the stone left the man's hand, the other party stuck out his head and took [the stone on the head], lo, this one is exempt."
C. [If] he threw the stone into his own courtyard and killed him,
D. if the victim had every right to go into there, [the other party] goes into exile.
E. And if not, he does not go into exile, as it is said, "As when a man goes into the forest with his neighbor" (Deut. 19:5) –
F. just as the forest is a domain in which both the victim and the one who inflicted injury have every right to enter,
G. so the courtyard belonging to the householder is excluded [from reference], since the victim had no right to go there.
2:3 I. One who bears enmity [for his victim] does not go into exile.
J. R. Yosé b. R. Judah says, "One who bears enmity [for his victim] is put to death,
K. "for he is in the status of one who is an attested danger."

L.   R. Simeon says, "There is one who bears enmity [for the victim] who goes into exile, and there is one who bears enmity who does not go into exile.

M.   "This is the governing principle: In any case in which one has the power to say, 'He killed knowingly,' he does not go into exile.

N.   "And if he has the power to say, 'He did not kill knowingly,' lo, this one goes into exile."

We shall see in Chapter Four the taxonomic power of intentionality; here the intersection of philosophy and religion in the principle that attitude is everything is illustrated in a single case. We distinguish among discrete actions, imposing a penalty for each one, when they are differentiated by intentionality, but we do not distinguish actions when these are carried on in a single spell of inadvertence; the case involves a religious taboo:

Mishnah-tractate Horayot

3:7   A.   A Nazirite who was drinking wine all day long is liable on only one count.

B.   [If] they said to him, "Don't drink, don't drink!" yet he continued to drink,

C.   he is liable on each count.

3:8   A.   [If a Nazirite] was contracting corpse uncleanness all day long, he is liable on only one count.

B.   [If] they said to him, "Do not contract corpse uncleanness! Do not contract corpse uncleanness!" yet he continued to contract corpse uncleanness,

C.   he is liable on each count.

D.   [If] he was shaving himself all day long, he is liable on only one count.

E.   [If] they said to him, "Don't shave! don't shave!" yet he continued to shave, he is liable on each count.

F.   If someone was wearing a garment of diverse kinds (Lev. 19:19, Deut. 22:11) all day long, he is liable on only one count.

G.   [If] they said to him, "Don't put it on! don't put it on!" yet he took it off and then put it on, he is liable on each count.

Intention alone, however, does not suffice. A concrete action must accompany the formation of an intention; one can always change his mind. If someone wants to plant seeds in an already planted field, then the plants now in the field must be removed before new plants are sown, not afterward. The new plants may not be allowed to grow alongside the old ones, for, although the owner intends to remove the latter, he appears to be sowing diverse kinds,[2] thus, the appearance, not the actual growth, of diverse kinds determines liability. This is expressed in the following:

---

[2]Irving Mandelbaum, *A History of the Mishnaic Law of Agriculture: Kilayim* (Chico, 1982: Scholars Press for Brown Judaic Studies) p. 71.

M. Kilayim

2:1   A.   [Concerning] every seah [of one kind of seeds] which contains a quarter [-qab] of another kind – he shall lessen [the quantity of seeds of the other kind, so that those seeds form less than a quarter-qab].

2:5   A.   [If] his field was sown with carum or arum,

       B.   he should not sow on top of them,

       C.   for they produce [fruit] only [after] three years.

       D.   (1) Grain among which aftergrowths of woad came up, (2) and so the threshing floors [lit.: the place of the threshing floors] in which many kinds came up, (3) and so fenugreek which brought up [different] kinds of plants –

       E.   they do not require him to weed or cut down [some of them], they say to him, "Uproot everything, except for one kind."

But the same rule cuts in both directions. If one does not appear to want to grow diverse kinds, he is not required to weed out wild plants; if he starts to weed, he must then uproot the wild plants, for if he stops weeding, he appears to allow the diverse kinds to grow. It follows that action defines intention, for example, if one leaves diverse kinds and does not uproot them, he indicates he wants them to grow. One may allow diverse kinds to grow until he reaches them in the course of his work; once he reaches them, he must uproot them. We distinguish also between accidentally and unknowingly sowing diverse kinds in a vineyard, and who does does so accidently but knowingly. These points register in the following:

M. Kilayim

5:6   A.   He who sees vegetables [growing] in the vineyard and said, "When I shall reach it [the vegetables] I shall pluck it" –

       B.   it is permitted [the vegetables and surrounding vines are not sanctified].

       C.   [If he said,] "When I shall return I shall pluck it" –

       D.   if [in the meantime] it [the vegetables] increased [in size] by [one] two-hundred[th],

       E.   it is prohibited [the vegetables and the surrounding vines are sanctified].

These general observations suffice to show the range and power of the premise that intentionality governs throughout. Now to specific rulings and details of the same subject.

1.   Intentionality governs the effect of one's words or deeds. This is spelled out in the following language at M. Ber. 2:1A-C:

       A.   One who was reading [the verses of the Shema] in the Torah and the time for the recitation [of the Shema] arrived:

       B.   If he directed his heart [towards fulfilling the obligation to recite the Shema], he fulfilled his obligation [to recite].

C.   And if [he did] not [direct his heart], he did not fulfill his obligation.

It is taken for granted, therefore, that one's intention in reciting the words classifies the effect of the recitation: fulfillment of the obligation, or (mere) recitation of words of the Torah. The requirement of effective intentionality in reciting the Shema is such as to exempt the mourner from having to do so, since his mind is preoccupied (M. Ber. 3:1-2). It is not equally clear that making intention explicit through articulated pronunciation of the actual words makes any difference at all (M. Ber. 2:3):

A.   One who recited the Shema so softly that he could not hear it [still] fulfilled his obligation.
B.   R. Yosé says, "He did not fulfill his obligation."

The upshot is, intentionality governs, the character of the actual deed is less decisive, or the upshot thereof is subject to schism. But it is absolutely required to recite the Prayer with perfect intentionality (M. Ber. 2:4). Correct intentionality may even override incorrect action, where the incorrect action is the result of one's inability to do things otherwise (M. Ber. 4:5, 6). Prayer may be recited only in the proper frame of mind, a correct disposition, requisite respect (M. Ber. 5:1): "One may arise to say the Prayer only with a solemn frame of mind."

2.   God responds to the human will and intention, taking action at the very point at which the householder has taken an action that expresses his will and intent to effect ownership of the crop. So God feels and thinks the way the householder does, responding in invisible ways to the visible, material action that a householder takes in expression of his attitude, will, or intention. If a farmer clearly intends to retrieve a sheaf later on, then the intention is revealed through some clear action, and the forgotten sheaf law does not apply (M. Peah 6:1-2), in the view of the House of Shammai; the Hillelites maintain that the action of leaving the sheaf is decisive; we do not know that the farmer will ever retrieve the sheaf.

3.   One's actions express one's intention. God pays close attention to the acts of the farmer, so that, as soon as the farmer has taken a given action – processing the produce as food – God enters his claim. Once the farmer has processed the grain, his action represents the expression of the farmer's exclusive ownership: "This arouses the intense interest of God."[3]

---

[3]Roger Brooks, *Support for the Poor in the Mishnaic Law of Agriculture: Tractate Peah* (Chico, 1983: Scholars Press) p. 51.

4. God is cognizant of the standing and character of one who forms an intention concerning what is material; the intangible considerations govern, so that if the physical requirements of the law are met, but the status of the one who forms the effective intention is inappropriate, then the physical character means nothing; intentionality overrides material considerations. Throughout, we observe, there is a perfect correspondence between the householder's claim on the crop and God's (Brooks, p. 72), therefore also, between the character or morphology of the householder's attitudes and will and God's. If someone other than the owner does an action, the act is null; the matter of intentionality and action rests upon the power and right of the one who forms the intent or takes the action; these, too, do not work *ex opere operato:*

M. Peah

2:7   A.   [As regards] a field which (1) gentiles harvested [without the permission of the Israelite owner], (2) thieves harvested, (3) ants destroyed, (4) or which wind or cattle broke down –

       B.   [the produce of such a field] is exempt [from designation as peah].

       C.   [if a farmer] had harvested half [of his field], and thieves [then] harvested [the remaining] half –

       D.   [the produce which the farmer harvests] is exempt [from designation as peah], since the [farmer's] obligation [to designate] peah applied only to the [produce which he left] standing, [and which thieves later harvested].

5. If someone takes an action that conveys a clear intention concerning some later point, that action establishes effective intention, and dictates the disposition of a case, so the House of Shammai. The House of Hillel maintain that what one does is decisive, without reference to what one intends in so doing; we cannot be certain that later on the person ever will do what the present action suggests he intends to do. This dispute is expressed in the following:

M. Peah

6:1   E.   [If] each of the sheaves of a field [contains] a single qab, but one [sheaf contains] four qabs, and [the worker] forgets [this latter sheaf] –

       F.   the House of Shammai say, "It is not [subject to the restrictions of the] forgotten sheaf," [because the sheaf is distinguished from the other sheaves in the field, and so the householder will not forget it] –

       G.   but the House of Hillel say, "[It is subject to the restrictions of the] forgotten sheaf," [for according to the House of Hillel, all sheaves, regardless of distinction, are treated alike; cf. M. 6:2C].

6. Heaven responds to human intentionality. If one takes up doubtfully tithed produce intending to eat it, he is liable to tithe it; even if he changes his mind, the liability he has incurred remains. If he does not intend to eat the produce, merely picking it up does not impose the obligation to tithe. Human intentionality produces a heavenly response, in particular, when the human being does a deed to warrant heaven's interest:

M. Demai

3:3 A. He who finds produce in the road and took it to eat it, and [then] decided to put [it] aside
B. should not put [it] aside until he has tithed [it].
C. But if he originally took it so that it should not perish,
D. he is exempt [from tithing it].

7. Intentionality figures in the ordering of things. How man wants things to be, and how man perceives things to be, governs how they are held to be. It is man through his powers of observation who decides what is orderly and what is confused; there is no established, immutable order. Everything is relative to human perceptions, and man creates order in line with his perceptions of the world around him (Mandelbaum, p. ix). Since God recognizes confusion and insists on division and order, God's perceptions are comparable to man's. Since human thought or attitude and human action affect susceptibility of objects to uncleanness or its opposite, holiness, the exact correspondence of human and divine intellect is at the foundations of not only this tractate but many others. The law does not work *ex opere operato,* but wholly depends upon the circumstances of the householder's intentionality as expressed in his deed. The givens of the law contain numerous principles that make that conception concrete. The primacy of intentionality over actuality is shown, among many instances, in the following law:

M. Kilayim

9:5 A. Clothes dealers sell [garments of diverse kinds] in their usual manner
B. provided that they do not intend, in a hot sun, [for the garments to protect them] from the hot sun, or in the rain, [for the garments to protect them] from the rain.
C. And the more scrupulous ones tie [the garments of diverse kinds] on a stick.
9:6 A. Tailors sew [garments of diverse kinds] in their usual manner,
B. provided that they do not intend, in a hot sun, [for the garments to protect them] from the hot sun, or in the rain, [for the garments to protect them] from the rain.
C. And the more scrupulous ones sew [while sitting] on the ground [with the garments resting on the ground as well].

Observance of the laws of diverse kinds makes Israel holy, there being a correlation between order and holiness (Mandelbaum, *Kilayim*, p. 2). This is the conception of the priestly code: man is to restore the world from its present condition of chaos to its original, orderly state and so to make the world ready once again for sanctification (Mandelbaum, p. 3). What is important to the priestly code is that the world should be returned from its present condition of confusion to its original, ordered state, as God had created it; the Mishnah underlines man's power to impose order upon the world, a capacity untouched by historical events (Mandelbaum, p. 4). The Mishnah regards man as able to impose order on a world in chaos and so participate in the process of creation. So the Mishnah maintains that it is man, not fixed, material rules, who decides what is orderly and what is confused, a conception P does not know (Mandelbaum, p. 3).

8. The attitude of the owner of a substance subject to more than a single classification dictates the operative classification for that object. If the owner (the priest) regards the substance as food, it must be treated as food, even though the substance may not customarily be used for that purpose. A man's own intention determines the status of consecration, one way or another:

M. Terumot

11:5   A.   [As regards] the pits of produce in the status of heave-offering –
       B.   when he [the priest] keeps them, they are forbidden [for consumption by nonpriests].
       C.   But if he throws them out, they are permitted.
       D.   And so [in the case of] the bones of Holy Things [animal-offerings] –
       E.   when he keeps them, they are forbidden [to nonpriests] –
       F.   but if he throws them out, they are permitted.
       G.   Coarse bran [from grain in the status of heave-offering] is permitted [for consumption by nonpriests].
       H.   Fine bran from fresh [wheat in the status of heave-offering] is forbidden [to nonpriests].
       I.   But [fine bran] from old [wheat in the status of heave-offering] is permitted.
       J.   [The priest] may treat heave-offering just as he treats unconsecrated produce [he may throw out the parts he does not normally eat],
       K.   One who prepares fine flour [from wheat in the status of heave-offering], deriving a qab or two from each seah [of wheat], may not destroy the residue [which is edible].
       L.   Rather, he places it in a concealed place.

9. God responds to human intentions and notices the human actions that convey the intentionality of a situation. God's attitudes are the same as man's. What a person takes for his own benefit, where God

has a claim, is something God, too, will want. The action of the farmer tells God the intention that is in play. If the farmer refrains from eating produce in the field as if it were his own, God's prior claim does not come into play. If he overreaches his privilege, either by making a meal of the produce in his field or by claiming to be its sole owner, he loses his privilege to eat it altogether until he tithes.[4] The intentionality of the householder is the governing consideration. Jaffee (p. 120): "If we can establish that a householder has decided to use a specific batch of produce in a meal, that produce may no longer be used even as a snack unless it is first tithed... once the intention to make a meal of produce has been formulated, we interpret all subsequent acts of eating as expressions of that original intention. The produce, now deemed to have been appropriated by the householder, must be tithed, before it is consumed." This is shown in the following, which makes the point that produce, prepared as if it were to be part of a meal, will indeed be so used; the householder's actions shown his intentions and guide in determining whether he has imposed upon himself the obligation to tithe (Jaffee, p. 121). Once the intention to use produce in a meal has been formulated – the moment at which untithed produce is designated for use on the Sabbath – the produce is liable to the removal of tithes, without regard to when or how it is actually used (Jaffee, p. 125). An indication of intent is the action that one takes, as in the following, where the case is a very concrete one:

M. Maaserot

4:5   A.   One who husks barley removes the husks [from the kernels] one by one, and eats [without tithing].
      B.   But if he husked [a few kernels] and placed [them] in his hand, he is required [to tithe].
      C.   One who husks parched kernels of wheat sifts [the kernels] from hand to hand, and eats [without tithing] .
      D.   But if he sifted [the kernels] and placed [them] inside his shirt, he is required [to tithe].

10. Priests cannot claim their dues whenever they choose; God has no active role in establishing when the produce must be tithed. God plays a passive role, only responding to human actions and intentions; God's claims are only reflexes of those very claims on the part of Israelite farmers; God's interest in his share of the harvest is first provoked by the desire of the farmer for the ripened fruit of his

---

[4]Martin S. Jaffee, *Mishnah's Theology of Tithing: A Study of Tractate Maaserot* (Chico, 1981: Scholars Press for Brown Judaic Studies) p. 4.

labor; his claim to that fruit becomes binding only when the farmer makes ready to claim his own rights to its use (Jaffee, pp. 4-5).

11. God recognizes the intentionality of an individual and judges the action done by that individual in accord with what is intended. A given action may be penalized or not, by heaven or by earthly action, in response to the intention of the one who does it. God therefore is fully informed of what people are thinking when they take various actions, and individual actions are known to heaven and the attitude conveyed in them is assessed by heaven:

M. Shabbat

2:5   A.   He who puts out a lamp because he is afraid of gentiles, thugs, a bad spirit,

      B.   or if it is so that a sick person might sleep,

      C.   is exempt [from liability to punishment].

      D.   [If he did so] to spare the lamp, the oil, the wick,

      E.   he is liable.

      F.   And R. Yosé exempts [him from liability to punishment] in all instances except for [one who does so to spare] the wick,

      G.   because he [thereby] makes [it into] charcoal.

This means that actions bear no intrinsic character, for example, being prohibited or permitted, but are judged only relative to the intention that produces them. The consideration of intentionality in classifying an action is expressed in so many words in the following:

M. Shabbat

22:3   A.   A person breaks a jar to eat dried figs from it,

      B.   on condition that he not intend [in opening the jar] to make it into a utensil.

      C.   "But they do not pierce the plug of a jar," the words of R. Judah.

      D.   And sages permit it.

      E.   And they do not pierce it on the side.

      F.   And if it was pierced, one should not put wax on it,

      G.   because he would [have to] spread it over [which is a prohibited act] –

12. It is possible by an act of intention to change the physical circumstances that affect a person. If one cannot physically correct a situation that violates the law, he may do so by an act of intentionality:

M. Pesahim

3:7   A.   He who goes to slaughter his Passover lamb, to circumcise his son, or to eat the betrothal meal at his father-in-law's house,

      B.   and remembers that he has left some leaven in his house,

      C.   if he can go back and remove it and go on to do his religious duty, let him go back and remove it.

D.   But if not, let him nullify it in his heart.

E.   [If he was going] to help against an invasion or to save someone from drowning in a river, from thugs, from a fire, or from a suddenly collapsed house, let him nullify it in his heart.

F.   [If he was going] to enjoy the festival rest on a pleasure jaunt, let him go back immediately [and remove the leaven].

Improper intentionality invalidates an otherwise validly performed act.

13. The issue of intentionality enters into the evaluation of the use of language. God cares about the honor that is owing to human beings and takes that into account in assessing the validity of vows. Hence if a person is able to say that he would not have brought into disrepute people deserving of honor, including himself, God does not regard such a vow as binding:

M. Nedarim

9:9   A.   They unloose a vow for a man by reference to his own honor and by reference to the honor of his children.

B.   They say to him, "Had you known that the next day they would say about you, 'That's the way of So-and-so, going around divorcing his wives,'

C.   "and that about your daughters they'd be saying, 'They're daughters of a divorcée! What did their mother do to get herself divorced' [would you have taken a vow]?"

D.   And [if] he then said, "Had I known that things would be that way, I should never have taken such a vow,"

E.   lo, this [vow] is not binding.

14. An act committed with the intention of sinning that in fact is not a sin is not culpable. Intentionality takes effect only when the facts of the matter conform to the intention:

M. Nazir

4:3   A.   A woman who took a vow as a Nazir but nonetheless went around drinking wine and contracting corpse uncleanness –

B.   lo, this one receives forty stripes.

C.   [If] her husband annulled the vow for her, but she did not know that her husband had annulled it for her and nonetheless continued to go around drinking wine and contracting corpse uncleanness,

D.   she does not receive forty stripes.

E.   R. Judah says, "If she does not receive forty stripes, nonetheless, she should receive punishment for disobedience."

15. A valid act can be carried out only by one who knows precisely what he is doing and also has the power to do what he is doing. A person who has not got the power to act, or who is not aware, or who has not formed the correct intention, or who cannot express the correct

intention, cannot carry out a valid action: the following is only one illustration of how this principle works:

M. Gittin

2:6 A. [If] a minor received [the writ of divorce from the husband,] and then passed the point of maturity,

B. a deaf-mute and he regained the power of speech,

C. a blind man and he regained the power of sight,

D. an idiot and he regained his senses,

E. a gentile and he converted,

F. [it remains] invalid.

G. But [if it was received from the husband] by one of sound senses who then lost the power of speech and then regained his senses,

H. by one who had the power of sight and who was blinded but then recovered the power of sight,

I. by one who was sane and then became insane and regained his sanity, it is valid.

J. This is the general principle: In any case in which the agent at the outset and at the end was in full command of his senses, it is valid.

16. Intentionality is limited by the facts of the case as well. One may consecrate something to no effect. The sacred takes effect not automatically, *ex opere operato*, but only when appropriate, that is, when what is subject to sanctification in fact can become sanctified. This is because God has a stake in the matter as well, and God's intentionality, as much as humanity's, plays its part in the assessment of a situation:

M. Zebahim

9:1 A. The altar sanctifies that which is appropriate to it.

B. R. Joshua says, "Whatever is appropriate to the altar fires, if it has gone up [onto the fires], should not go down, since it is said, 'This is the burnt-offering – that which goes up on the hearth on the altar' (Lev. 6:9) – just as the burnt-offering, which is appropriate to the altar fires, if it has gone up, should not go down, so whatever is appropriate to the altar fires, if it has gone up, should not go down."

C. Rabban Gamaliel says, "Whatever is appropriate to the altar, if it has gone up, should not go down. As it is said, 'This is the burnt-offering on the hearth on the altar' (Lev. 6:2) – just as the burnt-offering, which is appropriate to the altar, if it has gone up, should not go down, so whatever is appropriate to the altar, if it has gone up, should not go down."

D. The difference between the opinion of Rabban Gamaliel and the opinion of R. Joshua is only the blood and the drink-offerings.

E. For Rabban Gamaliel says, "They should not [having been placed on the altar] go down."

F. And R. Joshua says, "They should go down."

Proper procedures must always prevail, and these govern where one has formulated matters in an improper way. One must conform to the Torah, even though one's action is votive and not obligatory. Whatever one has said, he must conform to accepted usage. If one vowed to bring an offering in some form other than normal, he is obligated to do things in the correct manner:

M. Menahot

12:3   A.   [He who says,] "Lo, I pledge myself [to bring] a meal-offering made of barley," [in any case] must bring one made of wheat.

        B.   [He who says, "Lo, I pledge myself to bring a meal-offering made] of meal," must bring one made of fine flour.

        C.   [He who says, "Lo, I pledge myself to bring a meal-offering] without wine and frankincense," must bring one with oil and frankincense.

        D.   [He who says, "Lo, I pledge myself to bring a meal-offering made of] a half-tenth," must bring one made of a whole tenth.

        E.   [He who says, "Lo , I pledge myself to bring a meal-offering made of a tenth and a half-tenth," brings one made of two [whole] tenths [of an ephah of fine flour].

        F.   R. Simeon declares free [of the obligation to bring a meal-offering in any of the foregoing cases], for he has not volunteered [a freewill meal-offering] in the way in which people volunteer [to make a freewill meal-offering].

17. What is permitted when done in innocence is forbidden when done with an improper motive:

M. Bekhorot

5:3   A.   He who slit the ear of the firstling –

        B.   "lo, this should never be slaughtered [by reason of a blemish]," the words of R. Eliezer.

        C.   And sages say, "When another blemish will appear in it, it is slaughtered on its account."

        D.   M^CSH B: An old ram, with its hair dangling. A quaestor saw it.

        E.   He said, "What sort of thing is this?"

        F.   They said to him, "It is a firstling. And it is slaughtered only if there is a blemish on it."

        G.   He took a dagger and slit its ear.

        H.   And the case came before sages, and they declared it permitted.

        I.   He saw that they permitted [it] and went and tore the ears of other firstlings.

        J.   And they declared [them] prohibited.

        K.   One time children were playing in the field, and they tied the tails of lambs to one another. And the tail of one of them split off. And lo, it was a firstling.

        L.   And the case came before sages, and they declared it permitted.

        M.   They saw that they declared it permitted, and they went and tied together the tails of other firstlings.

        N.   And they declared [them] prohibited.

This repertoire, its breadth in topic and depth in effect suffices, to make the point that a principal premise of theology, expressed in normative law, maintains intention is the governing consideration.

B. The Yoke of the Kingdom of Heaven and the Commandments

The second, and equally pervasive and decisive, premise of the religious attitudes and theological convictions of our sages of blessed memory, beyond the correspondence of God's and humanity's emotional repertoire and modes of reasoning and range of attitudes, is that God wants something of humanity in general, but of Israel in particular, and that is, acceptance of God's will. God has made humanity free to choose; has informed humanity of what God wants; and responds to the freely made choices of the human being. The will of God is conveyed in the Torah, and the response of humanity to God takes the form of carrying out or defying the commandments of the Torah. These convictions take the mythic form of talk of accepting "the yoke of the kingdom of heaven" and "the yoke of the commandments." The law of the Mishnah and the exegesis of the Midrash compilations go over these matters.

"The yoke of the kingdom of heaven" represents a metaphor for the conception that Israel forms a supernatural people governed by God; "the yoke of the commandments" speaks of the religious duties that that people are to carry out. This theological principle encompasses a wide range of specific premises concerning right conduct under God's will; the status of Israel; where and when the kingdom of heaven takes place; and the like.

1. Israel accepts daily the rule of the Kingdom of heaven and the rule of the commandments (M. Ber. 2:2H-I):

    H. Said R. Joshua b. Qorha, "Why does [the passage of] Shema precede [that of] And it shall come to pass [if you keep my commandments]?

    I. "So that one may first accept upon himself the yoke of the kingdom of heaven and afterwards may accept the yoke of the commandments."

2. God intervenes on an ad hoc basis, and events or locations in which such an intervention has taken place are carefully commemorated (B. Ber. 9:1). Natural phenomena, too, represent divine intervention or result from God's action (M. Ber. 9:2). A variety of events involving the individual's private life are noteworthy occasions, marked by an appropriate response in a blessing. Noteworthy events, requiring the recitation of a blessing, are unfavorable as much as favorable ones (M. Ber. 9:5).

3.   Study of the Torah outweighs all other meritorious actions, and that
      is the study of God's rules for the life of Israel:

M. Peah

1:1   A.   These are things which have no [specified] measure:
       B.   (1) [the quantity of produce designated as] peah, (2) [the quantity of
             produce given as] first fruits, (3) [the value of] the appearance-
             offering, (4) [the performance of] righteous deeds, (5) and [time
             spent in] study of Torah.
       C.   These are things the benefit of which a person enjoys in this world,
             while the principal remains for him in the world to come:
       D.   (1) [deeds in] honor of father and mother, (2) [performance of]
             righteous deeds, (3) and [acts which] bring peace between a man
             and his fellow.
       E.   But the study of Torah is as important as all of them together.

4.   The covenant is spelled out in so many words, and obedience to the
      law is on account of the covenant. God and Israel are bound in the
      same way by the same covenant, and Israel is confident of what God
      will do by reason of the covenant; here is a concrete, halakhic
      expression of the centrality of the covenant in the relationship of God
      and Israel, in the citizenship of Israel in God's kingdom:

       A.   During the afternoon of the last festival day [of Passover during the
             fourth and seventh years of the Sabbatical cycle, the farmers] would
             recite the confession [Deut. 26:13-15, stating that they have properly
             distributed or destroyed all consecrated produce from their
             domain, cf. M. M.S. 5:6]....

M. M.S.

5:13   A.   Look down from your holy dwelling place in heaven –
        B.   we did what you required of us, now you do what you promised
              us.
        C.   Look down from your holy dwelling place in heaven and bless your
              people Israel –
        D.   with sons and daughters.
        E.   And the earth which you gave us –
        F.   with dew and rain and with offspring of cattle,
        G.   As you vowed to our fathers [to give them] a land flowing with
              milk and honey –
        H.   in order to give the fruit a [sweet] taste.

5.   The kingdom of God takes place not in location but in time.
      Specifically, the kingdom of heaven takes place on the Sabbath and
      on Holy Days, which are carefully differentiated from ordinary days.
      God's oversight of conduct on the Sabbath is detailed. What counts
      is not only cessation of labor but preservation of the clear lines of
      demarcation between domains. On ordinary days, these lines of
      demarcation are null; on holy days, they descend and bear

consequence and are not to be violated. The advent of holy time therefore marks the point at which the differentiation of space along lines deemed intrinsic or natural takes effect. At that point, therefore, people may not transport objects from one domain to the other, as a mark of the distinction between domains and the proper differentiation of all things by their species or types. This is expressed in the following:

M. Shabbat

1:1   A.   [Acts of]transporting objects from one domain to another [which violate] the Sabbath (1) are two, which [indeed] are four [for one who is] inside, (2) and two which are four [for one who is] outside.

      B.   How so?

      C.   [If on the Sabbath] the beggar stands outside and the householder inside,

      D.   [and] the beggar stuck his hand inside and put [a beggar's bowl] into the hand of the householder,

      E.   or if he took [something] from inside it and brought it out,

      F.   the beggar is liable, the householder is exempt.

      G.   [If] the householder stuck his hand outside and put [something] into the hand of the beggar,

      H.   or if he took [something] from it and brought it inside,

      I.   the householder is liable, and the beggar is exempt.

      J.   [If] the beggar stuck his hand inside, and the householder took [something] from it,

      K.   or if [the householder] put something in it and he [the beggar] removed,

      L.   both of them are exempt.

      M.   [If] the householder put his hand outside and the beggar took [something] from it,

      N.   or if [the beggar] put something into it and [the householder] brought it back inside,

      O.   both of them are exempt.

The sanctity of the Sabbath changes the order of being, all things being restricted to the intrinsic or inherent purpose for which they were created; on the Sabbath things may serve only that purpose and no other; an object that serves a purpose illicit on the Sabbath may not even be touched.

6.   People form part of the tableau of sanctification, doing so by taking their proper places – at home, in their village – and staying there for the span of holy time. Where people eat is where they live. With whom they eat defines the community of which they form a proprietary constituent. There is a clear relationship between the advent of holy time, the selection of a place in which to eat a meal (if only fictively), and the taking up of a particular place of residence for that occasion. The duty of the human being in holy time is to situate

himself and his family in some appropriate place and to take up permanent residence at that place, signified by eating his food there. The perfection of the holy day in part is represented by all persons, as much as all things, being at rest, in their proper place, eating where they should. The condition of sanctification, then, is, in part, that things be in their proper place, in right array before the Creator. The interplay between time and space then forms the premise; God has determined that, at the advent of the holy time, persons and things must be where they belong, and, as we already have seen, be used for that for which they were created. The indicative gesture of self-location is eating a meal.

7. The kingdom of heaven forms a continuum with this world. All things are hierarchically ordered by classes as to their sanctification, and when Holy Things are changed from one classification to another, it must be to a higher, not a lower, classification:

M. Megillah

3:1 A. Townsfolk who sold (1) a street of a town buy with its proceeds a synagogue.

B. [If they sold] (2) a synagogue, they buy an ark.

C. [If they sold] (3) an ark, they buy wrappings.

D. [If they sold] (4) wrappings, they buy scrolls [of the prophets or writings].

E. [If they sold] (5) scrolls, they buy a Torah scroll.

F. But if they sold (5) a Torah scroll, they should not buy scrolls.

G. [If they sold] (4) scrolls, they should not buy wrappings.

H. [If they sold] (3) wrappings, they should not buy an ark.

I. [If they sold] (2) an ark, they should not buy a synagogue.

J. [If they sold] (1) a synagogue, they should not buy a street.

K. And so with the surplus [of the proceeds of any of] these.

L. "They do not sell that which belongs to the public to a private person,

M. "because they thereby diminish its level of sanctity," the words of R. Judah.

N. They said to him, "If so, [they should] not [sell] from a large town to a small one."

8. What sort of king is God? God is a ruler who joins justice and mercy. Justice marks God's government of the world. There is an exact balance between a person's actions and the fate that is meted out, and that pertains to both sinners and saints:

M. Sotah

1:7 A. By that same measure by which a man metes out [to others], they mete out to him:

B. She primped herself for sin, the Omnipresent made her repulsive.

C. She exposed herself for sin, the Omnipresent exposed her.

     D.   With the thigh she began to sin, and afterward with the belly, therefore the thigh suffers the curse first, and afterward the belly.

     E.   (But the rest of the body does not escape [punishment].)

1:9   A.   And so is it on the good side:

     B.   Miriam waited a while for Moses, since it is said, "And his sister stood afar off" (Ex. 2:4), therefore, Israel waited on her seven days in the wilderness, since it is said, "And the people did not travel on until Miriam was brought in again" (Num. 12:15).

     C.   Joseph had the merit of burying his father, and none of his brothers was greater than he, since it is said, "And Joseph went up to bury his father... and there went up with him both chariots and horsemen" (Gen. 50:7,9).

     D.   We have none so great as Joseph, for only Moses took care of his [bones].

     E.   Moses had the merit of burying the bones of Joseph, and none in Israel was greater than He, since it is said, "And Moses took the bones of Joseph with him" (Ex. 13:19).

     F.   We have none so great as Moses, for only the Holy One blessed be He took care of his [bones], since it is said, "And he buried him in the valley" (Deut. 34:6).

     G.   And not of Moses alone have they stated [this rule], but of all righteous people, since it is said, "And your righteousness shall go before you. The glory of the Lord shall gather you [in death]" (Isa. 58:8).

9.   Doing the commandments brings heavenly response and blessing, and not doing them produces heavenly response and the holding back of blessings; keeping the commandments bears a this-worldly result:

M. Qiddushin

1:10   A.   Whoever does a single commandment – they do well for him and lengthen his days.

     B.   And he inherits the Land.

     C.   And whoever does not do a single commandment – they do not do well for him and do not lengthen his days.

     D.   And he does not inherit the Land.

     E.   Whoever has learning in Scripture, Mishnah, and right conduct will not quickly sin, since it is said, "And a threefold cord is not quickly broken" (Qoh. 4:12). And whoever does not have learning in Scripture, Mishnah, and right conduct has no share in society.

That is especially the case for one of the the most important of the commandments, which is study of the Torah. Study of the Torah yields long-term benefits both in this world and the next world:

M. Qiddushin

4:14   L.   R. Nehorai says, "I should lay aside every trade in the world and teach my son only Torah.

M.   "For a man eats its fruits in this world, and the principal remains for the world to come.

N.   "But other trades are not that way.

O.   "When a man gets sick or old or has pains and cannot do his job, lo, he dies of starvation.

P.   "But with Torah it is not that way.

Q.   "But it keeps him from all evil when he is young, and it gives him a future and a hope when he is old...."

Study of the Torah and mastery thereof transform relationships; study of the Torah brings a person into the kingdom of heaven and the world to come. The master of Torah takes precedence over the father, since the latter gives physical life but the former, the life of the world to come; studying the Torah creates supernatural relationships:

M. Baba Mesia

2:11 A.   [If he has to choose between seeking] what he has lost and what his father has lost,

B.   his own takes precedence.

C.   ...What he has lost and what his master has lost,

D.   his own takes precedence.

E.   ...What his father has lost and what his master has lost, that of his master takes precedence.

F.   For his father brought him into this world.

G.   But his master, who taught him wisdom, will bring him into the life of the world to come.

H.   But if his father is a sage, that of his father takes precedence.

I.   [If] his father and his master were carrying heavy burdens, he removes that of his master, and afterward removes that of his father.

J.   [If] his father and his master were taken captive,

K.   he ransoms his master, and afterward he ransoms his father.

L.   But if his father is a sage, he ransoms his father, and afterward he ransoms his master.

10.   Israel, of course, is the locus of the kingdom of God, since to Israel the Torah is given. "Israel" is a supernatural category, for Israel consists of all those who are born in Israel, except for those who deny the principles of the faith. The categories are defined in terms of belief: affirming a given doctrine, denying another. That fact bears in its wake the implication that Israel as a social entity, encompassing each of its members, is defined by reference to matters of correct doctrine. All "Israelites" – persons who hold the correct opinion – then constitute "Israel." Here is an "Israel" that, at first glance, is defined not in relationships but intransitively and intrinsically. What this means, therefore, is that Israel is not a social entity at all like other social entities but an entity that finds definition, as to genus and not species, elsewhere.

M. Sanhedrin

10:1   A.   All Israelites have a share in the world to come,

      B.   as it is said, "your people also shall be all righteous, they shall inherit the land forever; the branch of my planting, the work of my hands, that I may be glorified" (Isa. 60:21).

      C.   And these are the ones who have no portion in the world to come:

      D.   He who says, the resurrection of the dead is a teaching which does not derive from the Torah, and the Torah does not come from heaven; and an Epicurean.

      E.   R. Aqiba says, "Also: He who reads in heretical books,

      F.   "and he who whispers over a wound and says, 'I will put none of the diseases upon you which I have put on the Egyptians, for I am the Lord who heals you' (Ex. 15:26)."

      G.   Abba Saul says, "Also: He who pronounces the divine Name as it is spelled out."

Israel is defined inclusively: to be "Israel" is to have a share in the world to come. "Israel" then is a social entity that is made up of those who share a common conviction, and that "Israel" therefore bears an other-worldly destiny. Other social entities are not so defined within the Mishnah – and that by definition! – and it must follow that (an) "Israel" in the conception of the authorship of the Mishnah is *sui generis*, in that other social entities do not find their definition within the range of supernatural facts pertinent to "Israel"; an "Israel" is a social group that endows its individual members with life in the world to come; an "Israel"[ite] is one who enjoys the world to come. Excluded from this "Israel" are "Israel"[ite]s who within the established criteria of social identification exclude themselves. The power to define by relationships does not run out, however, since in this supernatural context of an Israel that is *sui generis*, we still know who is "Israel" because we are told who is "not-Israel," now, specific nonbelievers or sinners. These are, as we should expect, persons who reject the stated belief.

10:2   A.   Three kings and four ordinary folk have no portion in the world to come.

      B.   Three kings: Jeroboam, Ahab, and Manasseh.

      C.   R. Judah says, "Manasseh has a portion in the world to come,

      D.   "since it is said, 'And he prayed to him and he was entreated of him and heard his supplication and brought him again to Jerusalem into his kingdom' (2 Chr. 33:13)."

      E.   They said to him, "To his kingdom he brought him back, but to the life of the world to come he did not bring him back."

      F.   Four ordinary folk: Balaam, Doeg, Ahitophel, and Gehazi.

Not only persons, but also classes of Israelites are specified, in all cases contributing to the definition of (an) Israel. The excluded classes of

Israelites bear in common a supernatural fault, which is that they have sinned against God.

C. Words Form the Bridge from Humanity to God

Speech is enchanted and bears supernatural power. The words people say embody their intentionality in an irrevocable form; words form the bridge between earth and heaven; words constitute forms of action. God therefore hears and responds to prayer; the proper formulation of documents that engage heaven's interest, for example, those that affect a woman's status of consecration to a given man, likewise express this same conception. So, too, vows and oaths that people take are heard by heaven and bind the person who uses that language. God responds to what people say and to what they feel. The principle here may be expressed in a very simple way. Statements are performative and heaven enforces them. Since Scripture provides for pledges of valuation, these are effective; but they pertain only to persons of a determinate classification and of sound senses:

Arakhim

1:1 A. All pledge the valuation [of others] and are subject to the pledge of valuation [by others],

B. vow [the worth of another] and are subject to the vow [of payment of their worth by another]:

C. priests and Levites and Israelites, women and slaves.

D. A person of doubtful sexual traits and a person who exhibits traits of both sexes vow [the worth of another] and are subject to the vow [of payments of their worth by another], pledge the valuation [of others], but are not subject to the pledge of valuation by others,

E. for evaluated is only one who is certainly a male or certainly a female.

F. A deaf-mute, an imbecile, and a minor are subject to the vow [of payment of their worth by another], and are subject to the pledge of valuation by others, but do not vow the worth, and do not pledge the valuation, of others,

G. for they do not possess understanding.

H. One who is less than a month old is subject to the vow [of payment of worth by another], but is not subject to the pledge of valuation.

It follows that people are responsible for what they say, and God holds them to their use of binding expressions. Words spoken in anger bear consequence of a practical order. But vows made in error or under constraint are not binding, because we regard such vows as impaired at the outset and never having been valid. A vow to be binding must express in words the exact, and appropriate or binding, intent of the one who takes the vow. Hence we assess the act by reference to the circumstance or intent:

Mishnah-tractate Nedarim

3:1   A.   Four [types of] vows did sages declare not binding: (1) Vows of incitement, (2) vows of exaggeration, (3) vows made in error, and (4) vows [broken] under constraint.

       B.   Vows of incitement: How so?

       C.   [If] one was selling something and said, "Qonam if I chop the price down for you to under a sela," and the other says, "Qonam if I pay you more than a sheqel" –

       D.   [then] both of them agree at three denars.

       E.   R. Eliezer b. Jacob says, "Also: He who wants to force his fellow by a vow to eat with him says, 'Any vow which I am going to vow is null' – so long as he is mindful at the moment of his vow."

Now to specific cases.

1. God hears what people say, and therefore seemly speech, as much as proper behavior or restraint, is taken into account on the Sabbath. There are actions or words one may not do, not by reason of a specific, principled prohibition, but only by appeal to what us unseemly or inappropriate:

M. Shabbat

23:1   A.   A man [on the Sabbath] asks for jugs of wine or oil from his fellow,

       B.   provided that he does not say to him, "Lend [them] to me."

       C.   And so a woman [borrows] loaves of bread from her neighbor.

       D.   And if one does not trust the other, he leaves his cloak with him and settles with him after the Sabbath.

2. God hears and answers the specific prayers of specific persons, responding to the circumstance and character of each, as well as to the timing of the prayer. But it does not pay to pray for something out of season, that is, beyond the limits of nature. These are the givens of the tractate overall, as evidenced in its opening statements:

M. Taanit

1:1   A.   When do they include the mention of the powers of rain [in the Prayer]?

       B.   R. Eliezer says, "On the first day of the Festival [of Tabernacles]."

       C.   R. Joshua says, "On the last day of the festival."

       D.   Said to him R. Joshua, "Since rain is only a sign of a curse when it comes on the festival itself, why should one mention it?"

       E.   Said to him R. Eliezer, "I, too, have said so not for the purpose of asking [for rain] but only of mentioning restoring the wind and bringing down the rain: [That is,] in its due season."

       F.   He said to him, "If so, one should always make mention of it."

God's particular response to the circumstance of the one who prays, and the attitude that he brings to the prayer, is attested by the requirement for the position of prayer leader for a fast:

3. Since God hears and answers prayer, the correct prayers must be said, lest the entire community be harmed by incorrect prayer. Anyone who singles himself out in any way is not to lead the community in prayer. Special concern is expressed to avoid implying that there are two domains in heaven:

4:9   A.   He who says, "May the good folk bless you," lo, this is the way of heresy.
      B.   [He who says] "Even to a bird's nest do your mercies extend" –
      C.   "May your name be remembered for good" –
      D.   "We give thanks, we give thanks" – they silence him.
      E.   He who uses euphemisms in the pericope of the prohibited relationships [Lev. 18] they silence him.
      F.   He who says, "'And you shall not give any of your seed to make them pass through fire to Molech' means, 'And you shall not give of your seed to make it pass to heathendom'" – they silence him with a rebuke.

It follows that language is performative and always affective.

M. Shabuot

4:13 A.   (1) "I impose an oath on you," (2) "I command you," (3) "I bind you" – lo, these are liable.
      B.   "By heaven and earth" – lo, these are exempt.
      C.   (1) "By [the name of] Alef-dalet [Adonai]" or (2) "Yud-he [Yahweh]," (3) "By the Almighty," (4) "By Hosts," (5) "By him who is merciful and gracious," (6) "By him who is long-suffering and abundant in mercy," or by any other euphemism –
      D.   lo, these are liable.

Language may function *ex opere operato*. Thus, when assessing an oath, we pay attention to a formulation that provides an exegesis of the operative language. We treat as binding vows that do not carry with them their own exegesis. If there is a possibility of interpreting a vow as valid or invalid and the vow carries no specification, it is treated as valid.

D. The Sanctity of the Land of Israel and the People of Israel

Besides the language that people use, another locus of enchantment is a particular territory, the Land of Israel. The promise of the Land forms a critical part of the covenant; God undertakes to the patriarchs to provide them with the holy land, and the measure of Israel's success in keeping its part of the covenant lies in Israel's possession of the land. So land, no less than language, forms a central religious category that the rabbis take for granted, and upon which sizable theological constructions are built. The Land of Israel is enchanted, different from all other territory, enjoying a unique relationship to God and to the people, Israel. God sanctified the land by giving it to the chosen people as an exclusive possession. Israel works the Land and handles the produce in accord with God's wishes.

It follows that, by the covenant recorded in the Torah, God owes Israel sustenance to keep the promise he made to all Israelites who live in the Land (Brooks, p. 19), "So God alone determines what grain should be given to the poor and separates this from those crops that the householder is about to reap and take as his own. The householder is entirely excluded from this process; he must not interfere in God's allotment." God owns the Land of Israel, and shares partnership in the Land with the Israelite farmer. All are supposed to share equally in the bounty of the Land of Israel (cf. Brooks, *Peah*, p. 1). The needy are entitled to a share, and the householder must give part of the produce to them. They receive other parts of the crop by means of accident, for example, loss or neglect of part of the produce is deemed a mark of designation of what is lost for the poor's entitlement. The poor are in the status of priests, eating what no other Israelite may eat (Brooks, p. 17). God makes certain landless castes or classes have their share of the food that they need. This God does by assigning to them part of what is coming to God. God's share comes from tenant farmers – that is the standing of the Israelite householder throughout. The Land of Israel is holy, and Israel's living on that particular land imparts holiness to the land on which they live, but also marks Israel as holy. The land is enchanted, therefore, just as much as language is enchanted.

1. God owns the Land of Israel. What is said concerning givens of the law pertains as much to theology; God is the material, concrete, practical owner of the Holy Land, and that fact accounts for the sanctification of the Land. Gentiles have absolutely no rights of ownership to the Holy Land and their crops are not subject to tithing. A tenant farmer leasing from a gentile tithes the rental as if it were his own produce (M. Dem. 6:2).[5] Israel imparts sanctity; its presence and its perceptions determine the rule. The sanctity of the seventh year depends on the actions and will of the people of Israel, who are instruments of sanctification.[6]

M. Shebiit

6:1 A. Three provinces [are delineated] with regard to [the laws of] the Sabbatical year:

---

[5]Richard S. Sarason, *A History of the Mishnaic Law of Agriculture. Section Three. A Study of Tractate Demai. Part One. Commentary* (Leiden, 1979: E.J. Brill) p. 202.
[6]Louis E. Newman, *The Sanctity of the Seventh Year: A Study of Mishnah-Tractate Shebiit* (Chico, 1983: Scholars Press for Brown Judaic Studies) p. 19.

B.   (1) All [of the land] which was occupied by those who returned from Babylonia [the area] from the Land of Israel [in the south] to Kezib [in the north]:

C.   [That which grows of itself in this region] may not be eaten, and [the land of this region] may not be cultivated.

D.   (2) All [of the land] which was occupied by those who came out of Egypt, [the area] from Kezib to the river [the brook of Egypt, in the south], and [from Kezib] to Amana [in the north]:

E.   [That which grows of itself in these regions] may be eaten, but [the land of these regions] may not be cultivated.

F.   (3) [The land] from the river and from Amana and beyond:

G.   [That which grows of itself in these regions] may be eaten, and [the land of these regions] may be cultivated.

Israelites, by dwelling on the land, make it holy if they have lived in an area for a longer period of time, that area is holier than others (Newman, p. 19).

2.   God remains lord of the Land of Israel: "...Historical catastrophe has left the sacred economy of Israel undisturbed. While the temple is gone, the Land remains holy and its fruit is still under the claim of God" (Jaffee, p. 5). "Nowhere do the framers of Maaserot expect or allow for unilateral or uncontrollable actions proceeding from the initiative of God... his status as Lord depends upon the action of his remaining people. that is the whole point of linking God's claim upon the tithes to the social rhythms of the agricultural enterprise. Those who impose upon themselves the task of reconstructing the human and social fabric of Israelite life make effective the holiness of the Land and make real the claims of its God" (Jaffee, p. 6).

3.   The Land of Israel has a special claim on the people of Israel, who have the right to move there and cannot be removed from there, and the same is so for Jerusalem. On the hierarchy of sanctification, these places of course are at the pinnacle:

M. Ketubot

13:11   A.   All have the right to bring up [his or her family] to the Land of Israel, but none has the right to remove [his or her family] therefrom.

B.   All have the right to bring up to Jerusalem, but none has the right to bring down –

C.   all the same are men and women.

E. Random Events or Chance Express God's Will

Nothing happens by chance; all things express God's will. Therefore, if something happens apparently randomly, that is to be taken as a mark of how God wants things to come out. An example of the operation of chance is as follows: heave-offering must be separated in a random, accidental fashion, and not by an act of selection. A person may not ascertain the quantity of the produce or take a predetermined and measured amount; the process must include an aspect of chance:

M. Terumot

1:7   A.   They do not separate heave-offering by (1) a measure [of volume], or by (2) weight, or by (3) a count [of the number of pieces of fruit being separated as heave-offering].

       B.   But he separates the heave-offering of (1) [produce] which has been measured, of (2) that which has been weighed, and of (3) that which has been counted.

       C.   They do not separate heave-offering in a basket or in a vessel which [hold a known] measure.

       D.   But he separates heave-offering in them [if they are] one-half or one-third part [filled].

       E.   He may not separate heave-offering in [a basket which holds one] seah, [if it is] one-half part [filled], since the half thereof is a [known] measure.

It follows that what happens "by accident" in fact carries out God's will and purpose. Brooks, *Peah*, p. 18, states, "Only when accident separates grain from a normal crop is the food deemed to have been set aside by God for the poor. We therefore speak of produce that is set aside without any identifiable cause. Since neither the householder, his workers, nor anyone else has acted to identify which produce within a crop is to be designated, we know that God alone has reserved this particular food for the poor. Whether it is the grain that happens to grow in the rear corner of the field or the stalks that by chance fall aside from the edge of the farmer's sickle, all this food apportioned seemingly by accident must be left for the poor. So the framers of the Mishnah believe that God alone determines what produce falls into the category of poor-offerings. In fact, the deepest expression of God's wishes for the produce of his Land is carried in the random separation of a small amount of food. This random character is reflected likewise in the designation of produce for the priests. For example, when a farmer designates heave-offering from the produce he has collected at his threshing floor, he declares that the heave-offering is isolated in one part of the pile. When he lifts out this produce, whatever he grabs immediately takes on the status of heave-offering. He may not measure this produce or attempt to designate any specific grain." Gleanings are defined, therefore, as what falls by accident; it is set aside at random and that is how we know it is God's gift to the poor. The farmer plays no role in determining what produce falls into the status of gleanings (Brooks, p. 71). This is expressed as follows:

M. Peah

4:10 A. What [produce is subject to the law of] gleanings [cf. Lev. 19:9-10]?

B. That which falls [to the ground] during the harvest.

C. If one was harvesting and harvested an armful [of produce], or plucked a handful [of produce],

D. and a thorn pricked him so that [the produce he was holding] fell to the ground [before he had fully grasped it] –

E. lo, [this produce] belongs to the householder, [for only produce which falls to the ground while in the possession of the harvester is subject to the law of gleanings].

F. [Produce which falls from] within the [harvester's] hand, or [from] within the sickle, [produce of which the harvester had taken possession,]

G. [belongs] to the poor.

H. [Produce which falls from] the back of the [harvester's] hand, or [from] the back of the sickle,

I. [belongs] to the householder, [for the harvester had not yet taken possession].

J. [Produce which falls from] the tip of the [harvester's] hand, or [from] the tip of the sickle, [such that it is unclear whether or not the harvester had taken possession] –

K. R. Ishmael says, "[Such produce belongs] to the poor."

L. R. Aqiba says, "[It belongs] to the householder."

Gleanings are never the householder's private property, so they are exempt from tithing (Brooks, p. 72). This point further arises when we deal with the forgotten sheaf, M. Peah 5:7-7:2. Here again, the sheaf that is forgotten by definition is accidentally forgotten; it cannot be hidden or concealed by the poor, either. What is subject to constraint is untouched by the law. Chance is the sole criterion, and if an identifiable cause is in play to make the householder forget the sheaf, the sheaf does not belong to the poor (Brooks, p. 87).

M. Peah

5:7 A. A sheaf which (1) workers forgot, but which the householder did not forget, (2) which the householder forgot, but which the workers did not forget, (3) [or if] poor people stood in front [of a sheaf] or covered it with straw [in order to hide it so that the workers would forget it],

B. lo, this [sheaf] is not [subject to the restrictions of the] forgotten sheaf, [for either the poor received it by deception, or it was never forgotten by both the worker and the householder] [cf, Deut. 24:19-22].

The same conception pertains to defective clusters: only those grapes that fall for no apparent reason are subject to the law (M. Peah 7:3) (Brooks, p. 121). If the householder dropped produce under constraint, the poor have no claim on it; only what falls at random is subject to God's claim in behalf of the poor (Brooks, ibid.).

The householder plays no active role in identifying the produce designated as poor-offerings (Brooks, p. 19). He merely leaves grain unharvested, accidentally drops some stalks as gleanings, forgets to collect some sheaves. The farmer does nothing purposive, so Brooks: "God alone determines which particular grain must be given to the poor and separates this food from the remainder of the crop... the farmer is forbidden to dispense the offerings, lest he put them to his own purposes, not God's. So the householder has no part at all in separating poor-offerings." This is expressed as follows:

M. Peah

1:4   A.   They stated a general principle concerning [the designation of produce as] peah:

        B.   Whatever is: (1) Edible, (2) privately owned, (3) grown from the ground, (4) harvested as a crop, (5) and can be preserved in storage, is subject to [designation as] peah.

        C.   Grain and legumes are included in this general principle.

Brooks notes, "The law governs only produce of the Land, which is God's exclusive property. When Israelite farmers claim it as their own and grow food on it, they pay for using God's earth; they leave a portion of the yield unharvested as peah and give this food over to God's chosen representatives, the poor. The underlying theory is that householders are tenant farmers, who pay taxes to their landlord, God."

F. The Duality of the Torah

That the Torah comes to Israel in two media, oral and written, is a given; the media by which the oral part of the Torah is given its permanent, verbal formulation is less critical. That the premise of the rabbis is that they possess that oral part of the Torah is everywhere in play. Scripture forms the basis of some, but not all, accepted practices and rules. There are traditions that are external to Scripture but that are valid. There are traditions that are to be taught only to people qualified to learn them:

M. Hagigah

1:8   A.   The absolution of vows hovers in the air, for it has nothing [in the Torah] upon which to depend.

        B.   The laws of the Sabbath, festal-offerings, and sacrilege – lo, they are like mountains hanging by a string,

        C.   for they have little Scripture for many laws.

        D.   Laws concerning civil litigations, the sacrificial cult, things to be kept cultically clean, sources of cultic uncleanness, and prohibited consanguineous marriages have much on which to depend.

        E.   And both these and those [equally] are the essentials of the Torah.

M. Hagigah

2:1 A. They do not expound upon the laws of prohibited relationships [Lev. 18] before three persons, the works of creation [Gen. 13] before two, or the Chariot [Ezek. 1] before one,

   B. unless he was a sage and understands of his own knowledge.

   C. Whoever reflects upon four things would have been better off had he not been born:

   D. what is above, what is below, what is before, and what is beyond.

   E. And whoever has no concern for the glory of his Maker – would have been better off had he not been born.

G. Israel and the Nations

The rabbis understand as a given that the nations do not have the Torah, and by their own intention declined to accept it. That fact accounts for every detail of Israel's place among the nations, the nations' treatment of Israel, and the present history and future destiny of both the nations and Israel. The basic fact of the relationship between Israel and the gentiles is that the gentiles are not subject to the laws of the Torah; none may benefit from a sin that an Israelite has committed against the Torah:

2:3 A. Leaven belonging to a gentile which has remained over Passover –

   B. one is permitted to derive benefit from it.

   C. But that of an Israelite –

   D. one is prohibited to derive benefit from it,

   E. since it is said, "Let it not be seen with you" (Ex. 13:7).

2:4 A. A gentile who lent money to an Israelite on the security of his [the Israelite's] leaven –

   B. after Passover, it is permitted [for an Israelite] to derive benefit from it.

   C. And an Israelite who lent money to a gentile on the security of his leaven

   D. after Passover, it is prohibited [for an Israelite] to derive benefit from it.

Israel belongs in the Land of Israel, and the nations do not. If gentiles possess the holy land, that is not how the Torah intends things to be; Israel's own failures account for the anomaly of gentile presence in the Land. Gentiles have no right of ownership to the Land, therefore what is subject to gentiles' intentionality or actions is unaffected by the same:

M. Peah

4:6 A. [As regards] a gentile who had harvested his field, and then converted –

   B. [the produce he had harvested is] exempt from [the restrictions of] gleanings, the forgotten sheaf, and peah, since these are designated during the harvest, i.e. , before the gentile converted, so that his crop never became subject].

C. R. Judah obligates [such a man] to [the law of the] forgotten sheaf,

D. since [the law of the] forgotten sheaf applies only once he binds [the sheaves, i.e., after the gentile had converted and the produce has become subject].

Thus only Israelites exercise effective actions and intentions in dealing with the Land; what gentiles do falls outside of the Torah. Only an Israelite's crop is subject to the agricultural taxes. Gentiles are assumed as a matter of course to have sexual relations with animals, to fornicate, to murder, and the like, as well as to practice idolatry:

Mishnah-tractate Abodah Zarah

2:1 A. They do not leave cattle in gentiles' inns,

B. because they are suspect in regard to bestiality.

C. And a woman should not be alone with them,

D. because they are suspect in regard to fornication.

E. And a man should not be alone with them, because they are suspect in regard to bloodshed.

It is absolutely forbidden for Israelites to make use of whatever has served for idolatry, and that pertains especially to wine; all wine that is open is assumed to have yielded a libation and may not be utilized in any way:

2:4 A. "Skins of gentiles and their jars, with Israelite wine collected in them –

B. "they are prohibited, and the prohibition affecting them extends to deriving benefit from them at all," the words of R. Meir.

C. And sages say, "The prohibition affecting them does not extend to deriving benefit from them."

D. "Grape pits and grape skins belonging to gentiles are prohibited, and the prohibition affecting them extends to deriving any benefit from them at all," the words of R. Meir.

E. And sages say, "[If] they are moist, they are forbidden. If they are dry, they are permitted."

H. History: Its Meaning and Divisions

I find nothing relevant to this category. The famous passage at Mishnah-tractate 9:15 cited above does not change that judgment, since it is a singleton, bearing no premises that engage the treatment of any other problem or topic in the Mishnah.

II. The Tosefta, Tractate Abot, and the Earlier Midrash Compilations: Sifra, Sifré to Numbers, and Sifré to Deuteronomy

A. Intentionality

1. Once one has formed an improper intention, that intention takes over and invalidates the consequence rite, however briefly it was in effect:

Tosefta to Mishnah-tractate Parah

4:14   A.   An *'am ha ares* who said, "These utensils have I brought for my purification, and I changed my mind concerning them and decided to use them for my heave-offering" – since they were designated [for a baser purpose] in the possession of the *'am ha ares* [even] for one moment, lo, these are unclean.

2.   Intentionality has no bearing upon substances the classification of which is determined by their physical characteristics. It can classify only when there is a choice:

Tosefta to Mishnah-tractate Tohorot

2:5   A.   Honey which oozes from the hive of bees receives uncleanness as liquid.

      B.   [If] one gave thought to it as food, it receives uncleanness as food.

      C.   Oil is neither food nor liquid.

      D.   [If] one gave thought to it to make use of it as food and not as liquid his intention is of no effect.

      E.   Blood which congealed is neither food nor liquid.

      F.   [If] one gave thought to it to make use of it as food, it receives uncleanness as food. And [if one gave thought to use it as] liquid his intention is null.

      G.   The honey of palms is neither food nor liquid.

      H.   [If] one gave thought to it to make use of it for food, it receives uncleanness as food.

      I.   And [if one gave thought to it to use it] for liquid, his intention is null.

      J.   And as to all other fruit juice, [it is] neither food nor liquid.

      K.   [If] one gave thought to it, whether for liquid or for food, his intention is null.

      L.   Snow is neither food nor liquid. If one gave thought to it for food, his intention is null. For liquid – it receives uncleanness as liquid.

      M.   [If] part of it is made unclean, the liquid is made unclean.

      N.   [If] part of it is made unclean, the whole of it is not made unclean.

      O.   [If] part of it is clean, the whole of it is clean.

3.   We differentiate among sins by reason of the attitude that accompanies them; those done deliberately differ in character and penalty from those done inadvertently:

Sifra to Aharé Mot 2

      E.   Scripture says, "[because of the uncleannesses of the people of Israel] and because of their transgressions," and "transgressions" refers to acts of rebellion [that is, sins done deliberately].

      F.   And so Scripture uses the word, "The king of Moab has transgressed [deliberately] against me" (2 Kgs. 3:7).

      G.   And also: "Libnah likewise fell away at that time" (2 Kgs. 8:22, which uses the same word).

      H.   "Sins" ["all their sins"] fall into the category of acts of rebellion which are not subject to expiation through an offering.

4. It is the intentionality of the human being that renders objects into gods. If one treats an object as an idol, it is an idol:

Sifra Qedoshim XCV

I.9   A.   "Do not turn to idols or make for yourselves molten gods":

       B.   "To begin with, they are idols. But if you turn to them, you make them into gods."

5. Intentionality is specific; the right attitude is defined in specific and concrete terms. For example, the correct attitude for the service of God is to do so unconditionally and without expectation of reward; selflessly; one should make what God wants into what he wants:

Tractate Abot

1:3   Antigonus of Sokho received [the Torah] from Simeon the Righteous. He would say: Do not be like servants who serve the master on condition of receiving a reward, but [be] like servants who serve the master not on condition of receiving a reward. And let the fear of heaven be upon you.

Tractate Abot

2:4   He would say: Make His wishes into your own wishes, so that He will make your wishes into His wishes. Put aside your wishes on account of His wishes, so that He will put aside the wishes of other people in favor of your wishes.

B. The Yoke of the Kingdom of Heaven and the Commandments

1. Living in the kingdom of God, Israel is holy to God and holy like God: separate; Israel's vocation is to sanctify itself by accepting the yoke of the Torah's religious duties (commandments):

Sifra to Shemini CXXI

II.3   A.   "For I am the Lord who brought you up out of the Land of Egypt, to be your God; you shall therefore be holy, for I am holy" (Lev. 11:41-45):

       B.   Just as I am holy, so are you holy. Just as I am separate, so you be separate.

II.4   A.   "You shall not defile yourselves with any swarming things that crawls upon the earth":

       B.   Even though it does not reproduce through sexual activity.

II.5   A.   "For I am the Lord who brought you up out of the Land of Egypt":

       B.   It was on this stipulation that I brought you up out of the Land of Egypt, on the condition that you accept on yourselves the yoke of the religious duties.

       C.   For whoever accepts the yoke of the religious duties also affirms the exodus from Egypt, but whoever rejects the yoke of the commandments rejects the exodus from Egypt.

II.6   A.   "...To be your God":

       B.   whether you like it or not.

II.7   A.   "...You shall therefore be holy, for I am holy":

       B.   Just as I am holy, so are you holy. Just as I am separate, so you be separate.

2.   Humanity is made in the image of God, and the Torah is an act of divine grace, since it informs humanity that it is made in the image of God; so, too, with regard to Israel:

Tractate Abot

3:14   A.   R. Aqiba would say, "Precious is the human being, who was created in the image [of God]. It was an act of still greater love that it was made known to him that he was created in the image [of God]. As it is said, 'For in the image of God he made man' (Gen. 9:6).

       B.   "Precious are Israelites, who are called children to the Omnipresent. It was an act of still greater love that it was made known to them that they were called children to the Omnipresent, as it is said, 'You are the children of the Lord your God' (Deut. 14:1).

       C.   "Precious are Israelites, to whom was given the precious thing. It was an act of still greater love that it was made known to them that to them was given that precious thing with which the world was made, as it is said, 'For I give you a good doctrine. Do not forsake my Torah' (Prov. 4:2)."

3.   God is creator, merciful, judge, and is reliable to mete out punishment and reward as appropriate:

Sifra to Aharé Mot CXCIII

I.1   A.   ["The Lord spoke to Moses saying, 'Speak to the Israelite people and say to them, I am the Lord your God. You shall not copy the practices of the Land of Egypt where you dwelt, or of the land of Canaan to which I am taking you; nor shall you follow their laws. My rules alone shall you observe and faithfully follow my laws: I the Lord am your God. You shall keep my laws and my rules, by the pursuit of which man shall live: I am the Lord' (Lev. 18:1-30)."]

       B.   "The Lord spoke to Moses saying, 'Speak to the Israelite people and say to them, I am the Lord your God'":

       C.   "I am the Lord," for I spoke and the world came into being.

       D.   "I am full of mercy."

       E.   "I am judge to exact punishment and faithful to pay recompense."

       F.   "I am the one who exacted punishment from the generation of the Flood and the men of Sodom and Egypt, and I shall exact punishment from you if you act like them."

4.   God is faithful to protect Israel and reward the keeping of the commandments. But people may not obey by reason of stipulations or conditions that must be met; obedience must be totally gratuitous. God will respond to what is freely given by giving freely, but God cannot be coerced. Divine justice is inexorable:

Sifra to Emor CCXXVII

I.3　A.　"So you shall keep my commandments and do them: [I am the Lord]":

　　B.　This serves to assign to the commandments the duties of both keeping and doing them.

　　C.　"I am the Lord":

　　D.　Faithful to pay a reward.

I.4　A.　"And you shall not profane [my holy name]":

　　B.　I derive the implication from the statement, "you shall not profane," that sanctification is covered.

　　C.　And when Scripture says, "but I will be hallowed," the sense is, "Give yourself and sanctify my name."

　　D.　Might one suppose that that is when one is all alone?

　　E.　Scripture says, "among the people of Israel."

I.5　A.　In this connection sages have said:

　　B.　Whoever gives his life on condition that a miracle is done for him – no miracle will be done for him.

　　C.　But if it is not on condition that a miracle be done for him, a miracle will be done for him.

I.6　A.　"Who brought you out of the Land of Egypt":

　　B.　"I brought you out of the Land of Egypt on a stipulation that you be prepared to give yourselves to sanctify my name."

I.7　A.　"To be your God":

　　B.　like it or not.

I.8　A.　"I am the Lord":

　　B.　"I am faithful to pay a reward."

5.　The kingdom of heaven involves submission to its laws, the commandments. Intentionality to obey or intentionality to sin is critical. Rebellion against God takes place when those who know the Torah despise it; not hearkening means knowing that God is Lord and intentionally rebelling against him:

Sifra Behuqotai CCLXIV

I.1　A.　"But if you will not hearken to me [and will not do all these commandments, if you spurn my statutes and if your soul abhors my ordinances, so that you will not do all my commandments but break my covenant, I will do this to you: I will appoint over you sudden terror, consumption and fever that waste the eyes and cause life to pine away. And you shall sow your seed in vain, for your enemies shall eat it; I will set my face against you, and you shall be smitten before your enemies; those who hate you shall rule over you, and you shall flee when none pursues you. And if in spite of this you will not hearken to me, then I will chastise you again sevenfold for your sins, and I will break the pride of your power, and I will make your heavens like iron and your earth like brass; and your strength shall be spent in vain, for your land shall not yield its increase and the trees of the land shall not yield their fruit]":

B.   "But if you will not hearken to me" means, if you will not listen to the exposition of sages.

C.   Might one suppose that reference is made to Scripture [rather than sages' teachings]?

D.   When Scripture says, "and will not do all these commandments," lo, reference clearly is made to what is written in the Torah.

E.   Then how shall I interpret, "But if you will not hearken to me"?

F.   It means, if you will not listen to the exposition of sages.

6.   No one's merit is sufficient, and everyone must in the end throw himself upon God's mercy and grace:

Sifré to Deuteronomy to Waethanan XXVI

I.1   A.   "I pleaded with the Lord at that time, saying, ['O Lord, God, you who let your servant see the first works of your greatness and your mighty hand, you whose powerful deeds no god in heaven or on earth can equal! Let me, I pray, cross over and see the good land on the other side of the Jordan, that good hill country, and the Lebanon.' But the Lord was wrathful with me on your account and would not listen to me. The Lord said to me, 'Enough, never speak to me of this matter again! Go up to the summit of Pisgah and gaze about, to the west, the north, the south, and the east. Look at it well, for you shall not go across yonder Jordan. Give Joshua his instructions and imbue him with strength and courage, for he shall go across at the head of this people, and he shall allot to them the land that you may only see.' Meanwhile we stayed on in the valley near Beth-peor]" (Deut. 4:23-29):

B.   That is in line with this verse: "The poor uses pleading, but the rich answers impudently" (Prov. 18:23):

C.   Israel had two truly excellent leaders, Moses and David, king of Israel, and their deeds were sufficient to sustain the whole world. Nonetheless, they pleaded the Holy One, blessed be He, only for nought [but grace, without appealing to their own meritorious achievements].

D.   And that produces an argument *a fortiori*:

E.   If these two, whose deeds were sufficient to sustain the whole world, pleaded with the Holy One, blessed be He, only for nought [but grace, without appealing to their own meritorious achievements], one who is only no more than one thousand-thousand-thousandth or ten-thousand-ten-thousandth part of the disciples of their disciples should also plead with the Holy One, blessed be He, only for nought [but grace, without appealing to their own meritorious achievements].

7.   Imitating God means to be merciful and gracious to others; cleaving to the Torah is like cleaving to God:

Sifré to Deuteronomy to Eqeb XLIX

I.1   A.   "...Walking in all his ways, and holding fast to him, [the Lord will dislodge before you all these nations; you will dispossess nations greater and more numerous than you. Every spot on which your

> foot treads shall be yours; your territory shall extend from the wilderness to the Lebanon, and from the river, the Euphrates, to the Western Sea. No man shall stand up to you: the Lord your God will put the dread and the fear of you over the whole land in which you set foot, as he promised you]" (Deut. 11:22-25):

B. What are the ways of the Omnipresent?

C. "The Lord, God, merciful and gracious" (Ex. 34:6).

I.2   A. Scripture states, "And it shall come to pass that whoever shall be called by the name of the Lord shall be delivered" (Joel 3:5).

B. How is it possible for someone to be called by the name of the Omnipresent?

C. But since the Omnipresent is called "merciful," you, too, be merciful.

D. The Holy One, blessed be He, is called gracious, so you, too, be gracious.

E. For it is said, "The Lord, God, merciful and gracious" (Ps. 145:8).

F. And give gifts for nothing.

G. Just as the Omnipresent is called "Righteous," as it is said, "For the Lord is righteous, he loves righteousness" (Ps. 11:7), so you, too, be righteous.

H. The Omnipresent is called merciful: "For I am merciful, says the Lord" (Jer. 3:12), so you, too, be merciful.

I. That is why it is said, "And it shall come to pass that whoever shall be called by the name of the Lord shall be delivered" (Joel 3:5).

J. "Every one who is called by my name" (Isa. 43:7).

K. "The Lord has made every thing for his own purpose" (Prov. 16:4).

C. Words Form the Bridge from Humanity to God

While prayer is discussed, I find in this layer of the documents only a reprise of what is familiar from the prior writings.

D. The Sanctity of the Land of Israel and the People of Israel

1. God takes up residence in the Temple, which is where God and Israel meet; Israel's sin is atoned for; God forgives Israel in accepting the offerings:

Sifra to Shemini

2.   A. For all of the seven days of consecration, Moses would carry out the assigned tasks,

B. But the Presence of God did not come to rest on his account, until Aaron came and carried out the tacts of service in the priestly garments of the high priest.

C. Then the Presence of God came to rest on his account,

D. in line with this verse: "For today the Lord will appear to you."

2. Israel's claim to the holy land is eternal, because Israel was given the Torah to keep; Israel is to be separate from the nations; Israel should keep the Torah not by reason of desire but by reason of obligation:

Sifra to Qedoshim CCVII

II.3   A.   "And you shall not walk in the customs of the nation [which I am casting out before you]":

       B.   This refers to the Egyptians.

       C.   "...Which I am casting out before you":

       D.   This refers to the Canaanites.

II.4   A.   "...For they did all these things, [and therefore I abhorred them]":

       B.   This teaches that the Canaanites were flooded with these things.

       C.   "I sent them into exile only on account of these things."

II.8   A.   "I am the Lord your God who has separated you from the peoples":

       B.   "See how vast is the difference between you and the idolatrous nations!

       C.   "One of them fixes up his wife and hands her over to someone else [for sexual relations], a man fixes up himself and gives himself to someone else [for sexual relations]."

II.11   A.   "You shall be holy to me, for I the Lord am holy":

       B.   "Just as I am holy, so you be holy.

       C.   "Just as I am separate, so you be separate."

II.12   A.   "...And have separated you from the peoples, that you should be mine":

       B.   "If you are separated from the nations, lo, you are for my Name, and if not, lo, you belong to Nebuchadnezzar, king of Babylonia, and his associates."

II.13   A.   R. Eleazar b. Azariah says, "How do we know that someone should not say, 'I do not want to wear mixed fibers, I don't want to eat pork, I don't want to have incestuous sexual relations.'

       B.   "Rather: 'I do want [to wear mixed fibers, I do want to eat pork, I do want to have incestuous sexual relations.] But what can I do? For my father in heaven has made a decree for me!'

       C.   "So Scripture says, 'and have separated you from the peoples, that you should be mine.'

       D.   "So one will turn out to keep far from transgression and accept upon himself the rule of heaven."

3.   The Land of Israel is not only holier than, but also superior to all other lands:

Sifré to Deuteronomy to Eqeb XXXVII

III.2   A.   R. Judah says, "Now did the thirty-one kings who were in the past ever spend time in the Land of Israel?

       B.   "But it is as they do things in Rome now.

       C.   "For any king or ruler who did not acquire a portion in Rome says, 'I have never done a thing.'

       D.   "So, too, any king or ruler who has not acquired a palace or fortification in the Land of Israel says, 'I have accomplished nothing.'"

4.   God cares for all lands but looks out for them only because of his love for the Land of Israel in particular, and the same is so for the nations and Israel:

Sifré to Deuteronomy XI

I.1   A.   "It is a land which the Lord your God looks after, on which the Lord your God always keeps his eye, from year's beginning to year's end" (Deut. 11:10-12):

        B.   Does God look after that land alone? Does he not look after all lands?

        C.   For it is said, "...to cause it to rain on a land where no man is... to satisfy the desolate and waste ground" (Job 38:26-27).

        D.   Why then does Scripture say, "It is a land which the Lord your God looks after, [on which the Lord your God always keeps his eye, from year's beginning to year's end]" (Deut. 11:10-12)?

        E.   It is – as it were – that he cares only for that land, but on account of caring about that land, he cares also for all other lands as well.

I.2   A.   Along these same lines: "Behold, he who keeps Israel does not slumber or sleep" (Ps. 121:4).

        B.   Does God keep only Israel? Does he not keep everyone, for it is said, "In whose hand is the soul of every living thing and the breath of all mankind" (Job 12:10).

        C.   Why then does Scriptures say "Behold, he who keeps Israel does not slumber or sleep" (Ps. 121:4)?

        D.   It is – as it were – that he keeps Israel alone, but on account of keeping Israel, he also keeps everyone else along with them.

E. Random Events or Chance Express God's Will

I find nothing relevant.

F. The Duality of the Torah

1.   Through studying the Torah with sages, Israel knows God; God is best served through the study of the Torah and prayer:

Sifré to Deuteronomy to Eqeb XLI

III.2   A.   ["The words of the sages are as goads" (Qoh. 12:11):] Just as a goad guides an ox in its furrow to produce life-sustaining crops for its master,

         B.   so teachings of Torah guide a person's intellect to know the Omnipresent.

III.3   A.   And it is not as if one has heard it merely on the authority of the collegium of sages, but as if one has heard it from a formally constituted sanhedrin:

         B.   "...Masters of assemblies" (Qoh. 12:11),

         C.   and "assemblies" refers only to the sanhedrin,

         D.   as it is said, "Assemble to me seventy men of the elders of Israel" (Num. 11:16).

         E.   And it is not as if one has heard it merely from a formally constituted sanhedrin, but as if one has heard it from the mouth of Moses:

         F.   "Then his people remembered the days of old, the days of Moses" (Isa. 63:11).

         G.   And it is not as if one has heard it from Moses, but as if one has heard it from the mouth of the Omnipotent God:

H.   "They are given from one shepherd," "Give ear, shepherd of Israel, thou who leads Joseph like a flock" (Ps. 80:2), "Hear O Israel, the Lord our God, the Lord is one" (Deut. 6:4).

XLI

A.   "...And serving him [with all your heart and soul]":
B.   This refers to study [of the Torah].
C.   You say that it refers to study. But perhaps it refers only to actual service?
D.   Lo, Scripture says, "And the Lord God took the man and put him into the Garden of Eden to work it and to guard it" (Gen. 2:15).
E.   Now in the past what sort of work was there to do, and what sort of guarding was there to do?
F.   But you learn from that statement that "to work it" refers to study of the Torah, and "to guard it" refers to keeping the religious duties.
G.   And just as the service at the altar is called work, so study of the Torah is called work.

VI.2   A.   "...And serving him [with all your heart and soul]":
B.   This refers to prayer.
C.   You say that it refers to prayer. But perhaps it refers only to actual service?
D.   Lo, Scripture says, "With all your heart and with all your soul" (Deut. 11:13).
E.   Now is there a form of labor that is carried out only with the heart?
F.   Why then does Scripture say, "...and serving him [with all your heart and soul]?"
G.   This refers to prayer.

G. Israel and the Nations

1.   One who is subject to differentiations in cleanness or uncleanness stands at a higher level of sanctification than one who does not. Gentiles, who are not subject to uncleanness, do not afford protection against uncleanness; Israelites, who are subject to uncleanness, also afford protection against uncleanness:

Tosefta Negaim

7:9   A.   [If] one was standing inside and stretched his hand outside, and his fellow gave him his sandals and his rings in the palm of his hand, he and they are unclean forthwith.
B.   But if he had been dressed in them, he would have been clean until he had remained long enough to eat a piece of bread.
C.   [If] he was standing outside, with his sandals on his feet,
D.   and he stretched [his hand] inside,
E.   with his ring on his finger,
F.   and he stretched them [it] inside –
G.   R. Judah declares unclean forthwith.
H.   And sages say, "Until he will remain there [for an interval] sufficient for eating a piece of bread."
I.   They said to R. Judah, "When his entire body is unclean, he does not render what is on him unclean until he remains for a sufficient

time to eat a piece of bread. So when his entire body is not unclean, should he [not] render unclean what is on him before he remains for a time sufficient to eat a piece of bread?"

J. Said to them R. Judah, "The reason is that the power of that which is capable of becoming unclean is stronger to afford protection than is the power of the clean to afford protection.

K. "Israelites receive uncleanness and afford protection for clothing in the house afflicted with plague. But the gentile and the beast do not receive uncleanness and do not afford protection for clothing in the house afflicted with plague."

Uncleanness itself may also serve as a mark of sanctification. Books that were said through the Holy Spirit impart uncleanness to hands, those not, do not:

Tosefta Yadayim

2:14 A. R. Simeon b. Menassia says, "The Song of Songs imparts uncleanness to hands, because it was said by the Holy Spirit.

B. "Qohelet does not impart uncleanness of hands, because it is [merely] the wisdom of Solomon."

C. They said to him, "And did he write only this alone? Lo, it says, 'And Solomon uttered three thousand proverbs and his songs were a thousand and five' (1 Kgs. 5:12).

D. "And it says, 'Do not add to his words lest he rebuke you and you be found a liar' (Prov. 30:6)."

2:19 A. Said to them Rabban Yohanan b. Zakkai, "The preciousness of Holy Scriptures accounts for their uncleanness,

B. "so that a man should not make them into bedding for his cattle."

2. Uncleanness is a heavenly penalty imposed only on Israelites for certain moral sins:

Tosefta Negaim

6:7 D. He would come to the priest, and the priest says to him, "My son, go and examine yourself and return [from your evil ways].

E. "For plagues come only because of gossip, and leprosy comes only to those who are arrogant.

F. "And the Omnipresent judges man only in mercy."

G. Lo, they [plagues] come on his house: [If] He repents, it requires dismantling; and if not, it requires demolishing.

H. Lo, they appear on his clothing: [If] he repents, it requires tearing; and if not, it requires burning.

I. Lo, they appear on his body: [If] he repents, he repents; and if not, "Solitary shall he dwell; outside of the camp is his dwelling" (Lev. 13:46).

J. R. Simeon b. Leazar says in the name of R. Meir, "Even on the arrogant do plagues come, for so we find concerning Uzziah (2 Chr. 26:1-6)."

3. Gentiles are not eligible to bring a sin-offering, even if they inadvertently violate the religious duties that pertain to the children

of Noah; but Israelites, including proselytes and slaves (purchased as gentiles and converted) do have to do so:

Sifra Section Vayyiqra Dibura Dehobah

1.   A.   ["And the Lord said to Moses, 'Say to the people of Israel, "If any one sins unwittingly in any of the things which the Lord has commanded not to be done, and does any one of them...""' (Lev. 4:1-12):]

        B.   Israelites bring a sin-offering, but gentiles do not bring a sin-offering.

        C.   It is not necessary to say that [they do not have to bring a sin-offering for inadvertently violating] religious duties that were not assigned to the children of Noah, but even for violating religious duties concerning which the children of Noah were commanded, they do not have to bring a sin-offering on that account.

2.   A.   "Say to the people of Israel": I know that the sin-offering is owing only from Israelites.

        B.   How do I know that it is owing also from proselytes and bondmen?

        C.   Scripture says, "If any one [sins unwittingly]."

4.   The privilege of contracting uncleanness comes to Israel with the giving of the Torah. It was only from the giving of the Torah that Israel became subject to certain forms of uncleanness; prior to that time, these sources of uncleanness proved ineffective; gentiles are excluded from differentiated uncleanness altogether, being unclean only the way corpses are:

Sifra to Negaim CXXVII

II.1   A.   "When there will be" (Lev. 12:2) –

        B.   from the [time at which this law is] proclaimed [namely, Sinai] onward.

        C.   And is it not logical?

        D.   It [Scripture] has declared unclean with reference to those afflicted with flux [Lev. 15:1ff.: Zabim] and has declared unclean with reference to plagues.

        E.   Just as in the case of those afflicted with flux, it declared clear [such appearances of uncleanness as occurred] before the pronouncement [of the Torah], so in reference to plagues, it declared clear [such appearances of uncleanness as occurred] on them before the pronouncement.

Sifra to Zabim CLX

I.1   B.   Israelites are susceptible to uncleanness through flux, and gentiles are not susceptible to uncleanness through flux.

        C.   **And even if they [gentiles] are not susceptible to uncleanness through flux, they impart uncleanness like [K instead of B] Zabs.**

        D.   **And on their account they burn heave-offering.**

        E.   **And on their account are they [who touch gentiles] [T.2:1: *not*] liable for entering the sanctuary [while unclean on that account].**

F.   Since [Scripture speaks of] people of Israel, I know only that Israelites [are susceptible to uncleanness through flux]. How do I know that I should encompass proselytes and slaves?

G.   Scripture says, "Speak to the people of Israel and say to them, [When any] man [has a discharge from his body, the discharge is unclean" (Lev. 15:2)].

H.   "I know only that man [is susceptible to uncleanness through flux].

I.   "How do I know that I should encompass the woman and child?

J.   "Scripture says, 'any man' (Lev. 15:2)," the words of R. Judah.

K.   And R. Simeon [*sic!* b. b. Nid.: *Ishmael*] son of R. Yohanan b. Beroqah says, "Lo, Scripture says, '[When there will be] flux [from his body], his flux [will be unclean]' (Lev. 15:2).

L.   "[This refers both] to male and to female.

M.   "[In respect to] the male, [it means] any sort of male, whether adult or child, [with respect to] female, [it means] whether adult or child."

5.   Gentiles are not liable for actions carried on outside of the cult for which Israelites are culpable; proselytes and slaves are classed as Israel:

Sifra to Aharé Mot CLXXXVII

I.1   A.   ["And the Lord said to Moses, Say to Aaron and his sons and to all the people of Israel, This is the thing which the Lord has commanded. If any man of the house of Israel kills an ox or a lamb or a goat in the camp, or kills it outside the camp and does not bring it to the door of the tent of meeting, to offer it as a gift to the Lord before the tabernacle of the Lord, blood guilt shall be imputed to that man" (Lev. 17:1-7).]

B.   ["…The people of Israel":] The people of Israel are liable on the counts of slaughtering or offering up outside [of the Temple],

C.   but gentiles are not liable on the counts of slaughtering or offering up outside [of the Temple].

D.   And not this alone, but gentiles are permitted to make a high place anywhere and to make offerings to heaven.

I.2   A.   Since [Scripture refers to] "people of Israel," I know only that the law covers Israelites.

B.   How do I know that the law encompasses proselytes and slaves?

C.   Scripture says, "Say to them."

CLXXXIX

I.1   A.   "And you shall say to them, [Any man of the house of Israel or of the strangers that sojourn among them who offers a burnt-offering or sacrifice and does not bring it to the door of the tent of meeting, to sacrifice it to the Lord, that man shall be cut off from his people]" (Lev. 17:8-9):

B.   ["You shall say to them"] in accord with all that is stated in this passage.

C.   "…Israel": This refers to Israelites.

D.   "…Strangers": This refers to proselytes.

E.   "…That sojourn": Encompasses the wives of proselytes.

F.   "…Among them": Encompasses women and slaves.

6. Israel is holy, that is, separate, like God; the sanctification of Israel
    also represents the sanctification of God; but God remains sanctified
    even if Israel does not; it is Israel's task to imitate God:

Sifra to Qedoshim CXCV

I.1 A. "And the Lord said to Moses, Say to all the congregation of the
         people of Israel, You shall be holy, [for I the Lord your God am
         holy. Every one of you shall revere his mother and his father, and
         you shall keep my sabbaths; I am the Lord your God. Do not turn
         to idols or make for yourselves molten gods; I am the Lord your
         God]" (Lev. 19:1-4):
     B. This teaches that this chapter was stated in the assembly of all
         Israel.
     C. And why was it stated in the assembly of all Israel?
     D. It is because most of the principles of the Torah depend upon its
         contents.
I.2 A. "You shall be holy":
     B. "You shall be separate."
I.3 A. "You shall be holy, for I the Lord your God am holy":
     B. That is to say, "If you sanctify yourselves, I shall credit it to you as
         though you had sanctified me, and if you do not sanctify
         yourselves, I shall hold that it is as if you have not sanctified me."
     C. Or perhaps the sense is this: "If you sanctify me, then lo, I shall be
         sanctified, and if not, I shall not be sanctified"?
     D. Scripture says, "For I... am holy," meaning, I remain in my state of
         sanctification, whether or not you sanctify me.
     E. Abba Saul says, "The king has a retinue, and what is the task
         thereof? It is to imitate the king."

7. God's presence remains with Israel even when they are unclean;
    uncleanness comes about by reason of sin. So even though Israel
    sins, God's presence remains with them:

Sifré to Numbers I

X.1 A. "'[You shall put out both male and female, putting them outside the
         camp, that they may not defile their camp,] in the midst of which I
         dwell.' [And the people of Israel did so and drove them outside the
         camp, as the Lord said to Moses, so the people of Israel did]" (Gen.
         5:3-4).
     B. So beloved is Israel that even though they may become unclean, the
         presence of God remains among them.
     C. And so Scripture states, "...Who dwells with them in the midst of
         their uncleanness" (Lev. 16:16).
     D. And further: "...By making my sanctuary unclean, which
         [nonetheless] is in their midst " (Lev. 15:31).
     E. And it further says: "...That they may not defile their camp, in the
         midst of which I dwell" (Num. 5:3-4).
     F. And it further says, "You shall not defile the land in which you live,
         in the midst of which I dwell, for I the Lord dwell in the midst of
         the people of Israel" (Num. 35:34).

X.2　A.　R. Yosé the Galilean says, "Come and take note of how great is the power of sin.　For before the people had laid hands on transgression, people afflicted with flux and lepers were not located among them, but after they had laid hands on transgression, people afflicted with flux and lepers did find a place among them.

　　　B.　"Accordingly, we learn that these three events took place on one and the same day: [Transgression, the presence of those afflicted with flux, the development of leprosy among the people]."

X.3　A.　R. Simeon b. Yohai says, "Come and take note of how great is the power of sin.　For before the people had laid hands on transgression, what is stated in their regard?

　　　B.　"'Now the appearance of the glory of the Lord was like a devouring fire on the top of the mountain in the sight of the people of Israel' (Ex. 24:17).

　　　C.　"Nonetheless, the people did not fear nor were they afraid.

　　　D.　"But once they had laid hands on transgression, what is said in their regard?

　　　E.　"'And when Aaron and all the people of Israel saw Moses, behold, the skin of his face shone, and they are afraid to come near him' (Ex. 34:30)."

8.　The moment of the Exodus involved the most despicable generation of the most despicable nations, the Egyptians and the Canaanites:

Sifra Aharé Mot CXCIII

I.2　A.　And how do we know that there was never any nation among all of the nations that practiced such abominations, more than did the Egyptians?

　　　B.　Scripture says, "You shall not copy the practices of the Land of Egypt where you dwelt."

　　　C.　And how do we know that the last generation did more abhorrent things than all the rest of them?

　　　D.　Scripture says, "You shall not copy the practices of the Land of Egypt."

　　　E.　And how do we know that the people in the last location in which the Israelites dwelt were more abhorrent than all the rest?

　　　F.　Scripture says, "...Where you dwelt, you shall not do."

　　　G.　And how do we know that the fact that the Israelites dwelt there was the cause for all these deeds?

　　　H.　Scripture says, "You shall not copy... where you dwelt."

I.3　A.　How do we know that there was never a nation among all the nations that did more abhorrent things than the Canaanites?

　　　B.　Scripture says, "You shall not copy the practices... of the Land of Canaan [to which I am taking you; nor shall you follow their laws]."

　　　C.　And how do we know that the last generation did more abhorrent things than all the rest of them?

　　　D.　Scripture says, "You shall not copy the practices of the Land of Canaan."

　　　E.　And how do we know that the people in the place to which the Israelites were coming for conquest were more abhorrent than all the rest?

    F.   Scripture says, "...To which I am taking you."
    G.   And how do we know that it is the arrival of the Israelites that caused them to do all these deeds?
    H.   Scripture says, "Or of the land of Canaan to which I am taking you; nor shall you follow their laws."

9.   A gentile who keeps the Torah is in the status of the high priest:

Sifra to Aharé Mot CXCIV

II.15   A.   "...By the pursuit of which man shall live":
       B.   R. Jeremiah says, "How do I know that even a gentile who keeps the Torah, lo, he is like the high priest?
       C.   "Scripture says, 'By the pursuit of which man shall live.'"
       D.   And so he says, "'And this is the Torah of the priests, Levites, and Israelites,' is not what is said here, but rather, 'This is the Torah of the man, O Lord God' (2 Sam. 7:19)."
       E.   And so he says, "'Open the gates and let priests, Levites, and Israelites will enter it' is not what is said, but rather, 'Open the gates and let the righteous nation, who keeps faith, enter it' (Isa. 26:2)."
       F.   And so he says, "'This is the gate of the Lord. Priests, Levites, and Israelites...' is not what is said, but rather, 'The righteous shall enter into it' (Ps. 118:20).
       G.   And so he says, "'What is said is not, 'Rejoice, priests, Levites, and Israelites,' but rather, 'Rejoice, O righteous, in the Lord' (Ps. 33:1)."
       H.   And so he says, "It is not, 'Do good, O Lord, to the priests, Levites, and Israelites,' but rather, 'Do good, O Lord, to the good, to the upright in heart' (Ps. 125:4)."
       I.   "Thus, even a gentile who keeps the Torah, lo, he is like the high priest."

10.   The key to Israel's and the nations' status in God's sight is the conduct of the nations, their decisions in respect to God. Specifically, a number of closely related propositions account for matters. Israel consecrates itself by giving up idolatry in particular; God is reliable both in penalizing sin and in rewarding right behavior:

Sifra to Qedoshim CCVIII

I.2   A.   "Consecrate yourselves, therefore, and be holy":
      B.   This refers to the sanctification achieved through separation from idolatry.
      C.   Or perhaps it refers to the sanctification involved in carrying out out all religious duties?
      D.   When Scripture says, "You shall be holy" (Lev. 19:1), lo, we find reference to the sanctification involved in carryout out all the religious duties.
      E.   What then is the sense of the statement, "Consecrate yourselves, therefore, and be holy, for I am the Lord your God"?
      F.   This refers to the sanctification achieved through separation from idolatry.
I.3   A.   "...For I am the Lord your God":
      B.   I am the Judge for exacting penalty and faithful to pay a reward.

I.5 A. "I am the Lord who sanctifies you":

B. "Just as I am holy, so you be holy."

That explains why, who hates Israel hates God:

Sifré to Numbers LXXXIV

IV.1 A. "...And let them that hate you flee before you":

B. And do those who hate [come before] him who spoke and brought the world into being?

C. The purpose of the verse at hand is to say that whoever hates Israel is as if he hates him who spoke and by his word brought the world into being.

D. Along these same lines: "In the greatness of your majesty you overthrow your adversaries" (Ex. 15:7).

E. And are there really adversaries before him who spoke and by his word brought the world into being? But Scripture thus indicates that whoever rose up against Israel is as if he rose up against the Omnipresent.

And the reason derives from the character of the nations, that is, why they are the nations and not Israel. Specifically, Israel was chosen because the nations proved unworthy; Israel chose God as much as God chose Israel; the relationship is always reciprocal:

Sifré to Deuteronomy to Ha'azinu CCCXII

I.1 A. "For the Lord's portion is his people, [Jacob his own allotment]":

B. The matter may be compared to a king who had a field, which he handed over to tenant farmers.

C. The tenant farmers began to steal [the produce of the field that was owing to the king, so] he took it from them and handed it over to the children.

D. They began to conduct themselves worse than the earlier ones.

E. He took it from their children and handed it over to the children of the children.

F. They began to conduct themselves even worse than the earlier ones.

G. He had a son. He said to them, "Get out of what is mine. I don't want you in it. Give me my portion, which I may get it back."

H. So when our father, Abraham, came into the world, chaff came forth from him, Ishmael and all the children of Keturah.

I. When Isaac came into the world, chaff came forth from him, Esau and all the nobles of Edom.

J. They began to conduct themselves worse than the earlier ones.

K. When Jacob came along, no chaff came forth from him. All the sons that were born to him were proper people, as it is said, "And Jacob was a perfect man, dwelling in tents" (Gen. 25:27).

L. Whence will the Omnipresent regain his share? It will be from Jacob: "For the Lord's portion is his people, Jacob his own allotment."

M. And further: "For the Lord has chosen Jacob to himself" (Ps. 135:4).

I.2   A.   Still, the matter is not fully clear, for we do not know whether the Holy One, blessed be He, has chosen Jacob, or whether it is Jacob who chose the Holy One, blessed be He.

B.   Scripture says, "And Israel for his own treasure" (Ps. 135:4).

C.   Still, the matter is not fully clear, for we do not know whether the Holy One, blessed be He, has chosen Israel as his own treasure, or whether it is Israel who chose the Holy One, blessed be He.

D.   Scripture says, "And the Lord has chosen you to be his own treasure" (Deut. 14:2).

E.   And how on the basis of Scripture do we know that Jacob, for his part, chose him?

F.   As it is said, "Not like these is the portion of Jacob" (Jer. 10:16).

The condition of the nations, moreover, was brought about by their own actions. In fact, God offered the Torah to every nation; only Israel took it:

Sifré to Deuteronomy to Zot Habberakhah CCCXLIII

IV.1   A.   Another teaching concerning the phrase, "He said, 'The Lord came from Sinai'":

B.   When the Omnipresent appeared to give the Torah to Israel, it was not to Israel alone that he revealed himself but to every nation.

C.   First of all he came to the children of Esau. He said to them, "Will you accept the Torah?"

D.   They said to him, "What is written in it?"

E.   He said to them, "'You shall not murder' (Ex. 20:13)."

F.   They said to him, "The very being of 'those men' [namely, us] and of their father is to murder, for it is said, 'But the hands are the hands of Esau' (Gen. 27:22). 'By your sword you shall live' (Gen. 27:40)."

G.   So he went to the children of Ammon and Moab and said to them, "Will you accept the Torah?"

H.   They said to him, "What is written in it?"

I.   He said to them, "'You shall not commit adultery' (Ex. 20:13)."

J.   They said to him, "The very essence of fornication belongs to them [us], for it is said, 'Thus were both the daughters of Lot with child by their fathers' (Gen. 19:36)."

K.   So he went to the children of Ishmael and said to them, "Will you accept the Torah?"

L.   They said to him, "What is written in it?"

M.   He said to them, "'You shall not steal' (Ex. 20:13)."

N.   They said to him, "The very essence of their [our] father is thievery, as it is said, 'And he shall be a wild ass of a man' (Gen. 16:12)."

O.   And so it went. He went to every nation, asking them, "Will you accept the Torah?"

P.   For so it is said, "All the kings of the earth shall give you thanks, O Lord, for they have heard the words of your mouth" (Ps. 138:4).

Q.   Might one suppose that they listened and accepted the Torah?

R.   Scripture says, "And I will execute vengeance in anger and fury upon the nations, because they did not listen" (Mic. 5:14).

S. And it is not enough for them that they did not listen, but even the seven religious duties that the children of Noah indeed accepted upon themselves they could not uphold before breaking them.

T. When the Holy One, blessed be He, saw that that is how things were, He gave them to Israel.

11. Israel on earth and God in heaven correspond with one another and communicate in their comparability:

Sifré to Deuteronomy to Zot Habberakhah CCCLV

XVII.1 A. ["O Jeshurun, there is none like God, riding through the heavens to help you, through the skies in his majesty. The ancient God is a refuge, a support are the arms everlasting. He drove out the enemy before you. By his command: Destroy. Thus Israel dwells in safety, untroubled is Jacob's abode, in a land of grain and wine, under heavens dripping dew. O happy Israel! who is like you, a people delivered by the Lord, your protecting shield, your sword triumphant. Your enemies shall come cringing before you and you shall tread on their backs" (Deut. 33:24-29).]

B. "O Jeshurun, there is none like God":

C. The Israelites say, "There is none like God,"

D. and the Holy Spirit says, "O Jeshurun."

XVII.2 A. The Israelites say, "Who is like you, O Lord among the mighty" (Ex. 15:11).

B. And the Holy Spirit says, "Happy are you, Israel, who is like you" (Isa. 33:29).

XVII.3 A. The Israelites say, "Hear O Israel, the Lord our God, the Lord is one" (Deut. 56:4).

B. And the Holy Spirit says, "And who is like your people, Israel, a unique nation in the earth" (1 Chr. 17:21).

XVII.4 A. The Israelites say, "As an apple tree among the trees of the wood..." (Song 2:3).

B. And the Holy Spirit says, "As a lily among thorns" (Song 2:2).

XVII.5 A. The Israelites say, "This is my God and I will glorify him" (Ex. 15:2).

B. And the Holy Spirit says, "The people which I formed for myself" (Isa. 43:21).

XVII.6 A. The Israelites say, "For you are the glory of their strength" (Ps. 89:18).

B. And the Holy Spirit says, "Israel, in whom I will be glorified" (Isa. 49:3)

H. History: Its Meaning and Divisions

1. We distinguish three periods in human history: prior to Sinai, Sinai, and after Sinai, and different laws apply to each period, respectively:

Sifra to Emor CCXVII

II.1 A. "Say to them":

B. To those who are standing before Mount Sinai.

II.2 A. "If any one of all your descendants throughout your generations":

B. This teaches that the law applies for generations to come.

2. The exile was bad for Israel and Israel remained responsible for their sin when they were in exile:

Sifra Behuqotai 3

A. "...And brought them into the land of their enemies":

B. This is a good deal for Israel.

C. For the Israelites are not to say, "Since we have gone into exile among the gentiles, let us act like them."

D. [God speaks:] "I shall not let them, but I shall call forth prophets against them, who will bring them back to the right way under my wings."

E. And how do we know?

F. "What is in your mind shall never happen, the thought, 'Let us be like the nations, like the tribes of the countries, and worship wood and stone.' 'As I live,' says the Lord God, 'surely with a might hand and an outstretched arm and with wrath poured out, I will be king over you. [I will bring you out from the peoples and gather you out of the countries where you are scattered, with a mighty hand and an outstretched arm and with wrath poured out' (Ezek. 20:33)."

G. "Whether you like it or not, with or without your consent, I shall establish my dominion over you."

3. There will be an eschatological war of Gog and Magog, after which Israel will be saved and there will be no further period of subjugation:

Sifré to Numbers LXXVI

II.1 A. "[And when you go to war in your land] against the adversary who oppresses you, [then you shall sound an alarm with the trumpets]" (Num. 10:1-10):

B. Scripture speaks of the [eschatological] war of Gog and Magog.

C. You maintain that Scripture speaks of the [eschatological] war of Gog and Magog.

D. But perhaps it speaks only of any wars that are mentioned in the Torah?

E. Scripture says, "...That you may be remembered before the Lord your God, and you shall be saved from your enemies."

F. Thus you may argue: Go and find a war in which Israel is saved, but after which there is no period of subjugation?

G. You can find only the war of Gog and Magog.

H. And so Scripture says, "And the Lord will go forth and make war against those nations" (Zech. 14:3).

II.2 A. What is the meaning of [the phrase in that same context], "And the Lord will be king over all the earth"?

B. R. Aqiba says, "I know only that war is involved [at the end of history]. How do I know that there are also the troubles of blight and mildew, hard labor and ships floundering in the sea? Scripture says, '...Against the adversary who oppresses you,' referring to every sort of misfortune – may it not come into the world!"

4. Israel really controls its own destiny through its actions and attitudes:

Sifré to Deuteronomy to Ha'azinu CCCXXIII

I.1   A.   "Were they wise, they would think upon this, [gain insight into their future. How could one have routed a thousand or two put ten thousand to flight, unless their rock had sold them, the Lord had given them up? For their rock is not like our rock, in our enemies' own estimation]" (Deut. 32:19-31):

       B.   "If the Israelites would look upon the teachings of the Torah that I gave to them, no nation or kingdom would rule over them."

       C.   The meaning of "this" [in the base verse] is only Torah, in line with this verse: "This is the Torah that Moses set..." (Deut. 4:44).

I.2   A.   Another teaching concerning the phrase, "Were they wise, they would think upon this":

       B.   If the Israelites would look upon what their ancestor, Jacob, said to them, no nation or kingdom would rule over them.

       C.   And what did he say to them? "Accept upon yourselves the rule of heaven, and let one subdue the other in fear of heaven, and conduct yourselves with one another through acts of unrequited love."

III. The Later Midrash Compilations:
Genesis Rabbah, Leviticus Rabbah and Pesiqta deRab Kahana

A. Intentionality

I find nothing relevant to this topic.

B. The Yoke of the Kingdom of Heaven and the Commandments

1. The status of Israel depends upon Israel's acceptance of the commandments of the Torah. If Israel does what God commands, they then are Israel, and if not, they are not; all depends upon accepting the divinity of God:

Genesis Rabbah XLVI

IX.1   A.   "And I will give to you and to your descendants after you [the land of your sojournings, all the Land of Canaan, for an everlasting possession; and I will be their God]" (Gen. 17:8):

       B.   In this connection R. Yudan made five statements [imputing to God five propositions, which are now spelled out].

       C.   R. Yudan said, "[God said,] 'If your descendants accept my divinity, I shall be their patron God, and if not, I shall not be their patron God.

       D.   "'If your children enter the land, they will receive my divinity, and if they do not enter the land, they will not receive my divinity.

       E.   "'If your descendants accept circumcision, they will receive my divinity, and if not, they will not receive my divinity.

F. "'If your descendants accept circumcision, they will enter the land, and if not, they will not enter the land.' [So the cited verse yields a number of distinct conditions.]"

2. The mark of God's special love for Israel is the proliferation of the commandments, and that is because at the Sea Israel sanctified God's name:

Leviticus Rabbah II

IV.1 A. "Speak to the children of Israel" (Lev. 1:2).
B. R. Yudan in the name of R. Samuel b. R. Nehemiah: "The matter may be compared to the case of a king who had an undergarment, concerning which he instructed his servant, saying to him, 'Fold it, shake it out, and be careful about it!'
C. "He said to him, 'My lord, O king, among all the undergarments that you have, [why] do you give me such instructions only about this one?'
D. "He said to him, 'It is because this is the one that I keep closest to my body.'
E. "So, too, did Moses say before the Holy One, blessed be He, Lord of the Universe: 'Among the seventy distinct nations that you have in your world, [why] do you give me instructions only concerning Israel? [For instance,] "Command the children of Israel" (Num. 28:2), "Say to the children of Israel" (Ex. 33:5), "Speak to the children of Israel"' (Lev. 1:2).
F. "He said to him, 'The reason is that they stick close to me, in line with the following verse of Scripture: "For as the undergarment cleaves to the loins of a man, so have I caused to cleave unto me the whole house of Israel" (Jer. 13:11).'"

3. The purpose of the religious duties, or commandments, is only to refine or purify people through them:

Leviticus Rabbah XIII

III.1 A. "Every word of God is refined; he is a shield to those who take refuge in him" (Prov. 30:5).
B. Rab said, "The religious duties were handed over only to refine human beings through them."
C. Why so much [engagement]?
D. "He is a shield to those who take refuge in him" (Prov. 30:5) [and through the practice of religious duties gives people the opportunity to gain merit].

4. The demands of the Torah are reasonable and balanced; everything is fair and just, and for each prohibition there is a remission:

Leviticus Rabbah XXII

X.1 A. ["Who executes justice for the oppressed, who gives food to the hungry. The Lord permits what is forbidden" (Ps. 146:7).] "Who executes justice for the oppressed" refers to Israel, concerning whom is written, "Thus says the Lord, the children of Israel are oppressed" (Jer. 50:33).

B. "Who gives food to the hungry" (Ps. 146:7) refers to Israel, concerning whom it is written, "And he afflicted you and made you suffer hunger" (Deut. 8:3).

C. "The Lord permits what is forbidden" (Ps. 146:7): "What I forbade to you, I have permitted to you.

D. "I forbade the abdominal fat in the case of domesticated cattle but permitted it in the case of wild beasts.

E. "I forbade you to eat the sciatic nerve in a wild beast, but I permitted it to you in fowl.

F. "I forbade you beasts not killed through proper slaughter in the case of fowl, but I permitted the same in the case of fish."

X.2 A. R. Aha, R. Bisna, and R. Jonathan in the name of R. Meir: "More that I prohibited to you, I permitted to you.

B. "I forbade you to have sexual relations in the presence of menstrual blood, but I permitted you to have sexual relations despite the presence of hymeneal blood.

C. "I forbade you [to have sexual relations with] a married woman but I permitted you [to have sexual relations with] a captive woman [regardless of her marital status].

D. "I forbade you [to have sexual relations with] a brother's wife [or widow], but I permitted you [to marry] the deceased childless brother's widow.

E. "I forbade you to marry a woman along with her sister, but I permitted you to do so after the sister [you married] had died.

F. "I forbade you to wear a garment made of mixed species [wool and linen], but I permitted you to wear a linen cloak with show fringes made of wool.

G. "I forbade you to eat the meat of a pig, but I permitted you to eat the tongue of a fish [which tastes like pork].

H. "I forbade you to eat abdominal fat [of a beast], but I permitted you to eat ordinary fat.

I. "I forbade you to eat blood, but I permitted you to eat liver.

J. "I forbade you to eat meat with milk, but I permitted you to eat the cow's udder."

5. The numerous religious duties that have been assigned to Israel are marks of God's engagement with the life of Israel. The mark of the election of Israel is the commandments:

Pesiqta deRab Kahana XII

I.1 A. R. Judah bar Simon commenced discourse by citing the following verse: "*Many daughters show how capable they are, but you excel them all. [Charm is a delusion and beauty fleeting; it is the God-fearing woman who is honored. Extol her for the fruit of her toil and let her labors bring her honor in the city gate]* (Prov. 31:29-31):

B. "The first man was assigned six religious duties, and they are: Not worshipping idols, not blaspheming, setting up courts of justice, not murdering, not practicing fornication, not stealing.

C.   "And all of them derive from a single verse of Scripture: *And the Lord God commanded the man, saying, 'You may freely eat of every tree of the garden, [but of the tree of the knowledge of good and evil you shall not eat, for in the day that you eat of it you shall die]'* (Gen. 2:16).

D.   *"And the Lord God commanded the man, saying:* This refers to idolatry, as it is said, *For Ephraim was happy to walk after the command* (Hos. 5:11).

E.   *"The Lord:* This refers to blasphemy, as it is said, *Whoever curses the name of the Lord will surely die* (Lev. 24:16).

F.   *"God:* This refers to setting up courts of justice, as it is said, *God [in context, the judges] you shall not curse* (Ex. 22:27).

G.   *"The man:* This refers to murder, as it is said, *He who sheds the blood of man by man his blood shall be shed* (Gen. 9:6).

H.   *"Saying:* This refers to fornication, as it is said, *Saying, will a man divorce his wife...* (Jer. 3:1).

I.   *"You may freely eat of every tree of the garden:* This refers to the prohibition of stealing, as you say, *but of the tree of the knowledge of good and evil you shall not eat.*

J.   "Noah was commanded, in addition, not to cut a limb from a living beast, as it is said, *But as to meat with its soul – its blood you shall not eat* (Gen. 9:4).

K.   "Abraham was commanded, in addition, concerning circumcision, as it is said, *And as to you, my covenant you shall keep* (Gen. 17:9).

L.   "Isaac was circumcised on the eighth day, as it is said, *And Abraham circumcised Isaac, his son, on the eighth day* (Gen. 21:4).

M.   "Jacob was commanded not to eat the sciatic nerve, as it is said, *On that account the children of Israel will not eat the sciatic nerve* (Gen. 32:33).

N.   "Judah was commanded concerning marrying the childless brother's widow, as it is said, *And Judah said to Onen, Go to the wife of your childless brother and exercise the duties of a levir with her* (Gen. 38:8).

O.   "But as to you, at Sinai you received six hundred thirteen religious duties, two hundred forty-eight religious duties of commission [acts to be done], three hundred sixty-five religious duties of omission [acts not to be done],

P.   "the former matching the two hundred forty-eight limbs that a human being has.

Q.   "Each limb says to a person, 'By your leave, with me do this religious duty.'

R.   "Three hundred sixty-five religious duties of omission [acts not to be done] matching the days of the solar calendar.

S.   "Each day says to a person, 'By your leave, on me do not carry out that transgression.'"

C. Words Form the Bridge from Humanity to God

This topic is not discussed.

D. The Sanctity of the Land of Israel and the People of Israel

1. God had the right to assign the Land of Israel to Israel, because God made the entire world and is owner by right of all creation, so God can do what he wants with everything:

Genesis Rabbah I.II.1

1. A. R. Joshua of Sikhnin in the name of R. Levi commenced [discourse by citing the following verse]: "'He has declared to his people the power of his works, in giving them the heritage of the nations' (Ps. 111:6).

   B. "What is the reason that the Holy One, blessed be He, revealed to Israel what was created on the first day and what on the second?

   C. "It was on account of the nations of the world. It was so that they should not ridicule the Israelites, saying to them, 'Are you not a nation of robbers [having stolen the land from the Canaanites]?'

   D. "It allows the Israelites to answer them, 'And as to you, is there no spoil in your hands? For surely: "The Caphtorim, who came forth out of Caphtor, destroyed them and dwelled in their place" (Deut. 2:23)!

   E. "'The world and everything in it belongs to the Holy One, blessed be He. When he wanted, he gave it to you, and when he wanted, he took it from you and gave it to us.'

   F. "That is in line with what is written, '....in giving them the heritage of the nations, he has declared to his people the power of his works' (Ps. 111:6). [So as to give them the land, he established his right to do so by informing them that he had created it.]

   G. "He told them about the beginning: 'In the beginning God created...' (Gen. 1:1)."

E. Random Events or Chance Express God's Will

This subject does not make an appearance.

F. The Duality of the Torah

1. God consulted the Torah in creating the world; the Torah is the divine design of the world:

Genesis Rabbah I:I.2

2. If one wishes to know the secrets of creation, that person will study the Torah:

Genesis Rabbah I

VI.4 A. Said R. Judah bar Simon, "To begin with, when the world was being created, 'He reveals deep and secret things,' for it is written, 'In the beginning God created the heaven (Gen. 1:1).' But the matter was not spelled out.

   B. "Where then was it spelled out?

   C. "Elsewhere: 'Who stretches out the heaven as a curtain' (Isa. 40:22).

   D. "'....And the earth' (Gen. 1:1). But this matter, too, was not then spelled out.

E.   "Where then was it spelled out?
F.   "Elsewhere: 'For he says to the snow, "Fall on the earth" (Job 37:6).'
G.   "'And God said, Let there be light' (Gen. 1:3).
H.   "And this, too, was not spelled out.
I.   "Where then was it spelled out?
J.   "Elsewhere: 'Who covers yourself with light as with a garment' (Ps. 104:2)."

3. Accepting the Torah makes an ordinary human being into an Israelite. Then the proselyte becomes fully an Israelite, and his daughter may marry into the priesthood, if he studies the Torah and otherwise attains merit, like any other Israelite:

Genesis Rabbah LXX

V.1   A.   "...Will give me bread to eat and clothing to wear":
      B.   Aqilas the proselyte came to R. Eliezer and said to him, "Is all the gain that is coming to the proselyte going to be contained in this verse: '...And loves the proselyte, giving him food and clothing' (Deut. 10:18)?"
      C.   He said to him, "And is something for which the old man [Jacob] beseeched going to be such a small thing in your view namely, '...will give me bread to eat and clothing to wear'? [God] comes and hands it over to [a proselyte] on a reed [and the proselyte does not have to beg for it]."
      D.   He came to R. Joshua, who commenced by saying words to appease him: "'Bread' refers to Torah, as it is said, 'Come, eat of my bread' (Prov. 9:5). 'Clothing' refers to the cloak of a disciple of sages.
      E.   "When a person has the merit of studying the Torah, he has the merit of carrying out a religious duty. [So the proselyte receives a great deal when he gets bread and clothing, namely, entry into the estate of disciples].
      F.   "And not only so, but his daughters may be chosen for marriage into the priesthood, so that their sons' sons will offer burnt-offerings on the altar. [So the proselyte may also look forward to entry into the priests' caste. That statement will now be spelled out.]
      G.   "'Bread' refers to the showbread.'
      H.   "'Clothing' refers to the garments of the priesthood.'
      I.   "So lo, we deal with the sanctuary.
      J.   "How do we know that the same sort of blessing applies in the provinces? 'Bread' speaks of the dough-offering [that is separated in the provinces], 'while 'clothing' refers to the first fleece [handed over to the priest]."

G. Israel and the Nations

1. The prophets sent to Israel, for example, Moses, were of a different order entirely from those sent to the gentiles, and, from Moses forward, prophecy was taken away from the nations altogether:

Leviticus Rabbah I

XIII.1   A.   What is the difference between the prophets of Israel and those of the nations [= Gen. R. 52:5]?

       B.   R. Hama b. R. Haninah and R. Issachar of Kepar Mandi:

       C.   R. Hama b. R. Hanina said, "The Holy One, blessed be He, is revealed to the prophets of the nations of the world only in partial speech, in line with the following verse of Scripture: 'And God called [WYQR, rather than WYQR, as at Lev. 1:1] Balaam' [Num. 23:16]. On the other hand, [he reveals himself] to the prophets of Israel in full and complete speech, as it is said, 'And [the Lord] called (WYQR) to Moses' (Lev. 1:1)."

       D.   Said R. Issachar of Kepar Mandi, "Should that [prophecy, even in partial form] be [paid to them as their] wage? [Surely not, in fact there is no form of speech to gentile prophets, who are frauds]. [The connotation of] the language, 'And [God] called (WYQR) to Balaam' [Num. 23:16] is solely uncleanness. That is in line with the usage in the following verse of Scripture: 'That is not clean, by that which happens (MQRH) by night' [Deut. 23:11]. [So the root is the same, with the result that YQR at Num. 23:16 does not bear the meaning of God's calling to Balaam. God rather declares Balaam unclean.]

       E.   "But the prophets of Israel [are addressed] in language of holiness, purity, clarity, in language used by the ministering angels to praise God. That is in line with the following verse of Scripture: 'And they called (QR) one to another and said' (Isa. 6:3)."

2.   Israel and the nations of the world are comparable, but when a word applies to Israel, it serves to praise, and when the same word applies to the nations, it underlines their negative character. Both are called congregation, but the nations' congregation is desolate, and so throughout, as the context of the passage cited concerning the nations repeatedly indicates. The nations' sages are wiped out; the unblemished nations go down to the pit; the nations, called men, only work iniquity:

Leviticus Rabbah V

III.2   A.   "[If the whole congregation of Israel commits a sin unwittingly and the thing is hidden from the eyes of the assembly, and they do any one of the things which the Lord has commanded not to be done and are guilty, when the sin which they have committed becomes known, the assembly shall offer a young bull for a sin-offering and bring it before the tent of meeting;] and the elders of the congregation shall lay their hands [upon the head of the bull before the Lord]" (Lev. 4:13-15).

       B.   [Since, in laying their hands (SMK) on the head of the bull, the elders sustain (SMK) the community by adding to it the merit they enjoy,] said R. Isaac, "The nations of the world have none to sustain them, for it is written, 'And those who sustain Egypt will fall' (Ezek. 30:6).

C.   "But Israel has those who sustain it, as it is written: 'And the elders of the congregation shall lay their hands [and so sustain Israel]' (Lev. 4:15)."

III.3   A.   Said R. Eleazar, "The nations of the world are called a congregation, and Israel is called a congregation.

B.   "The nations of the world are called a congregation: 'For the congregation of the godless shall be desolate' (Job 15:34).

C.   "And Israel is called a congregation: 'And the elders of the congregation shall lay their hands' (Lev. 4:15).

D.   "The nations of the world are called sturdy bulls and Israel is called sturdy bulls.

E.   "The nations of the world are called sturdy bulls: 'The congregation of [sturdy] bulls with the calves of the peoples' (Ps. 68:31).

F.   "Israel is called sturdy bulls, as it is said, 'Listen to me, you sturdy [bullish] of heart' (Isa. 46:13).

G.   "The nations of the world are called excellent, and Israel is called excellent.

H.   "The nations of the world are called excellent: 'You and the daughters of excellent nations' (Ex. 32:18).

I.   "Israel is called excellent: 'They are the excellent, in whom is all my delight' (Ps. 16:4).

J.   "The nations of the world are called sages, and Israel is called sages.

K.   "The nations of the world are called sages: 'And I shall wipe out sages from Edom' (Obad. 1:8).

L.   "And Israel is called sages: 'Sages store up knowledge' (Prov. 10:14).

M.   "The nations of the world are called unblemished, and Israel is called unblemished.

N.   "The nations of the world are called unblemished: 'Unblemished as are those that go down to the pit' (Prov. 1:12).

O.   "And Israel is called unblemished: 'The unblemished will inherit goodness' (Prov. 28:10).

P.   "The nations of the world are called men, and Israel is called men.

Q.   "The nations of the world are called men: 'And you men who work iniquity' (Ps. 141:4).

R.   "And Israel is called men: 'To you who are men I call' (Prov. 8:4).

S.   "The nations of the world are called righteous, and Israel is called righteous.

T.   "The nations of the world are called righteous: 'And righteous men shall judge them' (Ezek. 23:45).

U.   "And Israel is called righteous: 'And your people – all of them are righteous' (Isa. 60:21).

V.   "The nations of the world are called mighty, and Israel is called mighty.

W.   "The nations of the world are called mighty: 'Why do you boast of evil, O mighty man' (Ps. 52:3).

X.   "And Israel is called mighty: 'Mighty in power, those who do his word' (Ps. 103:20).

3. Israel's suffering among the nations leads them to look upward to their father in heaven; it is good for Israel to be surrounded by enemies; Israel will be redeemed at the expense of its enemies:

Leviticus Rabbah XXIII

V.1   A.   R. Hanina son of R. Idi interpreted the verse to speak of the current generations:

       B.   "'Like a rose among thorns': Just as, when the north wind blows on the rose, it bends southward, and a thorn pricks it, and when the south wind blows, it bends northward, and a thorn pricks it, and all the while, the heart [of its stem] points upward,

       C.   "so even though Israel is enslaved among the nations of the world by surcharges, head taxes, and confiscations, nonetheless their heart points upward toward their father in heaven.

       D.   "So did David say, 'My heart is steadfast, O God, my heart is steadfast. I will sing and make melody!' [Ps. 57:8]. And what is further written? 'My eyes are always toward the Lord' (Ps. 25:15)."

V.2   A.   R. Abihu interpreted the cited verse to speak of the coming redemption:

       B.   "'Like a rose among thorns': Just as when a householder wants to pick a rose, he burns [the thorns] around it and plucks it,

       C.   "so: 'The Lord has commanded concerning Jacob that those who are around him should be his enemies' (Lam. 1:17).

       D.   "For example, Halamo [which is gentile, is enemy] to Naweh [which is Israelite], Susita to Tiberias, Qastra to Haifa, Jericho to Nauran, Lud to Ono.

       E.   "That is in line with the following verse of Scripture: 'This is Jerusalem. I have set her in the midst of the gentiles' (Ezek. 5:5).

       F.   "Tomorrow, when redemption comes to Israel, what will the Holy One, blessed be He, do to them? He will bring a flame and burn [the area] around [Israel].

       G.   "That is in line with the following verse of Scripture: 'And the peoples will be as burnings of lime, as thorns cut down that are burned in fire' (Isa. 33:12)."

4. The enmity of the nations assures God's forgiveness of Israel; he will not give them occasion to rejoice over the fall of Israel:

Leviticus Rabbah XXVII

VI.1   A.   "O my people, what have I done to you, in what have I wearied you? Testify against me" (Mic. 6:3).

       B.   Said R. Aha, "'Testify against me' and receive a reward, but 'Do not bear false witness' (Ex. 20:13) and face a settlement of accounts in the age to come."

VI.2   A.   Said R. Samuel b. R. Nahman, "On three occasions the Holy One, blessed be He, came to engage in argument with Israel, and the nations of the world rejoiced, saying, 'Can these ever [dare] engage in an argument with their creator? Now he will wipe them out of the world.'

B.   "One was when he said to them, 'Come, and let us reason together, says the Lord' (Isa. 1:18). When the Holy One, blessed be He, saw that the nations of the world were rejoicing, he turned the matter to [Israel's] advantage: 'If your sins are as scarlet, they shall be white as snow' (Isa. 1:18).

C.   "Then the nations of the world were astonished, and said, 'This is repentance, and this is rebuke? He has planned only to amuse himself with his children.'

D.   "[A second time was] when he said to them, 'Hear, you mountains, the controversy of the Lord' (Mic. 6:2), the nations of the world rejoiced, saying, 'How can these ever [dare] engage in an argument with their creator? Now he will wipe them out of the world.'

E.   "When the Holy One, blessed be He, saw that the nations of the world were rejoicing, he turned the matter to [Israel's] advantage: 'O my people, what have I done to you? In what have I wearied you? Testify against me' [Mic. 6:3]. 'Remember what Balak king of Moab devised' (Mic. 6:5).

F.   "Then the nations of the world were astonished, saying, 'This is repentence, and this is rebuke, one following the other? He has planned only to amuse himself with his children.'

G.   "[A third time was] when he said to them, 'The Lord has an indictment against Judah, and will punish Jacob according to his ways' (Hos. 12:2), the nations of the world rejoiced, saying, 'How can these ever [dare] engage in an argument with their creator? Now he will wipe them out of the world.'

H.   "When the Holy One, blessed be He, saw that the nations of the world were rejoicing, he turned the matter to [Israel's] advantage. That is in line with the following verse of Scripture: 'In the womb he [Jacob = Israel] took his brother [Esau = other nations] by the heel [and in his manhood he strove with God. He strove with the angel and prevailed, he wept and sought his favor]' (Hos. 12:3-4)."

5.   Israel's sin brings about its fate, but the gentiles who deliver the divine punishment themselves have sinned and will be punished, too:

Pesiqta deRab Kahana XIX

I.1   A.   *[You know what reproaches I bear, all my anguish is seen by you.] Reproach has broken my heart, my shame and my dishonor are past hope; I looked for consolation and received none, for comfort and did not find any* (Ps. 69:19-21):

B.   "The reproach that has broken us are the Ammonites and Moabites."

C.   You find that when sin had made it possible for the gentiles to enter Jerusalem, the Ammonites and Moabites came in with them.

D.   They came into the house of the holy of holies and took the cherubim and put them onto a bier and paraded them around the streets of Jerusalem, saying, "Did not the Israelites say, 'We do not worship idols'? See what they were doing."

E.   That is in line with this verse of Scripture: *Moab and Seir say, [Behold the house of Judah is like all the other nations]* (Ezek. 25:8).

F.   What did they say? "Woe, woe, all of them are as one."

G.   From that time the Holy One, blessed be He, said, *I have heard the shame of Moab and the blaspheming of the children of Ammon, who have shamed my people, the children of Israel, and aggrandized their border.... Therefore as I live, says the Lord of hosts, the God of Israel, surely Moab shall be as Sodom and the children of Amon as Gomorrah* (Zeph. 2:8-9).

H. History: Its Meaning and Divisions

1.   The condition of the natural world corresponds to the condition of the world of humanity, and the supernatural condition of Israel is attested in nature as well; this point recurs, but is registered here alone:

Genesis Rabbah II

I.1   A.   ["And the earth was unformed..." (Gen. 1:2):]

          B.   R. Judah b. R. Simon interpreted the verse as referring to coming generations, [as follows]:

          C.   "'The earth was unformed' refers to Adam, who was [Freedman:] reduced to complete nothingness [on account of his sin].

          D.   "'And void' refers to Cain, who sought to return the world to unformedness and void.

          E.   "'And darkness was upon the face of the deep' (Gen. 1:2) refers to the generation of Enosh: 'And their works are in the dark' (Isa. 29:15).

          F.   "'Upon the face of the deep' (Gen. 1:2) refers to the generation of the flood: 'On the same day were all the fountains of the great deep broken up' (Gen. 7:11).

          G.   "'And the spirit of God hovered over the face of the water' (Gen. 1:2): 'And God made a wind pass over the earth' (Gen. 8:1).

          H.   "Said the Holy One, blessed be He, 'For how long will the world make its way in darkness. Let light come.'

          I.   "'And God said, "Let there be light"' (Gen. 1:3). This refers to Abraham. That is in line with the following verse of Scripture: 'Who has raised up one from the earth, whom he calls in righteousness to his foot' (Isa. 41:23).

          J.   "'And God called the light day' (Gen. 1:3) refers to Jacob.

          K.   "'And the darkness he called night' (Gen. 1:30) refers to Esau.

          L.   "'And there was evening' refers to Esau.

          M.   "'And there was morning' refers to Jacob.

          N.   "'One day'– for the Holy One, blessed be He, gave him one day, and what is that day? It is the Day of Atonement. [Freedman, p. 17, n. 1: It is the one day over which Satan, symbolizing the wickedness of Esau, has no power.]"

II.1   A.   R. Simeon b. Laqish interpreted the verses at hand to speak of the empires [of the historical age to come].

          B.   "'The earth was unformed' refers to Babylonia, 'I beheld the earth and lo, it was unformed' (Jer. 4:23).

          C.   "'And void' refers to Media: 'They hasted [using the letters of the same root as the word for void] to bring Haman' (Est. 6:14).

D. "'Darkness' refers to Greece, which clouded the vision of the Israelites through its decrees, for it said to Israel, 'Write on the horn of an ox [as a public proclamation for all to see] that you have no portion in the God of Israel.'

E. "'...Upon the face of the deep' refers to the wicked kingdom [of Rome].

F. "Just as the deep surpasses investigation, so the wicked kingdom surpasses investigation.

G. "'And the spirit of God hovers' refers to the spirit of the Messiah, in line with the following verse of Scripture: 'And the spirit of the Lord shall rest upon him' (Isa. 11:2)."

The same point is made in a different way, when the creation of the world is shown as a paradigm for the actions and condition of humanity:

Genesis Rabbah III

VIII.1 A. Said R. Yannai, "At the beginning of the creation of the world the Holy One, blessed be He, foresaw the deeds of the righteous and the deeds of the wicked.

B. "'And the earth was unformed and void' refers to the deeds of the wicked.

C. "'And God said, "Let there be light"' refers to the deeds of the righteous.

D. "'And God saw the light, that it was good,' refers to the deeds of the righteous.

E. "'And God divided between the light and the darkness' means, [he divided] between the deeds of the righteous and the deeds of the wicked.

F. "'And God called the light day' refers to the deeds of the righteous.

G. "'And the darkness he called night' refers to the deeds of the wicked.

H. "'And there was evening' refers to the deeds of the wicked.

I. "'And there was morning' refers to the deeds of the righteous.

J. "'One day,' for the Holy One, blessed be He, gave them one day, [and what day is that]? It is the day of judgment."

2. The four kingdoms who have ruled the world up to now correspond to nature, and all four will give way to Israel's ultimate dominion:

Genesis Rabbah XVI

IV.1 A. R. Tanhuma in the name of R. Joshua b. Levi said to him, "In the future the Holy One, blessed be He, is destined to give a cup of bitterness to the nations to drink from the place from which this [river] goes forth. And what is the verse that so indicates? 'A river flowed out of Eden to water the garden' (Gen. 2:10).

B. "This refers to the four kingdoms, forming the counterpart to the four heads [into which the river is divided].

C. "'The name of the first is Pishon' (Gen. 2:11) refers to Babylonia, in line with this verse: 'And their horsemen spread (*pashu*) themselves' (Hab. 1:8). And it also responds to [Freedman:] the midget dwarf, who was smaller than a handbreadth [that is, Nebuchadnezzar].

D. "'It is the one which flows around the whole land of Havilah' [again, referring to Babylonia,] for [Nebuchadnezzar] came up and encompassed the entire Land of Israel, concerning which it is written, 'Hope you in God, for I shall yet praise him' (Ps. 42:6). [There is a play on the words for Havilah and hope.]

E. "'...Where there is gold' (Gen. 2:11) speaks of words of Torah, which are 'more to be desired than gold and than much fine gold' (Ps. 19:1). [Compare above, XVI:II.3.B. 'Actual gold, not something that symbolizes something else of great value'].

F. "'And the gold of that land is good' (Gen. 2:11) teaches that there is no Torah like the Torah of the Land of Israel, and there is no wisdom like the wisdom of the Land of Israel.

G. "'Bdellium and onyx stone are there' (Gen. 2:12) refers to Scripture, Mishnah, Talmud, supplementary teachings, and lore.

H. "'And the name of the second river is Gihon' refers to Media, for Haman [who was a Median] had [because of his deranged hatred of Israel] inflamed eyes like those of a serpent, on the count: 'On your belly (GHWNK) you will go, and dust you will eat all the days of your life' (Gen. 3:14).

I. "'It is the one which flows around the whole land of Cush' (Gen. 2:13). This allusion is to [Ahasueros, the Median, as in this verse]: 'Who reigned from India even to Cush' (Est. 1:1).

J. "'And the name of the third river is Tigris' (Gen. 2:14) refers to Greece, which was sharp and speedy in making evil decrees, saying to Israel, 'Write on the horn of an ox [as a public proclamation] that you have no share in the God of Israel.'"

3. Israel's history in the Land is comparable to Adam's history in Eden:

Genesis Rabbah XIX

IX.2 A. R. Abbahu in the name of R. Yosé bar Haninah: "It is written, 'But they are like a man [Adam], they have transgressed the covenant' (Hos. 6:7).

B. "'They are like a man,' specifically, like the first man. [We shall now compare the story of the first man in Eden with the story of Israel in its land.]

C. "'In the case of the first man, I brought him into the garden of Eden, I commanded him, he violated my commandment, I judged him to be sent away and driven out, but I mourned for him, saying "How..." [which begins the book of Lamentations, hence stands for a lament, but which, as we just saw, also is written with the consonants that also yield, "Where are you"].

D. "'I brought him into the garden of Eden,' as it is written, 'And the Lord God took the man and put him into the garden of Eden' (Gen. 2:15).

E. "'I commanded him,' as it is written, 'And the Lord God commanded...' (Gen. 2:16).

F. "'And he violated my commandment,' as it is written, 'Did you eat from the tree concerning which I commanded you' (Gen. 3:11).

G. "'I judged him to be sent away,' as it is written, 'And the Lord God sent him from the garden of Eden' (Gen. 3:23).

H.   "'And I judged him to be driven out.' 'And he drove out the man' (Gen. 3:24).

I.   "'But I mourned for him, saying, "How...."' 'And he said to him, "Where are you"' (Gen. 3:9), and the word for 'where are you' is written, 'How....'

J.   "'So, too, in the case of his descendants, [God continues to speak,] I brought them into the Land of Israel, I commanded them, they violated my commandment, I judged them to be sent out and driven away but I mourned for them, saying, "How...."'

K.   "'I brought them into the Land of Israel.' 'And I brought you into the land of Carmel' (Jer. 2:7).

L.   "'I commanded them.' 'And you, command the children of Israel' (Ex. 27:20). 'Command the children of Israel' (Lev. 24:2).

M.   "'They violated my commandment.' 'And all Israel have violated your Torah' (Dan. 9:11).

N.   "'I judged them to be sent out.' 'Send them away, out of my sight and let them go forth' (Jer 15:1).

O.   "'....And driven away.' 'From my house I shall drive them' (Hos. 9:15).

P.   "'But I mourned for them, saying, "How...."' 'How has the city sat solitary, that was full of people' (Lam. 1:1)."

4.   Israel and Adam are counterparts, but opposites; what Adam did not succeed in accomplishing, Israel realized in abundance: obedience to the Torah.

Genesis Rabbah XXIV

V.2   A.   Said R. Yudah, "The first man [Adam] was worthy to have the Torah given through him. What is the verse of Scripture that so indicates? 'This is the book of the generations of man' (Gen. 5:1). ['This book can be given over to man.']

      B.   "Said the Holy One, blessed be He, 'He is the creation of my hands, and should I not give it to him?' Then he reversed himself and said, 'I gave him no more than six commandments to follow, and he did not stand by them, so how can I now give him six hundred thirteen commandments, two hundred forty-eight commandments of things to do and three hundred sixty-five commandments of things not to do?'

      C.   "'And he said to man,' meaning, 'not-to-man' [reading the L before the consonants for 'man,' read as 'to man,' as though it bore the negative]. 'To man I shall not give it. And to whom shall I give it? To his children.' 'This is the book that belongs to the children of man' (Gen. 5:1)."

V.3   A.   Said R. Jacob of Kefar Hanan, "The first man was worthy to produce the twelve tribes. What is the verse of Scripture that so indicates? 'This is the book of man.'

      B.   "The word 'this' in Hebrew has consonants with the numerical value of twelve (ZH).

      C.   "Said the Holy One, blessed be He, 'He is the creation of my hands, and should I not give it to him?' Then he reversed himself and said,

'Two sons I gave him, and one of them went and killed his fellow.
How shall I then give him twelve?'

D. "'And he said to man,' (Job 28:27) meaning, 'not-to-man' [reading
the L before the consonants for man as though it bore the negative].
'To man I shall not give it. And to whom shall I give it? To his
children': 'This is the book that belongs to the children of man'
(Gen. 5:1)."

5. God responds to the devotion of Israel and remembers in behalf of a
later generation the achievements of an earlier one; God responds
especially to the devotion of those who are persecuted in his name:

Genesis Rabbah XXXIV

IX.4   A. "And when the Lord smelled the pleasing odor, [the Lord said in
his heart, 'I will never again curse the ground because of man, for
the imagination of man's heart is evil from his youth']" (Gen. 8:21):

B. He smelled the fragrance of the flesh of Abraham, our father,
coming up from the heated furnace.

C. He smelled the fragrance of the flesh of Hananiah, Mishael, and
Azariah, coming up from the heated furnace.

D. The matter may be compared to the case of a king, whose courtier
brought him a valuable present. It was a fine piece of meat on a
lovely plate [following Freedman].

E. His son came along and brought him nothing. His grandson came
along and brought him a present. He said to him, "The value of the
gift you brought is equivalent to the value of the gift your
grandfather brought."

F. So God smelled the fragrance of the sacrifice of the generation of
persecution.

6. The deeds of the patriarchs prefigure the history of Israel, and
actions they took shaped the future history of their descendents:

Genesis Rabbah XLIV

XV.1   A. Another matter: "Bring me a heifer three years old, [a she-goat three
years old, a ram three years old, a turtledove, and a young pigeon]"
(Gen. 15:9):

B. "Bring me a heifer three years old" refers to Babylonia, that
produced three [kings important in Israel's history],
Nebuchadnezzar, Evil Merodach, and Balshazzar.

C. "...A she-goat three years old" refers to Media, that also produced
three kings, Cyrus, Darius, and Ahasuerus.

D. "...A ram three years old" refers to Greece.

E. R. Eleazar and R. Yohanan:

F. R. Eleazar said, "Greece conquered every point on the compass
except for the east."

G. R. Yohanan said to him, "And indeed so, for is it not written, 'I saw
the ram pushing westward and northward and southward, and no
beasts could stand before him' (Dan. 8:4)?"

H. That indeed is the view of R. Eleazar, for the verse at hand does not
refer to the east.

       I.   "...A turtledove, and a young pigeon" (Gen. 15:9) refers to Edom. It was a turtledove that would rob.

7.   God informed Abraham about what would happen in the future history of Israel. Abraham in fact formulated what would happen to Israel in the future, making choices about his descendants' fate:

Genesis Rabbah XLIV

XVIII.1 A. "Then the Lord said to Abram, 'Know of a surety [that your descendants will be sojourners in a land that is not theirs, and they will be slaves there, and they will be oppressed for four hundred years; but I will bring judgment on the nation which they serve, and afterward they shall come out with great possessions']" (Gen. 15:13-14):

       B.   "Know" that I shall scatter them.

       C.   "Of a certainty" that I shall bring them back together again.

       D.   "Know" that I shall put them out as a pledge [in expiation of their sins].

       E.   "Of a certainty" that I shall redeem them.

       F.   "Know" that I shall make them slaves.

       G.   "Of a certainty" that I shall free them.

The same rule, that the actions of the patriarchs prefigure the future life of Israel, pertains also to the redemption of Israel and the resurrection of the dead:

Genesis Rabbah LVI

I.1   A.   "On the third day Abraham lifted up his eyes and saw the place afar off" (Gen. 22:4):

       B.   "After two days he will revive us, on the third day he will raise us up, that we may live in his presence" (Hos.16:2).

       C.   On the third day of the tribes: "And Joseph said to them on the third day, 'This do and live'" (Gen. 42:18).

       D.   On the third day of the giving of the Torah: "And it came to pass on the third day when it was morning" (Ex. 19:16).

       E.   On the third day of the spies: "And hide yourselves there for three days" (Josh 2:16).

       F.   On the third day of Jonah: "And Jonah was in the belly of the fish three days and three nights" (Jonah 2:1).

       G.   On the third day of the return from the Exile: "And we abode there three days" (Ezra 8:32).

       H.   On the third day of the resurrection of the dead: "After two days he will revive us, on the third day he will raise us up, that we may live in his presence" (Hos. 16:2).

       I.   On the third day of Esther: "Now it came to pass on the third day that Esther put on her royal apparel" (Est. 5:1).

       J.   She put on the monarchy of the house of her fathers.

       K.   On account of what sort of merit?

       L.   Rabbis say, "On account of the third day of the giving of the Torah."

M.   R. Levi said, "It is on account of the merit of the third day of Abraham: 'On the third day Abraham lifted up his eyes and saw the place afar off' (Gen. 22:4)."

8.   Israel and Rome are brothers and enemies, and they are comparable opposites:

Genesis Rabbah LXIII

VII.2   A.   "Two nations are in your womb, [and two peoples, born of you, shall be divided; the one shall be stronger than the other, and the elder shall serve the younger]" (Gen. 25:23):

     B.   There are two proud nations in your womb, this one takes pride in his world, and that one takes pride in his world.

     C.   This one takes pride in his monarchy, and that one takes pride in his monarchy.

     D.   There are two proud nations in your womb.

     E.   Hadrian represents the nations, Solomon, Israel.

     F.   There are two who are hated by the nations in your womb. All the nations hate Esau, and all the nations hate Israel.

     G.   [Following Freedman's reading:] The one whom your creator hates is in your womb: "And Esau I hated" (Mal. 1:3).

9.   The entire structure of Judaism was foreseen by Jacob in the well in the field, that is, the events of the exodus and the wandering in the wilderness; Zion; the Temple; the history of Israel under the three kingdoms; the disciples of sages in God's presence; the synagogue; Sinai; the Presence of God:

Genesis Rabbah LXX

VIII.2   A.   "As he looked, he saw a well in the field":

     B.   R. Hama bar Hanina interpreted the verse in six ways [that is, he divides the verse into six clauses and systematically reads each of the clauses in light of the others and in line with an overriding theme]:

     C.   "'As he looked, he saw a well in the field': This refers to the well [of water in the wilderness, Num. 21:17].

     D.   "'...And lo, three flocks of sheep lying beside it': Specifically, Moses, Aaron, and Miriam.

     E.   "'...For out of that well the flocks were watered': For from there each one drew water for his standard, tribe, and family."

     F.   "And the stone upon the well's mouth was great":

     G.   Said R. Hanina, "It was only the size of a little sieve."

     H.   [Reverting to Hama's statement:] "'...And put the stone back in its place upon the mouth of the well': For the coming journeys. [Thus the first interpretation applies the passage at hand to the life of Israel in the wilderness.]

VIII.3   A.   "'As he looked, he saw a well in the field': Refers to Zion.

     B.   "'...And lo, three flocks of sheep lying beside it': Refers to the three festivals.

C.   "'...For out of that well the flocks were watered': From there they drank of the holy spirit.

D.   "'...The stone on the well's mouth was large': This refers to the rejoicing of the house of the water drawing."

E.   Said R. Hoshaiah, "Why is it called 'the house of the water drawing'? Because from there they drink of the Holy Spirit."

F.   [Resuming Hama b. Hanina's discourse:] "'...And when all the flocks were gathered there': Coming from 'the entrance of Hamath to the brook of Egypt' (1 Kgs. 8:66).

G.   "'...The shepherds would roll the stone from the mouth of the well and water the sheep': For from there they would drink of the Holy Spirit.

H.   "'...And put the stone back in its place upon the mouth of the well': Leaving it in place until the coming festival. [Thus the second interpretation reads the verse in light of the Temple celebration of the Festival of Tabernacles.]

VIII.4 A.   "'...As he looked, he saw a well in the field': This refers to Zion.

B.   "'...And lo, three flocks of sheep lying beside it': This refers to the three courts, concerning which we have learned in the Mishnah: **There were three courts there, one at the gateway of the Temple mount, one at the gateway of the courtyard, and one in the chamber of the hewn stones [M. San. 11:2].**

C.   "'...For out of that well the flocks were watered': For from there they would hear the ruling.

D.   "The stone on the well's mouth was large': This refers to the high court that was in the chamber of the hewn stones.

E.   "'...And when all the flocks were gathered there': This refers to the courts in session in the Land of Israel.

F.   "'...The shepherds would roll the stone from the mouth of the well and water the sheep': For from there they would hear the ruling.

G.   "'...And put the stone back in its place upon the mouth of the well': For they would give and take until they had produced the ruling in all the required clarity." [The third interpretation reads the verse in light of the Israelite institution of justice and administration.]

VIII.5 A.   "'As he looked, he saw a well in the field': This refers to Zion.

B.   "'...And lo, three flocks of sheep lying beside it': This refers to the first three kingdoms [Babylonia, Media, Greece].

C.   "'...For out of that well the flocks were watered': For they enriched the treasures that were laid upon up in the chambers of the Temple.

D.   "'...The stone on the well's mouth was large': This refers to the merit attained by the patriarchs.

E.   "'...And when all the flocks were gathered there': This refers to the wicked kingdom, which collects troops through levies over all the nations of the world.

F.   "'...The shepherds would roll the stone from the mouth of the well and water the sheep': For they enriched the treasures that were laid upon up in the chambers of the Temple.

G.   "'...And put the stone back in its place upon the mouth of the well': In the age to come the merit attained by the patriarchs will stand [in defense of Israel].' [So the fourth interpretation interweaves the themes of the Temple cult and the domination of the four monarchies.]

VIII.6 A. "'As he looked, he saw a well in the field': This refers to the sanhedrin.

B. "'...And lo, three flocks of sheep lying beside it': This alludes to the three rows of disciples of sages that would go into session in their presence.

C. "For out of that well the flocks were watered': For from there they would listen to the ruling of the law.

D. "'...The stone on the well's mouth was large': This refers to the most distinguished member of the court, who determines the law decision.

E. "'...And when all the flocks were gathered there': This refers to disciples of the sages in the Land of Israel.

F. "'...The shepherds would roll the stone from the mouth of the well and water the sheep': For from there they would listen to the ruling of the law.

G. "'...And put the stone back in its place upon the mouth of the well': For they would give and take until they had produced the ruling in all the required clarity." [The fifth interpretation again reads the verse in light of the Israelite institution of legal education and justice.]

VIII.7 A. "'As he looked, he saw a well in the field': This refers to the synagogue.

B. "'...And lo, three flocks of sheep lying beside it': This refers to the three who are called to the reading of the Torah on weekdays.

C. "'...For out of that well the flocks were watered': For from there they hear the reading of the Torah.

D. "'...The stone on the well's mouth was large': This refers to the impulse to do evil.

E. "'...And when all the flocks were gathered there': This refers to the congregation.

F. "'...The shepherds would roll the stone from the mouth of the well and water the sheep': For from there they hear the reading of the Torah.

G. "'...And put the stone back in its place upon the mouth of the well': For once they go forth [from the hearing of the reading of the Torah] the impulse to do evil reverts to its place." [The sixth and last interpretation turns to the twin themes of the reading of the Torah in the synagogue and the evil impulse, temporarily driven off through the hearing of the Torah.]

10. Israel's rule will follow that of Rome; the Messiah will come when Rome falls, and Israel will take over:

Genesis Rabbah LXXXIII

IV.3 A. "Magdiel and Iram: These are the chiefs of Edom, that is Esau, the father of Edom, according to their dwelling places in the land of their possession" (Gen. 36:42):

B. On the day on which Litrinus came to the throne, there appeared to R. Ammi in a dream this message: "Today Magdiel has come to the throne."

C. He said, "One more king is required for Edom [and then Israel's turn will come]."

IV.4 A. Said R. Hanina of Sepphoris, "Why was he called Iram? For he is destined to amass [a word using the same letters] riches for the king-messiah."

B. Said R. Levi, "There was the case of a ruler in Rome who wasted the treasuries of his father. Elijah of blessed memory appeared to him in a dream. He said to him, 'Your fathers collected treasures and you waste them.'

C. "He did not budge until he filled the treasuries again."

11. The history of Israel among the nations is foreseen by prophecy and conveyed by apocalyptic. The nations at hand are Babylonia, Media, Greece, and Rome, time and again differentiated from the first three. The matter unfolds rather majestically, introducing first one theme – the nations' role in the history of Israel, their hostile treatment of Israel – and then the next, the food taboos, finally bringing the two themes together. We can identify each of the successive kingdoms with the four explicitly tabooed animals of Lev. 11:1-8: camel, rock badger, hare, pig. Then, as we see, the reasons for the taboo assigned to each of them are worked out, in a triple sequence of plays on words, with special reference to the secondary possibilities presented by the words for "chew the cud," "bring up GRH." So while the first impression is that a diverse set of materials has been strung together, upon a closer glance we see quite the opposite: a purposive and careful arrangement of distinct propositions, each leading to, and intensifying the force of, the next. That is why at the climax comes the messianic reference to Israel's ultimate inheritance of the power and dominion of Rome.

Leviticus Rabbah XIII

V.1 A. Said R. Ishmael b. R. Nehemiah, "All the prophets foresaw what the pagan kingdoms would do [to Israel].

B. "The first man foresaw what the pagan kingdoms would do [to Israel].

C. "That is in line with the following verse of Scripture: 'A river flowed out of Eden [to water the garden, and there it divided and became four rivers]' (Gen. 2:10). [The four rivers stand for the four kingdoms, Babylonia, Media, Greece, and Rome]."

V.3 A. "[There it divided] and became four rivers" (Gen 2:10) – this refers to the four kingdoms.

B. "The name of the first is Pishon (PSWN); [it is the one which flows around the whole land of Havilah, where there is gold; and the gold of that land is good; bdellium and onyx stone are there]" (Gen. 2:11-12).

C.   This refers to Babylonia, on account [of the reference to Babylonia in the following verse:] "And their [the Babylonians'] horsemen spread themselves (PSW)" (Hab. 1:8).

D.   [It is further] on account of [Nebuchadnezzar's being] a dwarf, shorter than ordinary men by a handbreadth.

E.   "[It is the one which flows around the whole land of Havilah" (Gen. 2:11).

F.   This [reference to the river's flowing around the whole land] speaks of Nebuchadnezzar, the wicked man, who came up and surrounded the entire Land of Israel, which places its hope in the Holy One, blessed be He.

V.4   A.   "The name of the second river is Gihon; [it is the one which flows around the whole land of Cush]" (Gen. 2:13).

B.   This refers to Media, which produced Haman, that wicked man, who spit out venom like a serpent.

C.   It is on account of the verse: "On your belly will you go" (Gen. 3:14).

V.5   A.   "And the name of the third river is Tigris (HDQL), [which flows east of Assyria]" (Gen. 2:14).

B.   This refers to Greece [Syria], which was sharp (HD) and frivolous (QL) in making its decrees, saying to Israel, "Write on the horn of an ox [= announce publicly] that you have no portion in the God of Israel."

C.   "Which flows east (QDMT) of Assyria" (Gen. 2:14).

V.6   A.   "And the fourth river is the Euphrates (PRT)" (Gen. 2:14).

B.   This refers to Edom [Rome], since it was fruitful (PRT), and multiplied through the prayer of the elder [Isaac at Gen. 27:39].

V.7   A.   (Gen. R. 42:2:) Abraham foresaw what the evil kingdoms would do [to Israel].

B.   "[As the sun was going down,] a deep sleep fell on Abraham; [and lo, a dread and great darkness fell upon him]" (Gen. 15:12).

C.   "Dread" (YMH) refers to Babylonia, on account of the statement, "Then Nebuchadnezzer was full of fury (HMH)" (Dan. 3:19).

D.   "Darkness" refers to Media, which brought darkness to Israel through its decrees: "To destroy, to slay, and to wipe out all the Jews" (Est. 7:4).

E.   "Great" refers to Greece.

F.   Said R. Judah b. R. Simon, "The verse teaches that the kingdom of Greece set up one hundred twenty-seven governors, one hundred and twenty-seven hyparchs, and one hundred twenty-seven commanders."

G.   And rabbis say, "They were sixty in each category."

H.   R. Berekhiah and R. Hanan in support of this position taken by rabbis: "'Who led you through the great terrible wilderness, with its fiery serpents and scorpions [and thirsty ground where there was no water]' [Deut. 8:15].

I.   "Just as the scorpion produces eggs by sixties, so the kingdom of Greece would set up its administration in groups of sixty."

J.   "Fell on him" (Gen. 15:12).

K.   This refers to Edom, on account of the following verse: "The earth quakes at the noise of their [Edom's] fall" (Jer. 49:21).

L.   There are those who reverse matters.

M.   "Fear" refers to Edom, on account of the following verse: "And this I saw, a fourth beast, fearful, and terrible" (Dan. 7:7).

N.   "Darkness" refers to Greece, which brought gloom through its decrees. For they said to Israel, "Write on the horn of an ox that you have no portion in the God of Israel."

O.   "Great" refers to Media, on account of the verse: "King Ahasuerus made Haman [the Median] great" (Est. 3:1).

P.   "Fell on him" refers to Babylonia, on account of the following verse: "Fallen, fallen is Babylonia" (Isa. 21:9).

V.9 A.   Moses foresaw what the evil kingdoms would do [to Israel].

B.   "The camel, rock badger, and hare" (Deut. 14:7). [Compare: "Nevertheless, among those that chew the cud or part the hoof, you shall not eat these: The camel, because it chews the cud but does not part the hoof, is unclean to you. The rock badger, because it chews the cud but does not part the hoof, is unclean to you. And the hare, because it chews the cud but does not part the hoof, is unclean to you, and the pig, because it parts the hoof and is cloven-footed, but does not chew the cud, is unclean to you" (Lev. 11:4-8).]

C.   The camel (GML) refers to Babylonia, [in line with the following verse of Scripture: "O daughter of Babylonia, you who are to be devastated!] Happy will be he who requites (GML) you, with what you have done to us" (Ps. 147:8).

D.   "The rock badger" (Deut. 14:7) – this refers to Media.

E.   Rabbis and R. Judah b. R. Simon.

F.   Rabbis say, "Just as the rock badger exhibits traits of uncleanness and traits of cleanness, so the kingdom of Media produced both a righteous man and a wicked one."

G.   Said R. Judah b. R. Simon, "The last Darius was Esther's son. He was clean on his mother's side and unclean on his father's side."

H.   "The hare" (Deut 14:7) – this refers to Greece. The mother of King Ptolemy was named "Hare" [in Greek: *lagos*].

I.   "The pig" (Deut. 14:7) – this refers to Edom [Rome].

J.   Moses made mention of the first three in a single verse and the final one in a verse by itself (Deut. 14:7, 8). Why so?

12. The past history of Israel serves as a metaphor for the human condition of the Israelite, facing a supernatural enemy, saved by God's favor. The Day of Atonement is a day of national salvation from enemies in this world and in the world above. This theory of the history of Israel is spelled out in an elaborate way in the following:

Leviticus Rabbah XXI

I.1 A.   "With this shall Aaron come [into the holy place: With a young bull for a sin-offering and a ram for a burnt-offering]" (Lev. 16:3).

B.   "The Lord is my light and my salvation; whom shall I fear? [The Lord is the stronghold of my life; of whom shall I be afraid?]" (Ps. 27:1).

    C.   R. Eleazar interpreted the cited verse to speak of [Israel at] the Red Sea:

    D.   "'My light': 'It gave light by night' (Ex. 14:20).

    E.   "'And my salvation': 'Stand firm and see the salvation of the Lord' (Ex. 14:13).

    F.   "'Whom shall I fear': 'Do not fear' (Ex. 14:13).

    G.   "'The Lord is the stronghold of my life': 'The Lord is my strength and song' (Ex. 15:2).

    H.   "'Of whom shall I be afraid': 'Trembling and fear fell on them' (Ex. 15:16).

    I.   "'When evildoers come near me to eat up my flesh, [my adversaries and foes shall stumble and fall]' (Ps. 27:2): 'And Pharaoh drew near' (Ex. 14:10).

    J.   "'To eat my flesh' (Ps. 27:2): 'Said the enemy, I shall pursue, I shall overtake [my lust shall be satisfied upon them]' (Ex. 15:9)."

13. God favors the pursued over the pursuer, the persecuted over the persecutor, and this is proven by the history of Israel:

Leviticus Rabbah XXVII

V.1   A.   "God seeks what has been driven away" (Qoh. 3:15).

    B.   R. Huna in the name of R. Joseph said, "It is always the case that 'God seeks what has been driven away' [favoring the victim].

    C.   "You find when a righteous man pursues a righteous man, 'God seeks what has been driven away.'

    D.   "When a wicked man pursues a wicked man, 'God seeks what has been driven away.'

    E.   "All the more so when a wicked man pursues a righteous man, 'God seeks what has been driven away.'

    F.   "[The same principle applies] even when you come around to a case in which a righteous man pursues a wicked man, 'God seeks what has been driven away.'"

V.2   A.   R. Yosé b. R. Yudan in the name of R. Yosé b. R. Nehorai says, "It is always the case that the Holy One, blessed be He, demands an accounting for the blood of those who have been pursued from the hand of the pursuer.

    B.   "Abel was pursued by Cain, and God sought [an accounting for] the pursued: 'And the Lord looked [favorably] upon Abel and his meal-offering' (Gen. 4:4).

    C.   "Noah was pursued by his generation, and God sought [an accounting for] the pursued: 'You and all your household shall come into the ark' (Gen. 7:1). And it says, 'For this is like the days of Noah to me, as I swore [that the waters of Noah should no more go over the earth]' (Isa. 54:9).

    D.   "Abraham was pursued by Nimrod, 'And God seeks what has been driven away': 'You are the Lord, the God who chose Abram and brought him out of Ur' (Neh. 9:7).

    E.   "Isaac was pursued by Ishmael, 'and God seeks what has been driven away': 'For through Isaac will seed be called for you' (Gen. 21:12).

F.   "Jacob was pursued by Esau, 'And God seeks what has been driven away': 'For the Lord has chosen Jacob, Israel for his prized possession' (Ps. 135:4).

G.   "Moses was pursued by Pharaoh, 'And God seeks what has been driven away': 'Had not Moses His chosen stood in the breach before Him' (Ps. 106:23).

H.   "David was pursued by Saul, 'And God seeks what has been driven away': 'And he chose David, his servant' (Ps. 78:70).

I.   "Israel was pursued by the nations, 'And God seeks what has been driven away': 'And you has the Lord chosen to be a people to him' (Deut. 14:2).

J.   "And the rule applies also to the matter of offerings. A bull is pursued by a lion, a sheep is pursued by a wolf, a goat is pursued by a leopard.

K.   "Therefore the Holy One, blessed be He, has said, 'Do not make offerings before me from those animals that pursue, but from those that are pursued: "When a bull, a sheep, or a goat is born"' (Lev. 22:27)."

14.   In the end of time God will give to Israel the dominions of those who have persecuted them:

Leviticus Rabbah XXVIII

IV.1   A.   "His harvest the hungry eat, and he takes it even without a buckler; and the thirsty pant after their wealth" (Job 5:5).

B.   "His harvest" refers to the four kingdoms (of Gen. 14:1).

C.   "The hungry eat" refers to our father, Abraham.

D.   "And he takes it even without a buckler" – without a sword, without a shield, but with prayer and supplications.

E.   This is in line with the following verse of Scripture: "He led forth his trained servants [empty handed, understanding the Hebrew word RK as empty], those born of his house, three hundred and eighteen" (Gen. 14:14).

F.   Said R. Simeon b. Laqish, "It was Eliezer alone [whom Abraham took with him]. And how do we know? [The numerical value of the letters that make up the Hebrew name] Eliezer adds up to three hundred and eighteen.

G.   "And the thirsty pant after their wealth" – who trampled on the wealth of the four kingdoms? It was Abraham and all those who were allied with him.

IV.2   A.   Another interpretation: "His harvest" refers to Pharaoh.

B.   "The hungry eat" refers to Moses.

C.   "And he takes it even without a buckler" – without a sword, without a shield, but with prayer and supplications.

D.   "And the Lord said to Moses, 'Why do you cry out to me?'" (Ex. 14:15).

E.   "And the thirsty pant after their wealth" – who trampled the wealth of Pharaoh? It was Moses and all those who were allied with him.

IV.3   A.   Another interpretation: "His harvest" refers to Sihon and Og.

B.   "The hungry eat" refers to Moses.

C. "And he takes it even without a buckler" – without a sword, without a shield, but with a [mere] word.

D. "And the Lord said to Moses, 'Be not afraid of him, because I have given him into your hand'" (Num. 21:34).

E. "And the thirsty pant after their wealth" – who trampled on the wealth of Sihon and Og? It was Moses and all those who were allied with him.

IV.4   A. Another interpretation: "His harvest" refers to the Canaanites.

B. "The hungry eat" refers to Joshua.

C. "And he takes it even without a buckler" – without a sword, without a shield, but with hailstones.

D. That is in line with the following verse of Scripture: "And as they fled before Israel, while they were going down the ascent of Beth-horon, the Lord threw down great stones from heaven upon them [as far as Azekah, and they died; there were more who died because of the hailstones than the men of Israel killed with the sword]" (Josh. 10:11).

E. "And the thirsty pant after their wealth" – who trampled upon the wealth of the Canaanites? It was Joshua and all those who were allied with him.

IV.5   A. Another interpretation: "His harvest" refers to Sisera.

B. "The hungry eat" refers to Deborah and Barak.

C. "And he takes it even without a buckler" – without a sword, without a shield, but [solely] by means of good deeds.

D. That is in line with the following verse of Scripture: "Was shield or spear to be seen among forty thousand in Israel?" (Jud. 5:8).

E. "And the thirsty pant after their wealth" – who trampled on the wealth of Sisera? It was Deborah and Barak and all those who were allied with them.

IV.6   A. Another interpretation: "His harvest" refers to Sennacherib.

B. "The hungry eat" refers to Hezekiah.

C. "And he takes it even without a buckler" – without a sword, without a shield, but [solely] through prayer.

D. "And Hezekiah the king and Isaiah ben Amoz, the prophet, prayed concerning this matter" (2 Chr. 32:20).

E. "And the thirsty pant after their wealth" – who trampled on the wealth of Sennacherib? It was Hezekiah and all those who were allied with him.

IV.7   A. Another interpretation: "His harvest" refers to Haman.

B. "The hungry eat" refers to Mordecai.

C. "And he takes it even without a buckler" – without a sword, without a shield, but solely with sack and ashes, as it is said, "Many lay in sackcloth and ashes" (Est. 4:3).

D. "And the thirsty pant after their wealth" – who trampled upon the wealth of Haman? It was Mordecai and Esther and all those who were allied with them.

IV.8   A. Said the Holy One, blessed be He, to Israel, "My children, I have fed you the harvest of the kingdoms. Take care that others not come and eat your harvest."

B. Therefore Moses admonished the Israelites, saying to them, "When you come into the land which I give you and reap its harvest, you

shall bring the sheaf of the first fruits of your harvest to the priest"
(Lev. 23:10).

15. God's principal habitation on earth was with humanity, but
gradually, as people sinned, God went up from one firmament to the
next, withdrawing from humanity; but with the coming of Israel's
patriarchs and prophets, God gradually returned to earth, finally
meeting humanity at Sinai:

Pesiqta deRab Kahana I

I.6 A. The principal locale of God's presence had been among the lower
creatures, but when the first man sinned, it went up to the first
firmament.

B. The generation of Enosh came along and sinned, and it went up
from the first to the second.

C. The generation of the flood [came along and sinned], and it went up
from the second to the third.

D. The generation of the dispersion [came along] and sinned, and it
went up from the third to the fourth.

E. The Egyptians in the time of Abraham our father [came along] and
sinned, and it went up from the fourth to the fifth.

F. The Sodomites [came along], and sinned, ...from the fifth to the
sixth.

G. The Egyptians in the time of Moses... from the sixth to the seventh.

H. And, corresponding to them, seven righteous men came along and
brought it back down to earth:

I. Abraham our father came along and acquired merit, and brought it
down from the seventh to the sixth.

J. Isaac came along and acquired merit and brought it down from the
sixth to the fifth.

K. Jacob came along and acquired merit and brought it down from the
fifth to the fourth.

L. Levi came along and acquired merit and brought it down from the
fourth to the third.

M. Kahath came along and acquired merit and brought it down from
the third to the second.

N. Amram came along and acquired merit and brought it down from
the second to the first.

O. Moses came along and acquired merit and brought it down to earth.

P. Therefore it is said, *On the day that Moses completed the setting up of
the Tabernacle, he anointed and consecrated it* (Num. 7:1).

16. The redemption of Israel is the counterpart to the fall of her enemies,
Amalek-Esau-Rome: one will fall by the hand of one who did fear
God, with the consequence interest in the contrast of Joseph and
Esau = Amalek. The salvation of Israel also marks the downfall of
Israel's enemies.

Pesiqta deRab Kahana III

XIII.1 A.   Remember *[what the Amalekites did to you on your way out of Egypt, how they met you on the road] when you were faint and weary [and cut off your rear, which was lagging behind exhausted; they showed no fear of God. When the Lord your God gives you peace from your enemies on every side, in the land which he is giving you to occupy as your patrimony, you shall not fail to blot out the memory of the Amalekites from under heaven]* (Deut. 25:17-19):

XIII.2 A.   ...*They showed no fear of God:* R. Phineas in the name of R. Samuel bar Nahman, "There is a tradition concerning the narrative that the seed of Esau will fall only by the hand of the sons of Rachel.

     B.   *"Surely the youngest of the flock shall drag them* (Jer. 49:20).

     C.   "Why does he refer to them as the youngest of the flock? Because they were the youngest of all the tribes.

     D.   "[Now we shall see the connection to the downfall of Esau = Amalek = Rome:] This one is called a youth, and that one is called young.

     E.   "This one is called a youth: *And he was a youth* (Gen. 37:2).

     F.   "And that one is called young: *Lo, I have made you the youngest among the nations* (Obad. 1:2).

     G.   "This one [Esau] grew up between two righteous men and did not act like them, and that one [Joseph] grew up between two wicked men and did not act like them.

     H.   "Let this one come and fall by the hand of the other.

     I.   "This one showed concern for the honor owing to his master, and that one treated with disdain the honor owning to his master.

     J.   "Let this one come and fall by the hand of the other.

     K.   "In connection with this one it is written, *And he did not fear God* (Deut. 25:18), and in connection with that one it is written, *And I fear God* (Gen. 42:18).

     L.   "Let this one come and fall by the hand of that one."

IV. The Latest Midrash Compilations: Song of Songs Rabbah, Ruth Rabbah, Esther Rabbah I, and Lamentations Rabbati, And The Fathers According to Rabbi Nathan

A. Intentionality

This set of writings has nothing on the topic of intentionality.

B. The Yoke of the Kingdom of Heaven and the Commandments

1.   Israel's merit lies in its faith in God, expressed in accepting the Torah and carrying out its rules:

Song of Songs Rabbah XX

I.1   A.   "As an apple tree among the trees of the wood":

     B.   R. Huna and R. Aha in the name of R. Yosé b. Zimra, "Just as in the case of an apple tree, everybody avoids it in extreme heat, since it has no shade in which to sit,

C.   "so the nations of the world fled from sitting in the shade of the
      Holy One, blessed be He on the day on which the Torah was given.
D.   "Might one suppose that the same was so of Israel?
E.   "Scripture states, 'With great delight I sat in his shadow,'
F.   "'I took delight in him and I sat.'
G.   "'I am the one who desired him, and not the nations of the world.'"

2.   Israel's beauty in God's eyes lies in its fulfillment of the obligations
     of the Torah; covenantal nomism defines Israel's relationship to God:

XLV

I.1   A.   "Behold, you are beautiful, my love, behold you are beautiful":
      B.   "Behold you are beautiful" in religious deeds,
      C.   "Behold you are beautiful" in acts of grace,
      D.   "Behold you are beautiful" in carrying out religious obligations of
            commission,
      E.   "Behold you are beautiful" in carrying out religious obligations of
            omission,
      F.   "Behold you are beautiful" in carrying out the religious duties of
            the home, in separating priestly ration and tithes,
      G.   "Behold you are beautiful" in carrying out the religious duties of
            the field, gleanings, forgotten sheaves, the corner of the field, poor
            person's tithe, and declaring the field ownerless.
      H.   "Behold you are beautiful" in observing the taboo against mixed
            species.
      I.   "Behold you are beautiful" in providing a linen cloak with woolen
            show fringes.
      J.   "Behold you are beautiful" in [keeping the rules governing]
            planting,
      K.   "Behold you are beautiful" in keeping the taboo on uncircumcised
            produce,
      L.   "Behold you are beautiful" in keeping the laws on produce in the
            fourth year after the planting of an orchard,
      M.   "Behold you are beautiful" in circumcision,
      N.   "Behold you are beautiful" in trimming the wound,
      O.   "Behold you are beautiful" in reciting the Prayer,
      P.   "Behold you are beautiful" in reciting the Shema,
      Q.   "Behold you are beautiful" in putting a mezuzah on the doorpost of
            your house,
      R.   "Behold you are beautiful" in wearing phylacteries,
      S.   "Behold you are beautiful" in building the tabernacle for the
            Festival of Tabernacles,
      T.   "Behold you are beautiful" in taking the palm branch and etrog on
            the Festival of Tabernacles,
      U.   "Behold you are beautiful" in repentance,
      V.   "Behold you are beautiful" in good deeds,
      W.   "Behold you are beautiful" in this world,
      X.   "Behold you are beautiful" in the world to come.

C. Words Form the Bridge from Humanity to God

I find nothing relevant to this topic.

D. The Sanctity of the Land of Israel and the People of Israel

I find nothing that requires attention here.

E. Random Events or Chance Express God's Will

This topic does not arise.

F. The Duality of the Torah

1. God is present where and when and among those by whom the Torah is studied, and a reward is given for the learning:

The Fathers According to Rabbi Nathan VIII

III.1   A.   In the case of three disciples in session and occupied with study of the Torah, the Holy One, blessed be He, credits it to them as if they formed a single band before him,

B.   as it is said, *He who builds his upper chambers in the heaven and has founded his band upon the earth, he who calls for the waters of the sea and pours them out upon the face of the earth, the Lord is his name* (Amos 9:6).

C.   Thus you have learned that in the case of three disciples in session and occupied with study of the Torah, the Holy One, blessed be He, credits it to them as if they formed a single band before him.

III.3   A.   In the case of an individual disciple in session and occupied with study of the Torah, his reward is received on high,

B.   as it is said, *Though he sit alone and keep silence, surely he has laid up [a reward] for him* (Lam. 3:28).

C.   The matter may be conveyed in a parable: To what is it comparable?

D.   To someone who had a young child, whom he left at home when he went out to the market. The son went and took a scroll and set it between his knees and sat and meditated on it.

E.   When his father came back from the marketplace, he said, "See my little son, whom I left when I went out to the marketplace. What has he done on his own! He has studied and taken the scroll and set it between his knees, going into session and meditating on it."

F.   So you have learned that even an individual disciple who has gone into session and occupied with study of the Torah, receives his reward received on high.

G. Israel and the Nations

1. Israel's condition among the nations is brought about by neglect of the Torah and religious duties:

Song of Songs Rabbah XXXV

I.2   A.   Said R. Levi, "Said the community of Israel before the Holy One, blessed be He, 'Lord of the world, in the past, you would give light for me between one night and the next night,

B.   "'between the night of Egypt and the night of Babylonia, between the night of Babylonia and the night of Media, between the night of Media and the night of Greece, between the night of Greece and the night of Edom.

C.   "'Now that I have fallen asleep [Simon:] neglectful of the Torah and the religious duties, one night flows into the next.'"

2.   The Torah is what distinguishes Israel from the nations, and the Torah is the mark of God's love for Israel; the nations have no share in the Torah and no medium for achieving atonement:

Song of Songs Rabbah CIX

I.1   A.   "Many waters":
      B.   This refers to the nations of the world: "Ah, the uproar of many peoples, that roar like the roaring of the seas" (Isa. 17:12).
      C.   "Cannot quench love":
      D.   The love with which the Holy One, blessed be He, loves Israel: "I have loved you, says the Lord" (Mal. 1:2).
      E.   "Neither can floods drown it":
      F.   This refers to the nations of the world: "In that day shall the Lord shave with a razor that is hired in the parts beyond the River... now therefore behold the Lord brings up upon them the waters of the River" (Isa. 7:20, 8:7).

3.   God's faithfulness endures, and evidence of that fact is the very condition of Israel among the nations:

Lamentations Rabbati LXXXVI

I.1   A.   "The steadfast love of the Lord never ceases, his mercies never come to an end":
      B.   Said R. Simeon b. Laqish, "Even though the Holy One, blessed be He, is angry with his servants, the righteous, in this world, in the world to come he goes and has mercy on them.
      C.   "That is in line with this verse: 'The steadfast love of the Lord never ceases, his mercies never come to an end.'"
I.2   A.   they are new every morning; great is your faithfulness":
      B.   Said R. Alexandri, "Because you renew us every morning, we know that 'great is your faithfulness.'"
      C.   R. Simon bar Abba said, "Because you renew us in the morning of the nations, we know that 'great is your faithfulness' to redeem us."

4.   The nations prosperity now is a sign of the certainty of Israel's redemption in time to come:

Lamentations Rabbati CXL

I.1   A.   "For Mount Zion which lies desolate; jackals prowl over it":
      B.   Rabban Gamaliel, R. Joshua, R. Eleazar b. Azariah, and R. Aqiba went to Rome. They heard the din of the city of Rome from a distance of a hundred and twenty miles.
      C.   They all begin to cry, but R. Aqiba began to laugh.
      D.   They said to him, "Aqiba, we are crying and you laugh?"
      E.   He said to them, "Why are you crying?"
      F.   They said to him, "Should we not cry, that idolators and those who sacrifice to idols and bow down to images live securely and prosperously, while the footstool of our God has been burned down

by fire and become a dwelling place for the beasts of the field? So shouldn't we cry?"

G. He said to them, "That is precisely the reason that I was laughing. For if those who outrage him he treats in such a way, those who do his will all the more so!"

H. History: Its Meaning and Divisions

1. Israel is like a woman now, but in the end of days will be like a man:

V

III.4   A.   R. Berekhiah in the name of R. Samuel b. R. Nahman said, "The Israelites are compared to a woman.

       B.   "Just as an unmarried women receives a tenth part of the property of her father and takes her leave [for her husband's house when she gets married], so the Israelites inherited the land of the seven peoples, who form a tenth part of the seventy nations of the world.

       C.   "And because the Israelites inherited in the status of a woman, they said a song in the feminine form of that word, as in the following: 'Then sang Moses and the children of Israel this song [given in the feminine form] unto the Lord' (Ex. 15:1).

       D.   "But in the age to come they are destined to inherit like a man, who inherits all of the property of his father.

       E.   "That is in line with this verse of Scripture: 'From the east side to the west side: Judah, one portion... Dan one, Asher one...' (Ezek. 48:7), and so throughout.

       F.   "Then they will say a song in the masculine form of that word, as in the following: 'Sing to the Lord a new song' (Ps. 96:1).

       G.   "The word 'song' is given not in its feminine form but in its masculine form."

III.5   A.   R. Berekiah and R. Joshua b. Levi: "Why are the Israelites compared to a woman?

       B.   "Just as a woman takes up a burden and puts it down [that is, becomes pregnant and gives birth], takes up a burden and puts it down, then takes up a burden and puts it down and then takes up no further burden,

       C.   "so the Israelites are subjugated and then redeemed, subjugated and then redeemed, but in the end are redeemed and will never again be subjugated.

       D.   "In this world, since their anguish is like the anguish of a woman in childbirth, they say the song before him using the feminine form of the word for song,

       E.   "but in the age to come, because their anguish will no longer be the anguish of a woman in childbirth, they will say their song using the masculine form of the word for song:

       F.   "'In that day this song [in the masculine form of the word] will be sung' (Isa. 26:1)."

2. The history of Israel in Egypt, at the Sea, at Sinai, and subjugated by the gentile kingdoms, ends when the redemption will come. The

entire message of history is contained within these theological statements:

Song of Songs Rabbah XVIII

I.1   A.   "I am a rose of Sharon, [a lily of the valleys]":
        B.   Said the community of Israel, "I am the one, and I am beloved.
        C.   "I am the one whom the Holy One, blessed be He, loved more than the seventy nations."

I.4   A.   Another explanation of the phrase, "I am a rose of Sharon":
        B.   Said the community of Israel, "I am the one, and I am beloved.
        C.   "I am the one who was hidden in the shadow of Egypt, but in a brief moment the Holy One, blessed be He, brought me together to Raamses, and I [Simon:] blossomed forth in good deeds like a rose, and I said before him this song: 'You shall have a song as in the night when a feast is sanctified' (Isa. 30:29)."

I.5   A.   Another explanation of the phrase, "I am a rose of Sharon":
        B.   Said the community of Israel, "I am the one, and I am beloved.
        C.   "I am the one who was hidden in the shadow of the sea, but in a brief moment I [Simon:] blossomed forth in good deeds like a rose, and I pointed to him with the finger [Simon:] [opposite to me]: 'This is my God and I will glorify him' (Ex. 15:2)."

I.6   A.   Another explanation of the phrase, "I am a rose of Sharon":
        B.   Said the community of Israel, "I am the one, and I am beloved.
        C.   "I am the one who was hidden in the shadow of Mount Sinai, but in a brief moment I [Simon:] blossomed forth in good deeds like a lily in hand and in heart, and I said before him, 'All that the Lord has said we will do and obey' (Ex. 24:7)."

I.7   A.   Another explanation of the phrase, "I am a rose of Sharon":
        B.   Said the community of Israel, "I am the one, and I am beloved.
        C.   "I am the one who was hidden and downtrodden in the shadow of the kingdoms. But tomorrow, when the Holy One, blessed be He, redeems me from the shadow of the kingdoms, I shall blossom forth like a lily and say before him a new song: 'Sing to the Lord a new song, for he has done marvelous things, his right hand and his holy arm have wrought salvation for him' (Ps. 98:1)."

3. God and Israel meet in history, at the Sea; and they meet in religious observances of holy time now, and finally, in the world to come:

Song of Songs Rabbah LXX

I.1   A.   The Israelites answer them, "'My beloved is all radiant and ruddy."
        B.   "Radiant": To me in the Land of Egypt,
        C.   "And ruddy": To the Egyptians.
        D.   "Radiant": In the Land of Egypt, "For I will go through the Land of Egypt" (Ex. 12:13).
        E.   "And ruddy": "And the Lord overthrew the Egyptians" (Ex. 14:27).
        F.   "Radiant": At the Sea: "The children of Israel walked upon dry land in the midst of the sea" (Ex. 14:29).
        G.   "And ruddy": To the Egyptians at the Sea: "And the Lord overthrew the Egyptians in the midst of the sea" (Ex. 14:27).
        H.   "Radiant": In the world to come.

I. "And ruddy": In this world.

I.2   A.   R. Levi b. R. Hayyata made three statements concerning the matter:

B.   "'Radiant': On the Sabbath.

C.   "'And ruddy': On the other days of the week.

D.   "'Radiant': On the New Year.

E.   "'And ruddy': On the other days of the year.

F.   "'Radiant': In this world.

G.   "'And ruddy': In the world to come.

4. Though Israel's history is marked by four successive gentile rulers, the fifth and final monarchy over Israel will be that of the Messiah:

Esther Rabbah I/I

I.3   A.   [Another interpretation of the verse,"And your life shall hang in doubt before you; night and day you shall be in dread, and have no assurance of your life":]

B.   Rab interpreted the verse to speak of the time of Haman.

C.   "'And your life shall hang in doubt before you': This speaks of the twenty-four hours from the removal of the ring.

D.   "'Night and day you shall be in dread': This speaks of the time that the letters were sent forth.

E.   "'And have no assurance of your life': This was when the enemies of the Jews were told to be 'ready against that day' (Est. 3:14)."

I.4   A.   "In the morning, you shall say, 'Would it were evening!' and at evening you shall say, 'Would it were morning!'":

B.   "In the morning," of Babylonia, "You shall say, 'Would it were evening!'"

C.   "In the morning," of Media, "you shall say, 'Would it were evening!'"

D.   "In the morning," of Greece, "you shall say, 'Would it were evening!'"

E.   "In the morning," of Edom, "you shall say, 'Would it were evening!'"

I.5   A.   Another interpretation of the verse: "In the morning, you shall say, 'Would it were evening!' and at evening you shall say, 'Would it were morning!'":

B.   "In the morning" of Babylonia, "you shall say, 'Would it were the evening of Media!'"

C.   "In the morning," of Media, "you shall say, 'Would it were evening of Greece!'"

D.   "In the morning," of Greece, "you shall say, 'Would it were evening of Edom!'"

E.   Why so? "because of the dread which your heart shall fear and the sights which your eyes shall see."

Nonetheless, God remains with Israel and will ultimately stand by them and redeem them from their enemies:

Esther Rabbah I/II

I.1   A.   Samuel commenced by citing the following verse of Scripture: "Yet for all that, when they are in the land of their enemies, I will not spurn them, neither will I abhor them so as to destroy them utterly and break my covenant with them, for I am the Lord their God; but I will for their sake remember the covenant with their forefathers, whom I brought forth out of the Land of Egypt in the sight of the nations, that I might be their God: I am the Lord" (Lev. 26:44-45):

B.   "'I will not spurn them': In Babylonia.
C.   "'Neither will I abhor them': In Media.
D.   "'So as to destroy them utterly': Under Greek rule.
E.   "'And break my covenant with them': Under the wicked kingdom.
F.   "'For I am the Lord their God': In the age to come.
G.   Taught R. Hiyya, "'I will not spurn them': In the time of Vespasian.
H.   "'Neither will I abhor them': In the time of Trajan.
I.   "'So as to destroy them utterly': In the time of Haman.
J.   "'And break my covenant with them': In the time of the Romans.
K.   "'For I am the Lord their God': In the time of Gog and Magog."

5.   God's omnipotence may be called into question by the behavior of the great empires, but that is only just for now. The history of Israel produces matched sets of relationships, with Rome and Iran; each relates to Israel in the same way. They serve to call into question Israel's faith in the power of God, by showing off their own power. Esau/Romulus and Remus pay back God's blessing by building temples to idols. Belshazzar, Vashti, and Iran do the same by oppressing Israel. Both intend to prove they are stronger than God. But God shows in the end who is the stronger. The empires display power, but God will display much greater power in time to come:

Esther Rabbah I/XVIII

IV.1   A.   It is written, "You have seen, for you behold trouble and vexation, to pay them back with your hand; unto you the helpless commits himself. You have been the helper of the fatherless" (Ps. 10:14).
B.   Said the community of Israel before the Holy One, blessed be He, "Lord of the world, 'you have seen' that the wicked Esau has come and is going to destroy the house of the sanctuary and exile the Israelites from their land and lead them away in iron collars.
C.   "'For you behold trouble and vexation, to pay them back with your hand': You caused your presence to dwell upon Isaac, so that he said to Esau, 'Behold, of the fat places of the earth shall be your dwelling... and by your sword you shall live' (Gen. 27:39).
D.   "'Unto you the helpless commits himself': 'Tomorrow he is going to come and take orphans and widows and lock them up in prison and say to them, "Let the one of whom it is written, 'He is the father of the fatherless and judge in behalf of widows' (Ps. 68:6) come and save you from my power.'"'
E.   "But truly 'You have been the helper of the fatherless':
F.   "There were two who were left as orphans to Esau, Remus and Romulus, and you allowed a she-wolf to give them suck, and in the end they went and built two enormous tents in Rome."

6. Calamities overtake Israel because of neglect of the Torah; so long as Israel studies the Torah and carries out its teachings, its future is secure. This theme is dominant in the document, and I do not catalogue every instance in which the premise of discussion goes over the present point.

Lamentations Rabbati II

I.10   A.   Said R. Abba bar Kahana, "There arose among the nations no philosophers like Balaam b. Beor and Oeonamos of Gadara.

       B.   "They said to them, 'Can we vanquish this nation?'

       C.   "They said to them, 'Go and make the rounds of their synagogues and schoolhouses. If children are chirping in loud voices, you cannot overcome them, but if not, you can overcome them.

       D.   "'For so did their Father promise them, saying to them, "The voice is the voice of Jacob, but the hands are the hands of Esau" (Gen. 27:22).

       E.   "'So long as the voice of Jacob chirps in the synagogues and schoolhouses, the hands are not the hands of Esau, and when his voice does not chirp in the synagogues and schoolhouses, the hands are the hands of Esau.'

       F.   "And so Scripture says, 'Therefore as stubble devours the tongue of fire' (Isa. 5:24).

       G.   "Now does stubble consume fire? But is it not the way of fire to consume stubble?

       H.   "So can you say, 'Therefore as stubble devours the tongue of fire' (Isa. 5:24)?

       I.   "But 'stubble' refers to the house of Esau, as it is said, 'And the house of Jacob shall be a fire, and the house of Joseph a flame, and the house of Esau stubble' (Obad. 18).

       J.   "'The tongue of fire' ['as stubble devours the tongue of fire' (Isa. 5:24)] refers to the house of Jacob, which is compared to fire: 'And the house of Jacob shall be a fire.'

       K.   "'And as the chaff if consumed in the flame' speaks of the house of Joseph, compared to flame: 'And the house of Joseph a flame.'

       L.   "'So their root shall be as rottenness' (Isa. 5:24): This refers to the patriarchs, who are Israelite's root.

       M.   "'And their blossom shall go up as dust' speaks of the tribes, who are Israel's blossoms.

       N.   "On what account?

       O.   "'Because they rejected the Torah of the Lord of hosts [and condemned the word of the Holy One of Israel' (Obad. 18)."

7. Israel's history in the land is the counterpart of Adam's history in Eden; with the destruction of Jerusalem in 586, Israel was driven out of Eden. But Israel can come back.

Lamentations Rabbati IV

I.1   A.   R. Abbahu in the name of R. Yosé bar Haninah commenced [discourse by citing this verse]: "*But they are like a man, they have* transgressed the covenant. *There they dealt treacherously against me"* (Hos. 6:7).

B.   *"They are like a man,* specifically, this refers to the first man [Adam]. [We shall now compare the story of the first man in Eden with the story of Israel in its land.]

C.   "Said the Holy One, blessed be He, 'In the case of the first man, I brought him into the garden of Eden, I commanded him, he violated my commandment, I judged him to be sent away and driven out, but I mourned for him, saying "How..."' [which begins the book of Lamentations, hence stands for a lament, but which also is written with the consonants that also yield, *Where are you*].

D.   "'I brought him into the garden of Eden,' as it is written, *And the Lord God took the man and put him into the garden of Eden* (Gen. 2:15).

E.   "'I commanded him,' as it is written, *And the Lord God commanded...* (Gen. 2:16).

F.   "'And he violated my commandment,' as it is written, *Did you eat from the tree concerning which I commanded you* (Gen. 3:11).

G.   "'I judged him to be sent away,' as it is written, *And the Lord God sent him from the garden of Eden* (Gen. 3:23).

H.   "'And I judged him to be driven out.' *And he drove out the man* (Gen. 3:24).

I.   "'But I mourned for him, saying, How....' *And He said to him, Where are you* (Gen. 3:9), and the word for 'where are you' is written, *How....*

J.   "'So, too, in the case of his descendants, [God continues to speak,] I brought them into the Land of Israel, I commanded them, they violated my commandment, I judged them to be sent out and driven away but I mourned for them, saying, *How....*'

K.   "'I brought them into the Land of Israel': *'And I brought you into the land of Carmel'* (Jer. 2:7).

L.   "'I commanded them': *'And you, command the children of Israel'* (Ex. 27:20). *'Command the children of Israel'* (Lev. 24:2).

M.   "'They violated my commandment': *'And all Israel have violated your Torah'* (Dan. 9:11).

N.   "'I judged them to be sent out': *'Send them away, out of my sight and let them go forth'* (Jer. 15:1).

O.   "'....And driven away': *'From my house I shall drive them'* (Hos. 9:15).

P.   "'But I mourned for them, saying, How...': *How lonely sits the city [that was full of people! How like a widow has she become, she that was great among the nations! She that was a princess among the cities has become a vassal. She weeps bitterly in the night, tears on her cheeks, among all her lovers she has none to comfort her; all her friends have dealt treacherously with her, they have become her enemies]* (Lam. 1:1-2)."

8.   God carefully planned the punishment of Israel, so that it would be tolerable, and this was in both political and human terms:

Lamentations Rabbati XLVIII

I.3   A.   Another interpretation of the word for "bound" in the verse, "My transgressions were bound into a yoke; by his hand they were fastened together":

    B.   Reading the word as though it were written to mean "consider carefully,"

    C.   he considered carefully how to bring evil upon me.

    D.   He thought, "If I send them into exile in the winter season, lo, all of them will die from cold. I shall send them into exile in the summer season, so that even if they sleep in the market places or on the roads, they will not be injured."

I.4   A.   Another interpretation of the word for "bound" in the verse, "My transgressions were bound into a yoke; by his hand they were fastened together":

    B.   Reading the word as though it were written to mean "consider carefully,"

    C.   he considered carefully how to bring evil upon me.

    D.   He thought, "If I send them into exile in the wilderness, they will die of hunger. I shall send them into exile by way of Armenia, where there are towns and cities, so that they can find food and drink."

God's punishment is very exact, the penalty fitting the crime with great precision, but that also brings assurance that the redemption that is coming will bring comfort in due proportion as well:

Lamentations Rabbati LVI

I.2   A.   "For my groans are many and my heart is faint":

    B.   You find that with every thing with which the Israelites sinned, they were smitten, and with that same thing they will be comforted. When they sinned with the head, they were smitten at the head, but they were comforted through the head.

    C.   When they sinned with the head: Let us make a head and let us return to Egypt (Num. 14:4).

    D.   ...They were smitten at the head: The whole head is sick (Isa. 1:5).

    E.   ...But they were comforted through the head: Their king has passed before them and the Lord is at the head of them (Mic. 2:13).

I.3   A.   When they sinned with the eye, they were smitten at the eye, but they were comforted through the eye.

    B.   When they sinned with the eye: [The daughters of Zion... walk]... with wanton eyes (Isa. 3:16).

    C.   ...They were smitten at the eye: My eye, my eye runs down with water (Lam. 1:16).

    D.   ...But they were comforted through the eye: For every eye shall see the Lord returning to Zion (Isa. 52:8).

I.4   A.   When they sinned with the ear, they were smitten at the ear, but they were comforted through the ear.

    B.   When they sinned with the ear: They stopped up their ears so as not to hear (Zech. 7:11).

    C.   ...They were smitten at the ear: Their ears shall be deaf (Mic. 7:16).

    D.   ...But they were comforted through the ear: Your ears shall hear a word saying, [This is the way] (Isa. 30:21).

V. General Observations

That a variety of religious attitudes and theological propositions comes to expression in the Mishnah is hardly surprising. The priority of intentionality, in which God and humanity intersect in shared attitudes, sentiments, and emotions, of course is the single most important religious conviction, which yields the theological proposition that God's and humanity's point of resemblance ("in our image, after our likeness") is to be defined in the matter of a shared structure of intellect and emotion and sentiment. This will find its counterpart in the law's premise that important actions in law realize or embody paradigms originally defined by God or, in response to God's instruction, the patriarchs and matriarchs or the prophet, Moses. The equally critical place accorded to the yoke of the kingdom of heaven and of the commandments hardly surprises, since it is here that the matter of attitude and will comes to concrete realization in action. The Torah then contains the will of God, and the commandments of the Torah spell out what is to be done; therefore study of the Torah forms a primary component in expressing the theology at hand.

Nor does the continuation of the theme of intentionality in the Tosefta's exposition require explanation, since that document falls entirely within the Mishnah's framework of thought. What is puzzling is that, outside of the framework of legal discussions, the critical and generative issue does not make an appearance, so far as I am able to discern. I find myself unable to point to a setting in the exegetical compilations, early, middle, and late, in which intentionality plays a part in the formation of a concrete idea, on the one side, or itself presents a critical consideration, on the other. For example, in considering Israel's history, to which the rabbis devoted such close attention and for which they formulated so remarkably cogent a body of doctrine, the intentionality of Israel scarcely appears as a mitigating consideration or as an aggravating circumstance for that matter. Intentionality proves a central issue in some documents, not through the documentary representation of the system as a whole. And if that is the case with what I conceive to be the single most important component of the Judaism that the rabbis (in some circumstances) take for granted, then we must wonder whether any important ideas form the premise of the documents that present us with whatever we know about Rabbinic Judaism.

When we come to "the yoke of the kingdom of heaven" and "...of the commandments," we reach the one premise that seems to me to operate throughout. Israel is conceived to be defined by reference to God's kingdom; Israel is Israel by reason of forming, realizing on earth, God's kingdom; when God rules, then Israel prospers. But God rules only when Israel willingly accepts God's rule and carries it out. God may intervene here and there; the supernatural dimension of ordinary life takes the measure of everyday affairs. But Israel's role in God's kingship, formulated in the Torah and defined in Torah study, is critical; God will not impose, but will only ratify the government that Israel has accepted for itself. God has set forth in the covenant the terms of God's dominion; Israel must freely accept those terms. These pertain to time, not space, circumstance, not situation. The circumstance of God's kingdom is the life of the holy people, Israel. The same general themes and propositions occur in the documents of scriptural exegesis as well, though the mythic formulation in terms of God's kingdom gives way to other images and media of expression altogether. But I see close continuity from document to document in this matter, for example, in the insistence that Israel's acceptance of God's rule must be gratuitous and not conditional, beseeching for grace, not an effort to compel God to do our will. The successive treatments of the topic emerge as variations on a theme, essentially cogent among themselves. I have presented only a small portion of the exegetical documents' treatments of God's kingdom, the commandments, covenant, and the Torah and study thereof. These suffice to show that here we deal with a fundamental idea, one that moves forward through the entire body of literature and takes form in many ways, all of them harmonious at the level of premise and presupposition.

That fact makes all the more puzzling the fact that premises that provoke deep thought and profound speculation in one area of the writings prove inert elsewhere. If the matter of intention falls into that category, we may not find surprising that the enchantment of language, the conception that God and humanity communicate in words, proves particular to some documents and does not take its place at the layer of premises throughout. Given the consequential position accorded to this premise throughout the law, I find it strange that in other contexts little is made of it; the way things can have worked out is illustrated by the premise of God's rule, which everywhere formed the basis of thought and produced a wide range of realizations. The premise that language forms the bridge to heaven, that words are performative, surely finds its place in those same deep layers of reflection; but it then surfaces only in some documents and turns out particular to a few topics. The same is so for the premise that the land, like language, is enchanted, and that the sanctification of land and language alike derives from its possession by holy Israel. The premise makes its appearance here and there, with some important points of expansion of the initially expressed convictions. But we cannot maintain that the premise that language and the land form principal arenas for God's rule and kingdom governs throughout.

And if that is so, all the more so with the conception that God's purpose is carried out by what humanity perceives to be random chance. That conception, which Scripture surely sustains on a broad scale, plays no ubiquitous role; it is a premise particular to the points at which the details make it relevant, therefore scarcely a systemic premise at all. The one point that occurs throughout, alongside the kingdom of God and related matters, is the theme of the duality of the Torah, on the one side, and the Torah's primary role in the formulation of Israel's life and destiny, on the other. This of course forms another mode of expressing the premise that God governs Israel, the Torah forming the medium of dominion, covenant, and grace, all three. Yet even here, we must notice, the theme is treated in diverse ways, and we cannot say that a common premise circulates from document to document, rather, a common topic, which is treated in diverse ways. For example, the Mishnah's premise, on the topic, is simply that the Torah comes to Israel in diverse media. The broader mythic framework, the claim that the Torah is God's plan for making creation, the conception that God is present among those who study the Torah, all of which I catalogued in the same rubric under the premise of the Torah as medium of grace, dominion, and covenant, come to expression only in later writings. So it is my definition of the generative premise, rather than the character of the evidence and the presuppositions that they yield, that wins for this topic a place among the premises of the documents overall.

The same is to be said for the general theme of Israel and the nations and the matter of history as the expression of God's program for Israel. On the one side, the premise of all documents is, the nations are not Israel by reason of their having rejected the Torah; they therefore are outside of the law, on the one side, and beyond the kingdom of God, on the other. That much forms a premise throughout. But not much else. That fact is underlined by the state of affairs with our final rubric, history, its meaning and divisions. While the Mishnah takes as a premise the division between Israel and the nations by reason of the Torah, the document does not then bring to concrete expression the presupposition that the relations between Israel and the nations find their measure in the nations' self-exclusion from the Torah or Israel's loyalty to it. The fact that the Mishnah can formulate rules that presuppose the division between holy Israel and the secular nations without introducing that division as the mode for explaining Israel's history (or even postulating that Israel has a history in the framework of the nations at all) is striking. It once more calls into question the notion that a fair corpus of premises come to expression here, there, and everywhere, on which account we gain access to the deepest levels of thought beneath the writings: the Judaism behind the texts overall. In the matter of history, in particular, we find that the premises we have identified prove as particular to the writings that bring them to concrete expression as does the notion of intentionality as the link between humanity and God.

4

Philosophical Premises

A single philosophical premise governs the Mishnah's method and message, which is that all things may be classified and ordered by classification. By philosophical premises, I mean, principles of thought, modes of analysis, and a range of premises that dictate the identification of problems and govern the mode of solving them that appeal not to revelation (the Torah) but to the nature of things. A philosophical problem concerns not Israel in particular but humanity in general; a philosophical mode of analysis seeks insight not in the exegesis of a verse of the Written Torah but in the prevailing consensus among persons of reason or common sense. Weighing possibilities on the basis of the observed order of nature, rather than settling questions on the strength of revealed truth, marks the philosophical, as against the theological, range of thought. As a matter of fact, we find in the documents under analysis a range of premises or presuppositions that are to be characterized as not theological, particular to Israel and resting on revealed truth, but philosophical, pertinent to the generality of humanity and appealing for proof to the observable traits of nature and the natural condition of affairs, respectively.

I. The Mishnah

The Mishnah itself employs a philosophical method to demonstrate in a philosophical manner a proposition important to philosophy of its setting. The Mishnah's philosophical method derives from the natural history of Aristotle and aims at the demonstration of the hierarchical classification of all things. It yields the proposition, familiar from Middle Platonism, that all things derive from one thing, and that one thing forms the goal of all things – philosophical monotheism. This the Mishnah demonstrates by showing in case after case that all things in place, in proper rank and position in the hierarchy of being, point to, stand for, one thing. The system and structure ask the questions philosophers ask, concerning the nature of things, and answer them in the way the philosophers answer them, through orderly sifting of data in the process of natural philosophy. In the Mishnah, many things are made to say one thing, which concerns the nature of being: teleologically hierarchized, to state matters in simple terms. The system of the Mishnah registers these two contrary propositions: many things are one, one thing is many. These propositions of course complement each other, because, in forming matched opposites, the two provide a complete and final judgment of the whole. For this philosophy rationality consists in hierarchy of the order of things. That rationality is revealed by the possibility always of effecting the hierarchical classification of all things: each thing in its taxon, all taxa in correct sequence, from least to greatest. A very limited sets of examples suffices to make these points concrete and begin the formulation of the catalogues of philosophical propositions required for the present analysis.

A. The Method of Hierarchical Classification

The purpose of classification is not only to find general rules covering multiple cases – what shares common taxonomic traits follows the same rule, what does not follows the opposite rule. It also is to hierarchize the classes that are established through such a process. Classification is for hierarchical purposes and forms correspondences, for example, between levels of uncleanness and layers of sanctification. There are gradations, or removes, of uncleanness; and there also are gradations, or levels, of sanctification or cleanness, and whatever is higher in the latter is more subject to the affect of the former; cf. M. Hagigah 2:3ff. as well.

11:4	A.	Whoever requires immersion in water according to the rules of the Torah renders unclean (1) Holy Things, (2) heave-offering, (3) unconsecrated food, (4) tithe, and (5) such a one is forbidden to enter the sanctuary.
	B.	After his immersion, he (1) renders Holy Things unclean, and (2) spoils the heave-offering," the words of R. Meir.
	C.	And sages say, "He spoils (1) the Holy Things and (2) the heave-offering."
	D.	And he is permitted to eat unconsecrated food and tithe.
	E.	And if he came to the sanctuary, whether before or after his immersion, he is liable.
11:5	A.	Whoever requires immersion in water according to the rules of the scribes (1) renders the Holy Things unclean and (2) spoils the heave-offering.
	B.	"And he is permitted in respect to unconsecrated food and tithe," the words of R. Meir.
	C.	And sages prohibit in the case of tithe.

	D.	After he has immersed, he is permitted for all of them.
	E.	And if he came to the sanctuary, whether before his immersion or after his immersion, he is free.
11:6	A.	Whoever requires immersion in water, whether according to the rules of the Torah or according to the rules of the scribes renders unclean (1) purification water, (2) purification ash, and (3) the one who sprinkles purification water –
	B.	in contact and in carrying,
	C.	and (4) the hyssop that has been made susceptible to uncleanness, (5) the water which has not been mixed, and (6) an empty utensil which is clean for the purification rite –
	D.	"In contact and carrying,"
	E.	the words of R. Meir.
	F.	And sages say, "In contact, but not in carrying."

What is most susceptible to uncleanness also is most holy, and what is insusceptible to gradations of uncleanness – beyond the range of classification altogether – lies outside of the system's purview and is of no consequence, for example, gentiles. Here is a good statement of what is at stake in the labor of hierarchical classification that plays so vital a role in the Mishnah. There is a hierarchy to be established in classifications of sources of uncleanness, with the more severe uncleanness marking a higher point in the list; the criterion of severity is the power of the given source of uncleanness to impart the status of uncleanness, for example, through various media, or to various things:

M. Kelim

1:1	A.	The Fathers of uncleannesses [are] (1) the creeping thing, and (2) semen [of an adult Israelite], and (3) one who has contracted corpse uncleanness, and (4) the leper in the days of his counting, and (5) sin-offering water of insufficient quantity to be sprinkled.
	B.	Lo, these render man and vessels unclean by contact, and earthenware vessels by [presence within the vessels' contained] airspace.
	C.	But they do not render unclean by carrying.
1:2	A.	Above them: (6) Carrion, and (7) sin-offering water of sufficient quantity to be sprinkled.
	B.	For they render man unclean through carrying, to make [his] clothing unclean.
	C.	But clothing is not made unclean through contact.

There are equivalent hierarchical classifications of sanctification:

1:6	A.	There are ten [degrees of] holiness:
	B.	(1) The land of Israel is holier than all lands.
	C.	And what is its holiness? For they bring from it the omer, and the first fruits, and the two loaves, which they do not bring (thus) from all lands.
1:7	A.	(2) The cities surrounded by a wall are more holy than it [the land].

B.   For they send from them the lepers, and they carry around in their midst a corpse so long as they like. [But once] it has gone forth, they do not bring it back.

1:8   A.   (3) Within the wall [of Jerusalem] is more holy than they.

B.   For they eat there lesser sanctities and second tithe.

C.   (4) The Temple mount is more holy than it.

D.   For Zabim, and Zabot, menstruating women, and those that have given birth do not enter there.

E.   (5) The rampart is more holy than it.

F.   For gentiles and he who is made unclean by a corpse do not enter there.

G.   (6) The court of women is more holy than it.

H.   For a tebul yom does not enter there, but they are not liable on its account for a sin-offering.

I.   (7) The court of Israel is more holy than it.

J.   For one who [yet] lacks atonement [offerings made in the completion of his purification rite] does not enter there, and they are liable on its account for a sin-offering.

What is at stake in matters of taxonomy is the ordering of the world in accord with its structure at the moment of creation. The lines of differentiation established at creation govern the delineation of batches of produce for the purpose of designating heave-offering. Heave-offering may be given for produce of the same genus or species in widely separated spots but under common ownership, but heave-offering may not be given for produce of diverse species under common ownership:

M. Terumot

2:4   A.   They may not separate heave-offering from [produce of one] kind for [produce] which is not of its same kind.

B.   And if he separated heave-offering [in this way] – that which he has separated is not [valid] heave-offering.

C.   All kinds of wheat are [considered] one [species];

D.   all kinds of figs, dried figs and [circles of] pressed figs are [considered] one [species] –

E.   so he separates heave-offering from one [kind of wheat, or figs] for another [kind].

Something that is created in a given category, for example, to serve a given purpose, must be permitted to serve that purpose and not any other, or not to go to waste. Produce in the status of heave-offering must be prepared in the customary way, so that all portions that normally are eaten are available for eating; it may not be prepared in such a way that edible portions would go to waste:

M. Terumot

11:1 A.   They may not put cakes of pressed figs or dried figs [in the status of heave-offering] in fish brine [in order to flavor that brine],

B.   since this ruins them [the figs, for use as food].

C. But they may put wine [in the status of heave-offering] in brine.
D. And they may not perfume oil [in the status of heave-offering, for it may not thereafter be eaten] –
E. But they may make wine [in the status of heave-offering] into honeyed wine.
F. They may not boil wine in the status of heave-offering,
G. since this diminishes its quantity.
H. R. Judah permits [one to cook wine], for this improves it [the flavor of the wine].

The principal mode of classification is through analogies. Things are like one another and follow the same rule. Or they are unlike, and so each follows the opposite rule from that governing the other. Analogical reasoning requires an exact match between analogies. If we can differentiate one case from another, then there is no analogy, and the rule for the one does not follow that governing the other.

Mishnah-tractate Besah

1:6 A. The House of Shammai say, "They do not bring dough-offering and priestly gifts to the priest on the festival day,
B. "whether they were raised up the preceding day or on that same day."
C. And the House of Hillel permit.
D. The House of Shammai said to them, "It is an argument by way of analogy
E. "The dough-offering and the priestly gifts [Deut. 18:3] are a gift to the priest, and heave-offering is a gift to the priest. Just as [on the festival day] they do not bring heave-offering [to a priest], so they do not bring these other gifts [to a priest]."
F. Said to them the House of Hillel, "No. If you have stated that rule in the case of heave-offering, which one [on the festival] may not designate to begin with, will you apply that same rule concerning the priestly gifts, which [on the festival] one may designate to begin with?"

If two things are analogous in all but one aspect, then the same rule governs both in all but that aspect:

Mishnah-tractate Besah

5:2 A. For (1) any act for which [people] are liable on grounds of Sabbath rest, for (2) optional acts, or for (3) acts of religious duty, on the Sabbath,
B. are they liable in regard to the festival day.
C. And these are the acts for which people are liable by reason of Sabbath rest:
D. (1) They do not climb a tree, (2) ride a beast, (3) swim in water, (4) clap hands, (5) slap the thigh, (6) or stamp the feet.
E. And these are the acts [for which people are liable] by reason of optional acts: (1) They do not sit in judgment, (2) effect a betrothal, (3) carry out a rite of halisah, (4) or enter into levirate marriage.

F.   And these are the acts [for which people are liable] by virtue of acts of religious duty: (1) They do not declare objects to be sanctified, (2) make a vow of valuation, (3) declare something to be herem, (4) or raise up heave-offering or tithe.

G.   All these actions on the festival have they declared [to be culpable], all the more so [when they are done] on the Sabbath.

H.   The sole difference between the festival and the Sabbath is in the preparation of food alone.

Classification may focus upon diverse traits, whether physical or functional. What is at stake in classification is accomplished without regard to the indicators that are invoked. For example, classification between unclean and clean may appeal to physical traits or the use of an object. Uncleanness is relative to the use or function of a utensil. A utensil that is useless, for example, that cannot serve as a receptacle, is insusceptible to uncleanness. When flat, the utensil is insusceptible, when formed into a receptacle, it is susceptible. An object that is useless is insusceptible; one that serves some purpose, if not its original one, remains susceptible. An object becomes susceptible when it is fully manufactured and no stage in the processing is lacking. If an object has a hole in it, then it may or may not be useful and so still susceptible; that depends upon how much the utensil still can hold:

Mishnah-tractate Kelim

2:1   A.   Vessels of wood, and vessels of leather, and vessels of bone, and vessels of glass:

B.   When they are flat, they are clean, and when they form receptacles, they are [susceptible of becoming] unclean.

C.   [If] they are broken, they are clean.

D.   [If] one went and made [new] vessels, they receive uncleanness from now and henceforth.

E.   [As to] vessels of clay and vessels of alum crystal, their [capacity to receive] uncleanness is alike.

F.   (1) They [both] become unclean and convey uncleanness by [their] contained airspace, and they impart uncleanness from their outer sides. (2) But they do not contract uncleanness from their outer parts.

G.   And breaking them is purifying them.

3:1   A.   The measure [of the perforation or hole] in a clay utensil to render it clean:

B.   That which is used for foods – its measure is with olives.

C.   That which is used for liquids – its measure is with liquids.

D.   That which is used for this and for that – they subject it to its more stringent [rule]: With olives.

If something no longer serves its original purpose but continues to serve some cognate purpose, it remains useful and therefore susceptible to uncleanness:

Mishnah-tractate Kelim

7:1   A.   The fire basket of householders which was diminished [to a distance of] less than three handbreadths [from the top] is unclean,

      B.   for one heats from the bottom and the pot boils from above.

      C.   [If it was hollowed out to] more than this [distance], it is clean.

      D.   [If] one placed stone or pebble [to fill up the hole],

      E.   [the basket remains] clean.

      F.   [If] one plastered it [the stone or pebble] with clay, it [the fire basket] receives uncleanness from now on.

The principle of distinguishing primary and secondary effects, or original and derivative cause, operates in the matter of classification, which joins within itself a large variety of secondary analytical or taxonomic principles. To give a concrete example: an article can lose its primary character through the breakage and replacement of its principal parts, so as to constitute a fundamentally new utensil. When those parts that give the original utensil its intrinsic character, carrying out its primary functions, have been replaced by new ones, then, even though the original utensil is superficially the same and in being, it has ceased to exhibit its primary character and is regarded as a new utensil, and the old one is as if it were broken:

Mishnah-tractate Kelim

18:5   A.   [As to] a bed which was unclean with midras uncleanness –

      B.   [if] a short side and two legs are removed,

      C.   it [still] is unclean.

      D.   [If] the long side and two legs [are removed],

      E.   [it] is clean.

      F.   R. Nehemiah declares unclean.

      G.   [If] one cut off two tongues at diagonally opposite corners, [or] cut off two legs at diagonally opposite corners by a square handbreadth, or diminished it [to] less than a handbreadth,

      H.   [it] is clean.

Classification and intention of course intersect throughout. When assessing usefulness, we are guided by the subjective opinions of ordinary people:

Mishnah-tractate Kelim

17:6   A.   The [measure] of the egg of which they have spoken – not a large, and not a small but a medium – sized [egg].

      B.   R. Judah says, "One brings the largest of the large [eggs] and the smallest of the small [eggs] and places them in water and divides [the volume of] the water."

      C.   Said R. Yosé, "And who will inform me which is largest and which is smallest? But everything is according to the opinion of the one who sees."

Intention to use an object imparts to the object the status of susceptibility; once it is ready for use, the owner's plan to use it suffices to complete the process. But if something is susceptible to uncleanness, it does not become insusceptible only by an act of intentionality, but solely if the owner does something to change the physical character of the object is its status changed:

Mishnah-tractate Kelim

25:9   C.   All the utensils descend into the power of their uncleanness with thought but do not ascend from the power of their uncleanness except by an act which changes them.

        D.   For the act cancels both an act and intention, but intention does not cancel either an act or intention.

Intentionality also plays a role in the determination of the classification of what can be eaten but ought not to be eaten, for example, carrion, which is fit for food but forbidden. Carrion of a clean bird conveys uncleanness as food only if someone has determined to eat it; that is what classifies it as food for the present purpose; it is not common to eat carrion, so intention is required. But it does not require an action to make the food susceptible to uncleanness; subject to proper intentionality, it is unclean in the first remove and conveys uncleanness on its own as a source of uncleanness:

1:1   A.   Thirteen matters regarding the carrion of the clean bird:

        B.   (1) It requires intention and does not require preparation.

        C.   And (2) it renders unclean with food uncleanness when it is the size of an egg,

        D.   and (3) [it conveys food uncleanness] when it is the size of an olive in the [eater's] gullet.

        E.   And (4) he who eats it requires waiting until sunset.

        F.   And (5) they are liable on its account for entering the sanctuary.

        G.   And (6) they burn heave-offering on its account.

        H.   And (7) he who eats a limb from the living [bird] from it is smitten with forty stripes.

Since classification deals not only with things but also relationships, we have to turn to the way in which the process is carried on in more abstract contexts. Classification extends to the analysis of actions; we may classify a single action in a variety of ways, with multiple consequences. A single action is divisible, involving a variety of distinct counts of culpability:

3:9   A.   There is one who ploughs a single furrow and is liable on eight counts of violating a negative commandment:

        B.   [Specifically, it is] he who (1) ploughs with an ox and an ass [Deut. 22:10], which are [2, 3] both Holy Things, in the case of (4) [ploughing] mixed seeds in a vineyard [Deut. 22:9], (5) in the

Seventh Year [Lev. 25:4], (6) on a festival [Lev. 23:7] and who was both a (7) priest [Lev. 21:1] and (8) a Nazirite [Num. 6:6] [ploughing] in a graveyard.

C. Hananiah b. Hakhinai says, "Also: He is [ploughing while] wearing a garment of diverse kinds" [Lev. 19:19, Deut. 22:11].

D. They said to him, "This is not within the same class."

E. He said to them, "Also the Nazir [B8] is not within the same class [as the other transgressions]."

One concrete example of the power of correct classification to dictate concrete behavior derives from the rule governing conduct on the Sabbath and festivals, that is, holy time, carefully differentiated from secular or ordinary time. Only what is designated in advance for use on the festival day may be utilized on that day. Food for use on the festival must be available and subject to designation, in fact or potentially, prior to the festival. That is the position of the House of Hillel in the following, which concerns an egg not made ready in advance for use on the festival day:

Mishnah-tractate Besah

1:1 A. An egg which is born on the festival day –

B. The House of Shammai say, "It may be eaten [on that day]."

C. And the House of Hillel say, "It may not be eaten."

The egg was born on the festival, so not made ready in advance. The House of Shammai hold the egg is part of the dam and therefore in its status; it was deemed ready, so, too, the egg; the Hillelites see the egg as distinct from the dam. In the following case, what is not certainly designated in advance of the holy day for use on the holy day may not be used on the holy day:

3:2 A. Nets for trapping a wild beast, fowl, or fish, which one set on the eve of the festival day –

B. one should not take [what is caught therein] out of them on the festival day,

C. unless one knows for sure that [creatures caught in them] were trapped on the eve of the festival day.

A further concrete example is readily adduced. What is meant for food must be preserved for that purpose and not wasted or destroyed. It may not be used for any other beneficial purpose; once the food is classified as second tithe, that classification takes over and defines all further use to which the food may be put:

M. M.S. 1:1

A. [As to produce in the status of] second tithe –

B.   (1) They do not sell it, (2) and they do not take it as a pledge, and (3) they do not give it in exchange [for other produce to be eaten as second tithe].

C.   And they do not reckon weight with it.

D.   And in Jerusalem, a man may not say to his friend: "Here is wine for you, now give me oil."

E.   And [this rule applies] likewise to all other [consecrated] produce.

F.   But they give [it] to each other as a gift

M. M.S. 1:2

A.   [As to] the tithe of cattle:

B.   (1) The [farmers] do not sell it [when the animal is] unblemished [and] alive; (2) and not [when the animal is] blemished, [whether it is] alive or slaughtered.

C.   (3) And they do not give it as a token of betrothal to women.

D.   [As to] the firstling [the first calves of the year's herd]:

E.   (1) They [the priests] sell it [when the animal is] unblemished [and] alive; (2) and [when the animal is] blemished, [whether it is] alive or slaughtered. (3) And they give it as a token of betrothal to women.

F.   They do not deconsecrate [produce in the status of] second tithe with (1) a poorly minted coin nor with (2) coin that is not [currently] circulating, nor with (3) money that is not in one's possession.

The matter of the right classification of all things extends into the Sabbath law. Objects may be used on the Sabbath only if they are designated for use on that day, and if not, they may not be handled lest they may be used. Those that serve a licit purpose on the Sabbath may be handled and used. Appurtenances of an object that may be handled on the Sabbath may be handled on the Sabbath, even though they are detached; objects normally used for purposes not done on the Sabbath but that may be used for licit purposes may be handled:

Mishnah-tractate Shabbat

17:1   A.   All utensils are handled on the Sabbath,

B.   and their [detached] doors along with them,

C.   even though they were detached on the Sabbath.

D.   For they are not equivalent to doors of a house,

E.   for the [latter] are not prepared [in advance of the Sabbath to be used].

17:2   A.   One handles (1), a hammer to split nuts,

B.   (2) an ax to chop off a fig,

C.   (3) a saw to cut through cheese,

D.   (4) a shovel to scoop up dried figs,

E.   (5) a winnowing shovel or (6) a fork to give something thereon to a child,

F.   (7) a spindle or (8) a shuttle staff to thrust into something,

G.   (9) a sewing needle to take out a thorn,

H.   (10) a sack-maker's needle to open a door.

Fragments of objects that may be handled may be handled, if they are still useful, even if they do not do the work they did when they were whole:

Mishnah-tractate Shabbat

17:5   A.   All utensils which are handled on the Sabbath – fragments deriving from them may be handled along with them,

          B.   on condition that they perform some sort of useful work [even if it is not what they did when they were whole]:

          C.   (1) Fragments of a kneading trough – to cover the mouth of a barrel,

          D.   (2) glass fragments – to cover the mouth of a flask.

          E.   R. Judah says, "On condition that they perform the sort of work which they did [when they were whole]: 1) "Fragments of a kneading trough – to pour porridge into them, (2) "glass fragments – to pour oil into them."

The power of classification is permanent. Animals that have been designated as holy for a particular purpose remain holy even though they are shifted from one to another holy purpose. In the case of animals designated for some offerings, for which a particular animal must be set aside for that one purpose alone, however, if the animal that has been designated for some other purpose is utilized, by the priest's own intentionality, for that purpose, the offering is a valid one, but the owner must meet his obligation by providing another animal. Intentionality therefore is in two parts: sanctification or designation of the beast as holy, and designation of the beast for a particular cultic purpose:

Mishnah-tractate Zebahim

1:1   A.   All animal-offerings which were slaughtered not for their own name are valid [so that the blood is tossed, the entrails burned, etc.],

        B.   but they do not go to the owner's credit in fulfillment of an obligation,

        C.   except for the Passover and the sin-offering –

Only the sin-offering, at all times, and the animal designated for use as a Passover-offering, at the time that that offering is prepared, are fit only if the animal is offered with the correct, specific intention for which it was originally designated. In all other cases, the beast remains a valid offering, though it does not serve the purpose for which the owner designated it. When sanctification, effected by an act that expresses the owner's intentionality, takes hold of the animal, the beast's status then governs, however the priest formulates the use of the beast within the menu of purposes for which animals can be sanctified; the sole exceptions involve the Passover; that must be offered from noon on the fourteenth of Nisan, and at that time, a beast designated for the Passover and suitable for that purpose that is offered for some other purpose is rendered unfit; at other times, it is just a peace-offering. But at that time, if the animal designated for the Passover is offered for some other purpose, the blood is not sprinkled; the rite is null.

Entire tractates work on the problem at hand, for example Mishnah-tractate Kilayim. This tractate formulates numerous problems around the conflict between appearance and actuality, setting forth cases to indicate which of the two principles governs; both positions are taken. The scriptural prohibitions against commingling different categories of plants, animals, and fibers are spelled out in three ways: [1] criteria for distinguishing among different classes; [2] defining what constitutes commingling of such distinct classes; [3] determining how to keep these categories separate and distinct from one another (Mandelbaum, p. ix). Man defines what constitutes a class and determines how to keep different classes distinct; Mandelbaum: "Man imposes upon an otherwise disorderly world limits and boundaries that accord with human perception of order and regularity.... What appears to man as orderly becomes identified with the objective order of the world." The commingling of different classes is prohibited only if the consequent mixture appears to man to contain a confusion of kinds, but not if the different kinds are arranged in an orderly manner; the Mishnah permits growing wheat and barley in the same field, if each kind is allowed a substantial amount of area and appears to be sown in a separate field unto itself (Mandelbaum, p. 3). If species are similar in appearance, they are not considered to be diverse kinds with one another; the field must not appear to be sown with diverse kinds, whether or not it is actually sown with seeds of different kinds (Mandelbaum, p. 27). Or, a field must not actually be sown with diverse kinds, without regard to its appearance. The following sustains the first of the two theories of the presupposition of the law before us:

M. Kilayim

1:5   A.   (1) A radish and a rape, (2) mustard and wild mustard, (3) a Greek gourd with an Egyptian [gourd] and the remusah,

        B.   even though they are similar to one another,

        C.   they are [considered] diverse kinds with one another.

1:6   A.   (1) A wolf and a dog, (2) a wild dog and a jackal, (3) goats and gazelles, (4) Nubian ibexes and fat-tailed sheep, (5) a horse and a mule, (6) a mule and an ass, (7) an ass and an Arabian onager,

        B.   even though they are similar to one another,

        C.   they are [considered] diverse kinds with one another.

The division between the theology of intentionality and the philosophy of classification, as we have seen, is provisional. In fact, the two matters flow together time and again. For example, since the intention with which a thing is made classifies it, what is intended for idolatry may not be used; what has been intended for some permissible purpose but then adapted for idolatrous purposes may be repaired and used; what one has removed from all idolatrous use may be used for Israelite purposes:

Mishnah-tractate Abodah Zarah

3:7   A.   There are three sorts of houses [so far as use as a shrine for idolatry is concerned]:

       B.   (1) A house which was built to begin with for the purposes of idolatry – lo, this is prohibited.

       C.   (2) [If] one stuccoed and decorated it for idolatry and renovated it, one removes the renovations.

       D.   (3) [If] one brought an idol into it and took it out – lo, this is permitted.

       E.   There are three sorts of stones:

       F.   (1) A stone which one hewed to begin with for a pedestal – lo, this is forbidden.

       G.   (2) [If] one plastered it and adorned it for an idol, and did something new to it –

       H.   one may remove that which he made which is new.

       I.   (3) [If] he set up an idol on [an existing] stone and then took it off, lo, this is permitted.

       J.   There are three kinds of asherahs:

       K.   (1) A tree which one planted to begin with for idolatry – lo, this is prohibited.

       L.   (2) [If] he chopped it and trimmed it for idolatry, and it sprouted afresh, he may remove that which sprouted afresh.

       M.   (3) [If] he set up an idol under it and then annulled it, lo, this is permitted,

We turn now to concrete examples of the foregoing principles.

1.   Recognition that one thing may fall into several categories and many things into a single one comes to expression, for the authorship of the Mishnah, in diverse ways. One of the interesting ones is the analysis of the several taxa into which a single action may fall, with an account of the multiple consequences, for example, as to sanctions that are called into play, for a single action. The right taxonomy of persons, actions, and things will show the unity of all being by finding many things in one thing, and that forms the first of the two components of what I take to be the philosophy's teleology.

Mishnah-tractate Keritot

3:9   A.   There is one who ploughs a single furrow and is liable on eight counts of violating a negative commandment:

       B.   [Specifically, it is] he who (1) ploughs with an ox and an ass [Deut. 22:10], which are (2, 3) both Holy Things, in the case of (4) [ploughing] mixed seeds in a vineyard [Deut. 22:9], (5) in the Seventh Year [Lev. 25:4], (6) on a festival [Lev. 23:7] and who was both a (7) priest [Lev. 21:1] and (8) a Nazirite [Num. 6:6] [ploughing] in a graveyard.

C. Hanania b. Hakhinai says, "Also: He is [ploughing while] wearing a garment of diverse kinds" [Lev. 19:19, Deut. 22:11].

D. They said to him, "This is not within the same class."

E. He said to them, "Also the Nazir [B8] is not within the same class [as the other transgressions]."

Here is a case in which more than a single set of flogging is called for. B's felon is liable to 312 stripes, on the listed counts. The ox is sanctified to the altar, the ass to the upkeep of the house (B2,3). Hanania's contribution is rejected since it has nothing to do with ploughing, and sages' position is equally flawed. The main point, for our inquiry, is simple. The one action draws in its wake multiple consequences. Classifying a single thing as a mixture of many things then forms a part of the larger intellectual address to the nature of mixtures. But it yields a result that, in the analysis of an action, far transcends the metaphysical problem of mixtures, because it moves us toward the ontological solution of the unity of being.

The real interest in demonstrating the unity of being lies not in things but in abstractions, and among abstractions *types* of actions take the centerstage. Mishnah-tractate Keritot works out how many things are really one thing. This is accomplished by showing the end or consequence of diverse actions to be always one and the same. The issue of the tractate is the definition of occasions on which one is obligated to bring a sin-offering and a suspensive guilt-offering. The tractate lists those sins that are classified together by the differentiating criterion of intention. If one deliberately commits those sins, he is punished through extirpation. If it is done inadvertently, he brings a sin-offering. In case of doubt as to whether or not a sin has been committed (hence: inadvertently), he brings a suspensive guilt-offering. Lev. 5:17-19 specifies that if one sins but does not know it, he brings a sin-offering or a guilt-offering. Then if he does, a different penalty is invoked, with the suspensive guilt-offering at stake as well. While we have a sustained exposition of implications of facts that Scripture has provided, the tractate also covers problems of classification of many things as one thing, in the form of a single sin-offering for multiple sins, and that problem fills the bulk of the tractate.

Mishnah-tractate Keritot 1:1, 2, 7, 3:2, 4

1:1 A. Thirty-six transgressions subject to extirpation are in the Torah....

1:2 A. For those [transgressions] are people liable, for deliberately doing them, to the punishment of extirpation,

B. and for accidentally doing them, to the bringing of a sin-offering,

C. and for not being certain of whether or not one has done them, to a suspensive guilt-offering [Lev. 5:17] –

D. "except for the one who imparts uncleanness to the sanctuary and its Holy Things,

E. "because he is subject to bringing a sliding scale-offering (Lev. 5:6-7, 11)," the words of R. Meir.

F. And sages say, "Also: [Except for] the one who blasphemes, as it is said, 'You shall have one law for him that does anything unwittingly' (Num. 15:29) – excluding the blasphemer, who does no concrete deed."

2. The recognition that one thing becomes many does not challenge the philosophy of the unity of all being, but confirms the main point. Why do I insist on that proposition? The reason is simple. If we can show that differentiation flows from within what is differentiated – that is, from the intrinsic or inherent traits of things – then we confirm that at the heart of things is a fundamental ontological being, single, cogent, simple, that is capable of diversification, yielding complexity and diversity. The upshot is to be stated with emphasis. *That diversity in species or diversification in actions follows orderly lines confirms the claim that there is that single point from which many lines come forth.* Carried out in proper order – [1] the many form one thing, and [2] one thing yields many – the demonstration then leaves no doubt as to the truth of the matter. Ideally, therefore, we shall argue from the simple to the complex, showing that the one yields the many, one thing, many things, two, four.

Mishnah-tractate Shabbat

1:1 A. [Acts of] transporting objects from one domain to another, [which violate] the Sabbath, (1) are two, which [indeed] are four [for one who is] inside, (2) and two which are four [for one who is] outside.

B. How so?

C. [If on the Sabbath] the beggar stands outside and the householder inside,

D. [and] the beggar stuck his hand inside and put [a beggar's bowl] into the hand of the householder,

E. or if he took [something] from inside it and brought it out,

F. the beggar is liable, the householder is exempt.

G. [If] the householder stuck his hand outside and put [something] into the hand of the beggar,

H. or if he took [something] from it and brought it inside,

I. the householder is liable, and the beggar is exempt.

J. [If] the beggar stuck his hand inside, and the householder took [something] from it,

K. or if [the householder] put something in it and he [the beggar] removed,

L. both of them are exempt.

M.   [If] the householder put his hand outside and the beggar took
      [something] from it,

N.   or if [the beggar] put something into it and [the householder]
      brought it back inside,

O.   both of them are exempt.

M. Shab. 1:1 classifies diverse circumstances of transporting objects
from private to public domain. The purpose is to assess the rules that
classify as culpable or exempt from culpability diverse arrangements.
The operative point is that a prohibited action is culpable only if one and
the same person commits the whole of the violation of the law. If two or
more people share in the single action, neither of them is subject to
punishment. At stake therefore is the conception that one thing may be
many things, and if that is the case, then culpability is not incurred by
any one actor. The Sabbath exposition appears so apt and perfect for the
present proposition that readers may wonder whether the authorship of
the Mishnah could accomplish that same wonder of concision of complex
thought more than a single time.

3.   Do we classify by appearances or by actualities? That is a recurrent
      problem in this Kilayim, which entertains the latter possibility but
      ordinarily prefers the former criterion. That ties in with the stress on
      the power of intention, as distinct from action, to govern the
      classification of things. This is spelled out in givens of theology, but
      it in fact is to be read as a free-standing, this-worldly issue. Here is a
      simple statement of matters:

M. Kilayim

9:2   A.   Silk and bast silk are not subject to [the laws of] diverse kinds,
       B.   but are prohibited for appearance's sake.

4.   We delineate the distinct forms of the same substance, for example,
      liquid, solid, and if we treat as the same thing the same substance in
      liquid and solid form, the act is invalid. On the other hand, we do
      not distinguish one solid form of a substance from another solid
      form of the same substance, nor does intentionality distinguish the
      physical traits of substances:

M. Terumot

1:8   A.   They may not separate oil as heave-offering for olives which have
             been crushed,
       B.   nor wine [as heave-offering] for grapes which have been trampled
             [but the processing of which has not yet been completed].
       C.   But if he [sic] separated heave-offering [in either of these fashions] –
       D.   that which he has separated is [valid] heave-offering.
       E.   But he must separate heave-offering again.

F.   The first [produce separated as heave-offering] imposes the status of heave-offering [upon other produce with which it is mixed], by itself [even if it falls into other produce apart from the second produce separated as heave-offering; cf. M. 3:11].
G.   And [nonpriests who accidentally eat it] are liable to the [added] fifth on its account.
H.   But this is not the case as regards the second [produce separated as heave-offering].

The heave-offering may not be separated from produce the preparation of which has been completed for that the preparation of which has not been completed; the pressing changes the form of the produce from solid to liquid, and so throughout (Peck, p. 71). What is deemed food and what is not deemed food are treated as distinct classes of produce, even of the same species. Cleanness or uncleanness constitutes a taxic indicator, and produce of the same species that is unclean is treated as a distinct category from that which is clean:

M. Terumot

2:2   A.   They do not separate heave-offering from that [produce] which is unclean for that which is clean.
B.   And if he separated heave-offering [in that manner] –
C.   [if he did it] unintentionally, that which he has separated is [valid] heave-offering;
D.   [but if he did it] intentionally, he has not done anything.
E.   And so [in the case of] a Levite who had [first] tithe from which heave-offering [of the tithe] had not been separated.
F.   [If he] was removing from it [heave-offering of the tithe for other clean first tithe], unintentionally, that which he has done is done [and valid];
G.   [but if he did it] intentionally, he has not done anything.
H.   R. Judah says, "If he knew about it [knew that the produce was unclean] from the beginning, even though [he forgot and his later actions were] unintentional, he has not done anything.

On the other hand, produce not contiguous but of the same species may be treated as a single batch for the present purpose; so physical location or propinquity by itself is null in the process of classification. Heave-offering thus may not be separated from produce of one genus for another, and distinct kinds must be kept separate.

5.   A principal concern of law is the classification of interstitial categories. The issue of classification involves, especially, what may fall into neither of two classes but is between the lines of them both. What is interstitial – between one status and another – requires special attention. This involves produce neither claimed by the farmer nor worthless, also food in transit from ripening in the field through the harvest season until it is brought home or sold in the

market. This is worked out through determining the intentions of the person who uses the food. What a person intends as a snack, however much, is so classified and may be eaten without tithing; what he intends to eat as a meal, however minimal, is a meal and may not be eaten until tithes are removed. All is determined by what the householder intends to do with the food. Intentions are inferred by what people actually do. Interstitiality covers spatial as well as temporal considerations, for example, the status of the courtyard of a house in regard to establishing that the farmer has produce produce home, as at M. Maaserot 3:5ff.:

M. Maaserot

3:5   A.   What type of courtyard is subject to [the law of] tithes [what kind of courtyard renders liable to tithes produce brought within it]?
      B.   R. Ishmael says, "A Tyrian courtyard,
      C.   "for household wares are kept [safely] within it."
      D.   R. Aqiba says, "Any [courtyard] which one [householder] opens but an other locks up is exempt [from the law of tithes]."
      E.   R. Nehemiah says, "Any [courtyard] in which a man eats unselfconsciously is subject [to the law of tithes]."
      F.   R. Yosé says, "Any [courtyard] into which [one] enters and no one inquires, 'What do you want?' is exempt [from the law of tithes]."
      G.   R. Judah says, "[If there are] two courtyards, one within the other,
      H.   "the inner [courtyard] is subject [to the law], while the other [courtyard] is exempt [from the law]."

6.   An interstitial question involves defining the language of the law, for example, if the law refers to planting, then is replanting an old tree equivalent to planting a new one? If the law refers to fruit, then what is the status of produce at various stages in its growth or ripening, for example, unripe berries, and what is the status of certain parts of fruit, for example, fruit pits?[1] In these cases, we deal with matters of doubt and interstitiality. First comes the issue of defining planting or replanting:

M. Hallah

1:3   A.   A tree which was uprooted together with the clump of earth [surrounding its roots],
      B.   [or a tree which] a river swept away together with the clump of earth [surrounding its roots] –
      C.   if it is able to live [from the clump alone and is replanted,] it is exempt [from the restriction of orlah].

---

[1]Howard Scott Essner, "The Mishnah Tractate Orlah: Translation and Commentary," in William S. Green, ed., *Approaches to Ancient Judaism* (Chico, 1981: Scholars Press for Brown Judaic Studies) p. 105.

      D.   But if not [if it could not live without being replanted], it is subject [after it is replanted, as if it were a new tree].

The matter is worked out by appeal to the rules of nature, that is, the natural facts governing the case. There is no appeal to the intentionality of the farmer here.

7.   Comparison and contrast yields the hierarchization of categories of things. When dealing with three or more categories, we compare and contrast the points in common among each set of two among the three, and that permits us to identify the indicative traits and to hierarchize the sets. Here is a complex essay in hierarchical classification, in which the indicative traits of classes are brought into juxtaposition for that purpose:

M. Hallah

2:1   A.   Heave-offering and first fruits –

      B.   (1) [nonpriests] are liable on their account [to suffer the] death [penalty, if they eat them intentionally], or [for restoring the principal and an] added fifth [if they eat them unintentionally; M. Hal. 1:9].

      C.   (2) And [they] are forbidden [as food] to commoners [nonpriests].

      D.   (3) And they are the property of the priests [M. Bik. 3:12].

      E.   (4) And they are neutralized [they become deconsecrated when mixed with unconsecrated produce] in [a ratio of] one [part of heave-offering or first fruits] to one hundred [parts of unconsecrated produce; M. Ter. 4:7]. (5) And [before they may be eaten], they require washing of the hands, and [in the case of one who has contracted uncleanness and immersed on that same day], the setting of the sun.

      F.   Lo, these [are restrictions which apply] to heave-offering and to first fruits but [which do] not [apply] to tithes.

2:2   A.   There are [restrictions which apply] to [second] tithe and to first fruits which [do] not [apply] to heave-offering.

      B.   For [second] tithe and first fruits

      C.   (1) require bringing [to the] place [Jerusalem];

      D.   (2) and they require [the recitation of the appropriate) confession;

      E.   (3) and they are prohibited [for consumption] by a mourner [whose dead relative has not yet been buried; Deut. 26:14, M. M.S. 5:8].

      F.   R. Simeon permits [such mourners to eat first fruits].

      G.   (4) And they are subject to [the law of] removal [Deut. 26:12ff., M. M.S.].

      H.   R. Simeon exempts [first fruits from the law of removal] [T. Bik. 1:7, M. M.S. 5:6].

      I.   (5) And in Jerusalem – [if they are mixed with unconsecrated produce] in any [portion], they [still] are forbidden for consumption [M. Or. 2:1],

      J.   (6) and in Jerusalem – [if they are used as seed], that which grows from them is prohibited for consumption,

K.   [and this prohibition applies] also to commoners [in the case of first fruits] and to cattle [in the case of second tithe].

L.   R. Simeon permits [the consumption, by commoners or cattle, of that which is mixed in Jerusalem with second tithe or first fruits and that which grows in Jerusalem from second tithe or first fruits].

M.   Lo, these [are restrictions which apply] to [second] tithe and to first fruits which [do] not [apply] to heave-offering.

2:3   A.   There are [restrictions which apply] to heave-offering and to tithe which [do] not [apply] to first fruits.

B.   For heave-offering and tithe

C.   (1) [which have not yet been separated] render prohibited [for consumption that which is on] the threshing floor [produce that had been completely processed];

D.   (2) and they have a [prescribed] quantity;

E.   (3) and [the laws governing them] are binding on any [kind of] produce;

F.   (4) [and these laws are binding] whether or not the Temple is standing;

G.   (5) and [they are separated] by sharecroppers, tenant farmers, holders of confiscated property, and by robbers [M. Ter. 1:1, M. M.S. 5:4, M. Bik. 1:2].

H.   Lo, these are [rules which apply] to heave-offering and to tithe but [do] not [apply] to first fruits.

2:4   A.   And there are [restrictions which apply] to first fruits which [do] not [apply] to heave-offering and tithe.

B.   For first fruits

C.   (1) are acquired [designated as first fruits] while [they are still] attached to the ground [unharvested] [M. Bik. 3:1];

D.   (2) and a person may designate his entire field [as] first fruits [M. Ter. 4:5, Hal. 1:9];

E.   (3) and he is responsible for [replacing] them [those first fruits which he has separated but could not offer; M. Bik. 1:8-9];

F.   (4) and they require a [peace]-offering [from the landowner; M. Bik. 3:3], singing [by the Levites; M. Bik. 3:4], waving [by the priest before the altar; M. Bik. 3:6], and staying overnight [in Jerusalem by the landowner; Deut. 16:7].

One could compose an account of the rules of classification from the cases given in the Mishnah, even though the cases themselves cover materials of not natural history but theological provenance. But here is a good example of the way in which natural history plays itself out in reference to its conventional subject matter:

M. Bikkurim

2:8   A.   A koy [a beast that falls into the taxon of a wild beast and also into that of a domesticated beast] –

B.   There are ways in which it is like a wild animal,

C.   and there are ways in which it is like a domesticated animal;

D.   and there are ways in which it is like [both] a domesticated animal and a wild animal;

	E.	and there are ways in which it is like neither a domesticated animal nor a wild animal.
2:9	A.	In what way is [a koy] like a wild animal?
	B.	(1) Its blood must be covered up like the blood of a wild animal [Lev. 17:13, M. Hul. 6:1ff.].
	C.	(2) And they may not slaughter it on a festival.
	D.	But if one slaughters it [on a festival], they do not cover up its blood [M. Bes. 1:2, M. Ed. 4:2].
	E.	(3) And its fat conveys carrion uncleanness like [the fat of] a wild animal [Lev. 7:24, M. Uqs. 3:9].
	F.	But its [own] uncleanness is in doubt.
	G.	And they do not redeem with it the firstborn of an ass [Ex. 13:13, M. Bek. 1:5].
2:10	A.	In what way is [a koy] like a domesticated animal?
	B.	(1) Its fat is forbidden [for consumption] as [is] the fat of a domesticated animal [Lev. 7:25].
	C.	But [those who eat it] are not subject to extirpation on its account [M. Ker. 1:1].
	D.	(2) And [the koy] may not be bought with [second]-tithe funds for consumption in Jerusalem [M. M.S. 1:3].
	E.	(3) And it is subject to [the priests' due of] the shoulder, cheeks, and stomach [Deut. 18:3, M. Hul. 10:1].
	F.	R. Eliezer exempts [it from the priests' due],
	G.	for the one who makes a claim on his fellow – upon [the claimant lies] the [burden of] proof [a priest who claims a share from a koy must prove that the koy is a domesticated animal].
2:11	A.	In what way is [a koy] like neither a domesticated animal nor a wild animal?
	B.	(1) It is forbidden under [the laws of] diverse kinds [to yoke it] either with a wild animal or with a domesticated animal [M. Kil. 1:6, 8:4].
	C.	(2) One who wills his wild animal or his domesticated animal to his son has not willed him a koy.
	D.	(3) If one said, Lo, may I be a Nazirite if this [animal] is a wild animal or a domesticated animal, [lo, he is a Nazirite] [M. Naz. 5:7].
	E.	But in all other ways, [the koy] is like [both] a wild animal and a domesticated animal.
	F.	And [thus] (1) it requires [ritual] slaughter [before it may be eaten] like both the wild animal and the domesticated animal [lit.: like this one and that one] –
	G.	And (2) it conveys uncleanness on account of [the laws of] the carrion and on account of [the laws of] a limb [cut off] from a living animal, as [do] both the wild and the domesticated animal [Lev. 11:8, M. Oh. 2:1].

8. Space is differentiated between public and private domain, with an interstitial domain, subject to traits of both public and private domain, recognized as well. The advent of holy time (the Sabbath) imparts consequence to that differentiation. In secular time, the distinction between public, neutral, and private domain is null. In

holy time, the distinction makes a difference. So – stating matters in gross terms – space is subject to temporal differentiation, but time is not subject to spatial differentiation. The specific difference is that in holy time, objects may not be transferred from space of one classification to space of the other, as expressed in the following vignette:

1:1   A.   [Acts of] transporting objects from one domain to another [which violate] the Sabbath (1) are two, which [indeed] are four [for one who is] inside, (2) and two which are four [for one who is] outside.
      B.   How so?
      C.   [If on the Sabbath] the beggar stands outside and the householder inside,
      D.   [and] the beggar stuck his hand inside and put [a beggar's bowl] into the hand of the householder,
      E.   or if he took [something] from inside it and brought it out,
      F.   the beggar is liable, the householder is exempt.
      G.   [If] the householder stuck his hand outside and put [something] into the hand of the beggar,
      H.   or if he took [something] from it and brought it inside,
      I.   the householder is liable, and the beggar is exempt.
      J.   [If] the beggar stuck his hand inside, and the householder took [something] from it,
      K.   or if [the householder] put something in it and he [the beggar] removed it,
      L.   both of them are exempt.
      M.   [If] the householder put his hand outside and the beggar took [something] from it,
      N.   or if [the beggar] put something into it and [the householder] brought it back inside,
      O.   both of them are exempt.

9.   Classification and hierarchization depends upon things remaining in their class, that is, for the purpose for which they were made. Substances and objects must on the Sabbath be used for the purpose that is distinctive to them, and may not be used for some other, extrinsic purpose. In holy time, the original and intrinsic purpose for which something is created is the sole legitimate purpose that that thing may serve. On the Sabbath, moreover, what is set aside for use on the Sabbath may be used on that day, but what is not designated for that distinct purpose may not be used on that day. This conception concerning the impact of enchanted time upon the utilization of things runs along the lines of the impact of enchanted time on the lines of spatial differentiation. What has a normal and available purpose must be allowed to carry out that purpose and may not, on the Sabbath, be prevented from serving its normal purpose. In the following case, the utensil may not be placed under

the lamp to catch the oil, since the oil cannot be used on the Sabbath, not having been designated for that purpose beforehand; with oil in it, the plate cannot be moved on the Sabbath. Otherwise, it may be moved on the Sabbath. By placing it under the lamp on the Sabbath, we have made it impossible to use the plate for its normal and available purpose:

Mishnah-tractate Shabbat

3:6   A.   [On the Sabbath] they do not put a utensil under a lamp to catch the oil.

        B.   But if one put it there while it is still day, it is permitted.

        C.   But they do not use any of that oil [on the Sabbath],

        D.   since it is not something which was prepared [before the Sabbath for use on the Sabbath].

10. There are genera divided into species. That fundamental distinction is expressed in diverse ways. We treat as a single genus of action those deeds that violate the Sabbath done by someone who does not even known about the Sabbath at all; those who know that there is a Sabbath but violates several Sabbath days in succession; and those who know that there is a Sabbath in principle but violate it in diverse ways. Under the first rubric, violation is of the genus, not the species, and, it follows, culpability is incurred on only a single count, for however many actions; in the second and third cases, violation is of various species, with culpability for each species:

Mishnah-tractate Shabbat

7:1   A.   A general rule did they state concerning the Sabbath:

        B.   Whoever forgets the basic principle of the Sabbath and performed many acts of labor on many different Sabbath days is liable only for a single sin-offering.

        C.   He who knows the principle of the Sabbath and performed many acts of labor on many different Sabbaths is liable for the violation of each and every Sabbath.

        D.   He who knows that it is the Sabbath and performed many acts of labor on many different Sabbaths is liable for the violation of each and every generative category of labor.

        E.   He who performs many acts of labor of a single type is liable only for a single sin-offering.

7:2   A.   The generative categories of acts of labor [prohibited on the Sabbath] are forty less one:

        B.   (1) He who sews, (2) ploughs, (3) reaps, (4) binds sheaves, (5) threshes, (6) winnows, (7) selects [fit from unfit produce or crops], (8) grinds, (9) sifts, (10) kneads, (11) bakes;

        C.   (12) he who shears wool, (13) washes it, (14) beats it, (15) dyes it;

        D.   (16) spins, (17) weaves,

        E.   (18) makes two loops, (19) weaves two threads, (20) separates two threads;

F.   (21) ties, (22) unties,

G.   (23) sews two stitches, (24) tears in order to sew two stitches;

H.   (25) he who traps a deer, (26) slaughters it, (27) flays it, (28) salts it, (29) cures its hide, (30) scrapes it, and (31) cuts it up;

I.   (32) he who writes two letters, (33) erases two letters in order to write two letters;

J.   (34) he who builds, (35) tears down;

K.   (36) he who puts out a fire, (37) kindles a fire;

L.   (38) he who hits with a hammer; (39) he who transports an object from one domain to another –

M.   lo, these are the forty generative acts of labor less one.

11.   The same principles concerning the division of space, at the advent of holy time, into the two types delineating by ownership and use, public and private domain, operates here too. But the legal premises of that metaphysical principle are far more carefully differentiated, and these have already been listed. The conception of the fictive fusion meal takes for granted that ownership may be represented by a symbolic action or object, given over by many individual householders to a common corporation formed of them all. This once more takes effect for the purpose of holy time (Sabbath, festival), having no this-worldly consequences of any kind:

8:1   A.   How do they prepare a shittuf [fictive fusion meal] for the Sabbath line?

B.   One puts down a jug [of food of some sort] and says, "Lo, this belongs to all the residents of my town,"

C.   "to whoever goes to the house of mourning" or "to the house of celebration."

D.   Whoever accepted for himself [a share in the ownership of this meal] while it was still day is permitted [to walk to the limit of two thousand cubits from the location of the shittuf].

E.   [But whoever accepts for himself ownership] after it gets dark is prohibited [from doing so], for they do not prepare an erub once it gets dark.

12.   Where two things are analogous, then they may be compared; the point of difference is the sole exception to the analogy, and in all other aspects, they remain the same, that is, subject to the same rule and part of the same class. Therefore the governing rule derives from the genus, and speciation only specifies exceptions to the prevailing rule:

Mishnah-tractate Megillah

1:4   A.   [If] they read the Scroll in the first Adar, and then the year was intercalated, they read it [again] in the second Adar.

B.   There is no difference between [the fourteenth or fifteenth of] the first Adar and [the same dates in] the second Adar except for the reading of the Scroll and giving gifts to the poor [which must be done in the second Adar, not in the first Adar, but in both Adars on the fourteenth or fifteenth, lamentations and fasts are prohibited].

1:5 A. There is no difference between a festival day and the Sabbath day except for preparing food alone [M. Bes. 5:2].

  B. There is no difference between the Sabbath and the Day of Atonement except that deliberately violating this one is punishable at the hands of an earthly court, while deliberately violating that one is punishable through extirpation.

1:6 A. There is no difference between one who is prohibited by vow from deriving [general] benefit from his fellow, and one who is prohibited by vow from deriving food from his fellow, except for setting foot in his house and using utensils of his which are not for preparing food [permitted in the former case].

  B. There is no difference between vows and freewill-offerings, except that for animals designated in fulfillment of vows one is responsible, while for animals set aside in fulfillment of freewill-offerings one is not responsible [should the animal be lost].

1:7 A. There is no difference between a Zab who suffers two appearances of flux and one who suffers three except for the requirement of an offering [for the latter] –

  B. There is no difference between a mesora who is shut up and one who has been certified except for the requirement to mess up the hair and tear the clothing.

  C. There is no difference between [a mesora] declared clean having been shut up and one declared clean having been certified [unclean] except for the requirement of shaving and of bringing a bird-offering.

1:8 A. There is no difference between sacred scrolls and phylacteries and mezuzot except that sacred scrolls may be written in any alphabet ["language"], while phylacteries and mezuzot are written only in square ["Assyrian"] letters.

13. Where for purposes of classification we invoke one analogy, we invoke all counterpart analogies as well. Since the surviving brothers are treated as analogous to, that is, enter into the status of, the deceased childless brother, so the same principle of analogy is extended to the deceased childless brother's co-wives as a whole. The status of one of the co-wives governs the status of them all, just as all of the brothers are available as levirs or for the rite of halisah. So there is a perfect consistency governing the operative analogies; if one analogy works to include, all covered are included; if one of the co-wives is excluded, all are in the same status and subject to the same rule:

Mishnah-tractate Yebamot

1:1 A. Fifteen women [who are near of kin to their deceased, childless husband's brother] exempt their co-wives, and the co-wives, from halisah and from levirate marriage, without limit.

The remainder of the exposition is not required to establish the premise that operates here.

14. Analogies carry weight, and when we deal with analogies, we interpret not the intent or the implicit sense but the actual meaning and wording of what is said. If one uses language that effects a change in the status of a thing, that language is valid. But if one uses language that in no way effects a change in the status of a thing, that language is null, even if one's intent is to forbid for himself the utilization of that thing. In the following case, we contrast language that speaks of sanctification with language that speaks of prohibition; the former changes the status of that subject to the formula, the latter does not:

Mishnah-tractate Nedarim

2:1   A.   And these [vows] are not binding [at all]:
        B.   [He who says,] "May what I eat of yours be unconsecrated food," "[Be like pig meat," "Like an idol," "Like hides pierced at the heart," "Like carrion," "Like terefah meat," "Like abominations," "Like creeping things," "Like the dough-offering of Aaron," or "Like his heave-offering,"
        C.   it is not binding.

15. The distinction between genus and species is of course broadly operative. The species is encompassed by language referring to the genus, but the genus is not covered by language referring to the species:

Mishnah-tractate Nedarim

3:6   A.   He who vows [not to gain benefit] from those who go down to the sea is permitted [to enjoy benefit] from those who dwell on dry land.
        B.   [He who vowed not to enjoy benefit] from those who dwell on dry land is prohibited [to enjoy benefit] from those who go down to the sea,
        C.   for those who go down to the sea are part of the generality of those who live on dry land.
        D.   [Those who go down to the sea includes] not the like of those who go from Acre to Jaffa but the one who sails out of sight of land.

Further analysis of the power of speciation and the distinction between the genus and species is in the following:

Mishnah-tractate Nedarim

6:1   A.   He who takes a vow not to eat what is cooked is permitted [to eat what is] roasted or seethed.

    B.   [If] he said, "Qonam if I taste cooked food," he is prohibited from eating what is loosely cooked in a pot but permitted to eat which is solidly cooked in a pot.
    C.   And he is permitted to eat a lightly boiled egg or gourds prepared in hot ashes.
6:2 A.   He who takes a vow not to eat what is cooked in a pot is prohibited only from what is boiled [therein].
    B.   [If] he said, "Qonam if I taste anything which goes down into a pot"' he is prohibited from eating anything which is cooked in a pot.

Speciation is accomplished through various taxic indicators, for example, solid versus liquid:

Mishnah-tractate Nedarim

6:7 A.   He who vows not to drink wine is permitted to eat a cooked dish which has the taste of wine.
    B.   [If] he said, "Qonam if I taste this wine," and it fell into a cooked dish, if there is sufficient [wine] to impart a flavor, lo, this is prohibited.
    C.   He who takes a vow not to eat grapes is permitted to drink wine.
    D.   [He who takes a vow not to eat] olives is permitted to have olive oil.
    E.   [If] he said, "Qonam! if I eat these olives or grapes," he is prohibited to eat them and what exudes from them.

The genus encompasses the species, but the species does not encompass the genus:

Mishnah-tractate Nazir

2:7 A.   [If one said,] "I will be a Nazir when a son is born to me," and a son was born to him, lo, this one is a Nazir.
    B.   [If[] a daughter, a child of unclear sexual traits, a childbearing the sexual traits of both sexes, is born to him, he is not a Nazir.
    C.   If he said, "When I see that a child is born to me, [I shall be a Nazir],"
    D.   even if a daughter, a child bearing unclear sexual traits [or] a child bearing the sexual traits of both sexes, is born to him, lo, he is a Nazir.

16. We distinguish among acts of the same kind, treating each as a separate incident, when these acts are separated from one another, for example, by an explicit statement; but if acts of the same kind are performed in a single, undifferentiated spell, for example, of inadvertence, then all are treated as one continuous action:

6:4 A.   A Nazir who was drinking wine all day long is liable only on one count.
    B.   [If] they said to him, "Don't drink it!" "Don't drink it!" and he continues drinking, he is liable on each and every count [of drinking].

C.   [If] he was cutting his hair all day long, he is liable only on a single count.

D.   [If] they said to him, "Don't cut it!" "Don't cut it!" and he continued to cut his hair, he is liable for each and every count [of cutting].

E.   [If] he was contracting corpse uncleanness all day long, he is liable on only one count.

F.   If they said to him, "Don't contract corpse uncleanness!" "Don't contract corpse uncleanness!" and he continued to contract corpse uncleanness, he is liable for each and every count.

The criteria of differentiation are diverse, but language is a major one.

17. Hierarchical classification may yield more than a single result; a given action may rank higher in one aspect and lower in another, and one of the requirements of classification is to compare and contrast matters of the same classification:

Mishnah-tractate Nazir

6:5   A.   Three things are prohibited to a Nazir: [Corpse] uncleanness, cutting the hair, and anything which goes forth from the grapevine [= M. 6:1A].

B.   A more strict rule applies to corpse uncleanness and haircutting than applies to that which comes forth from the grapevine.

C.   For corpse uncleanness and haircutting cause the loss of the days already observed, but [violating the prohibition against] that which goes forth from the vine does not cause the loss of the days already observed.

D.   A more strict rule applies to that which goes forth from the vine than applies to corpse uncleanness and haircutting.

E.   For that which goes forth from the vine allows for no exception, but corpse uncleanness and haircutting allow for exceptions,

F.   in the case of [cutting the hair for] a religious duty and in the case of finding a neglected corpse [with no one else to provide for burial, in which case, the Nazir is absolutely required to bury the corpse].

G.   A more strict rule applies to corpse uncleanness than to haircutting.

H.   For corpse uncleanness causes the loss of all the days previously observed and imposes the liability for an offering.

I.   But haircutting causes the loss of only thirty days and does not impose liability for an offering.

18. We differentiate species of a genus; but what is a single genus is undivided. Various actions may fall into a single classification and be punishable on a single count, if they are not differentiated; language effects the differentiation:

M. Shabuot

3:1   G.   "I swear that I won't eat," and he ate and drank – he is liable on only one count.

H.   "I swear that I won't eat and drink," and he ate and drank – he is liable on two counts.

3:2   A.   "I swear I won't eat,"
        B.   and he ate a piece of bread made of wheat, a piece of bread made of barley, and a piece of bread made of spelt – he is liable on one count only.
        C.   "I swear that I won't eat a piece of bread made of wheat, a piece of bread made of barley, and a piece of bread made of spelt," and he ate –
        D.   he is liable on each and every count.
3:3   A.   "I swear I won't drink," and he drank many different beverages –
        B.   he is liable on one count only.
        C.   "I swear that I won't drink wine, oil, and honey," and he drank –
        D.   he is liable on each and every count.

This motif is worked out time and again in the tractate, but the operative principle of differentiation is the same.

19. There are classifications the indicative traits of which are mutually exclusive: if A, then not B, if B, then not A. That principle of taxonomy is expressed in the following terms:

M. Hullin

1:5   A.   That which is valid in the case of turtledoves is invalid in the case of pigeons.
        B.   What is valid in the case of pigeons is invalid in the case of turtledoves.
        C.   The beginning of the brightening [of the neck feathers] in both this one and that one is invalid.
1:6   A.   What is valid [as a mode of killing] in the case of the [red] cow is invalid in the case of the calf [whose neck is to be broken].
        B.   What is valid in the case of the calf is invalid in the case of the cow.
        C.   What is valid in the case of priests is invalid in the case of Levites.
        D.   What is valid in the case of Levites in invalid in the case of priests.
        E.   What is clean [insusceptible to uncleanness] in the case of clay utensils is unclean [susceptible] in the case of all [other] utensils.
        F.   What is clean in the case of all [other utensils] is unclean in the case of the clay utensils.
        G.   What is clean in the case of wooden utensils is unclean in the case of metal utensils.
        H.   What is clean in the case of metal utensils is unclean in the case of wooden utensils.
        I.   What is liable [for tithes] in the case of bitter almonds is exempt [from tithes] in the case of sweet [almonds].
        J.   What is liable in the case of sweet ones is exempt in the case of bitter ones.

20. The problem of classification affects the potential and the actual. Do we classify what is going to happen as though it had already happened? What is actually in process is treated as if it had come about, but what is merely potential is not treated as fact:

M. Arakhin

1:4   A.   The woman who goes forth to be put to death –

      B.   they do not postpone [the execution] for her until she will give birth.

      C.   [If] she sat on the travailing stool, they postpone [the execution] for her until she will give birth.

      D.   The woman who is executed – they derive benefit from her hair.

4:3   A.   But in the case of offerings, the rule is not so.

      B.   Even if his father is about to die and leave him ten thousand,

      C.   [even if] his ship was at sea and [about to) arrive with ten thousand,

      D.   the sanctuary has no claim whatsoever on them.

In assessing a situation, we take account only of the facts prevailing at the time that the situation is assessed:

6:5   C.   Even though they have said: Slaves are sold with their clothing to improve their value,

      D.   so that if for him [the slave] a garment should be purchased for thirty denars, it improves his value by a maneh,

      E.   and so in the case of a cow: If they keep it for sale in a marketplace, it fetches a better price, and so in the case of a pearl: If they bring it up to a city, it fetches a better price –

      F.   the sanctuary [nonetheless] has a claim only in its own place and in its own time.

What is not actually in being is regarded as null and of no effect:

M. Temurah

1:3   A.   They do not substitute (1) limbs for foetuses, or foetuses for limbs,

      B.   or (2) limbs and foetuses for whole beasts, or whole beasts for them.

      C.   R. Yosé says, "They substitute limbs for whole beasts but not whole beasts for limbs."

      D.   Said R. Yosé, "And is it not so that in the case of animals which have been consecrated, he who says, 'The foot of this is a burnt-offering' – the whole beast is a burnt-offering?

      E.   "Also, when he will state, 'The foot of this is instead of that' – the whole of it should be a substitute in its stead."

21.   Things that fall into the same category also come under the same rule and so are deemed to form a single volume, for example, that which is required for the law to apply. Things that do not fall into the same category do not fall under the same rule and so do not join together to form a single quantity; and things that are alike in some ways but not others join together for the purposes of one law but not another:

M. Meilah

4:1   A.   Things consecrated for the altar join together with one another [for making up the requisite quantity – a perutah's worth – to be subject to] the law of sacrilege,

B. and to impose liability on their account for transgression of the laws of refuse, remnant and uncleanness.

C. Things consecrated for the upkeep of the house join together with one another [in regard to sacrilege].

D. Things consecrated for the altar and things consecrated for the upkeep of the house join together [for making up the quantity to be subject to] the law of sacrilege.

4:2 A. Five things in a burnt-offering join together [to form the requisite volume for liability to sacrilege]: (1) the meat, (2) the forbidden fat, (3) the fine flour, (4) the wine, and (5) the oil.

B. And six in the thank-offering [join together]: (1) the meat, (2) the forbidden fat, (3) the fine flour, (4) the wine, (5) the oil, and (6) the bread.

C. (1) Heave-offering, and (2) heave-offering of tithe, and (3) heave-offering of tithe of demai, and (4) dough-offering, and (5) first fruits join together

D. to impose a prohibition and to impose liability to the added fifth on their account.

4:3 A. All forms of refuse join together.

B. All forms of remnant join together.

C. All forms of carrion join together.

D. All forms of creeping things join together.

E. The blood of a creeping thing and its flesh join together.

F. A general principle did R. Joshua state, "All things that are alike in the [duration of] uncleanness of each and in the requisite measure of each join together.

G. "[If they are alike] (1) in [duration of] uncleanness but not in requisite measure, (2) in requisite measure but not in [duration of] uncleanness, (3) neither in [duration of] uncleanness nor in requisite measure,

H. "they do not join together [to form the volume that is necessary to convey uncleanness]."

22. An object falls into the classification for which it was originally destined, even though it later was changed in character. The water must be drawn or mixed by the use of a valid, cultically clean utensil. If the utensil after being manufactured was given a different character, for example, joined to the earth and therefore no longer a utensil, it still may be used:

M. Parah

5:7 A. The trough which is [hewn] in the rock –

B. (1) they do not draw with it, (2) they do not mix with it, (3) they do not sprinkle from it, (4) it does not require a tightly sealed stopper, and (5) it does not render an immersion pool unfit.

C. [If] it was a [movable] utensil, and one [then] joined it with plaster [to the ground] –

D. (1) they do draw with it, (2) they do mix with it, (3) they do sprinkle from it, (4) it does require a tightly sealed stopper, and (5) it renders unfit in the case of the immersion pool.

Changes in the volume of the same substance, for example, through shrinkage, may reclassify that substance:

M. Tohorot

3:4   A.   An egg's bulk of foodstuffs which one left in the sun and which shrank,

      B.   and so (1) an olive's bulk of corpse matter, (2) an olive's bulk of carrion and (3) a lentil's bulk of a creeping thing,

      C.   (4) an olive's bulk of refuse, (5) an olive's bulk of remnant, and (6) an olive's bulk of prohibited fat –

      D.   lo, they are clean.

      E.   And they are not liable on their account because of refuse, remnant, and uncleanness.

      F.   [If] one left them in the rain and they expanded, they are unclean,

      G.   and they are liable on their account [for transgression of the laws of I refuse, remnant, and uncleanness [Better: forbidden fat].

23. Something remains in its established classification until its essential condition changes and it is no longer suitable for its original purpose; what is subjected to intentionality is changed as to its status:

M. Tohorot

8:6   A.   A general rule did they state in connection with clean [foods]:

      B.   Whatever is set aside for human consumption – it is susceptible to uncleanness until it is unfit for food for a dog.

      C.   And whatever is not set aside for human consumption – it is insusceptible to uncleanness until it is designated for man.

      D.   How so?

      E.   A young pigeon which fell into the winepress, and one gave thought to it to bring it up for a gentile –

      F.   It is susceptible to uncleanness.

      G.   [And if one gave thought to bring it up] for a dog – it is insusceptible to uncleanness.

      H.   R. Yohanan b. Nuri declares it susceptible to uncleanness.

      I.   [If] a deaf-mute, an imbecile, or a minor gave thought to it, it is insusceptible to uncleanness.

      J.   If they brought it up, it is susceptible to uncleanness,

      K.   for they have the power of deed, but they do not have the power of [effective] intention.

B. The Message of the Taxonomic Power of Human Intentionality

While the matter of intentionality forms a critical component of the corpus of theological premises, it plays an equally critical role in the formulation of rules of classification and hierarchization. So while the Mishnah's authorship's discussion on intention works out several theories concerning God and God's relationship to humanity, the nature of the human will enters into the matter of classification, and so forms itself a decidedly philosophical topic. The human being is defined as not only sentient but also a volitional being, who can will with effect, unlike beasts and, as a matter of fact, angels (which do not, in fact, figure in the Mishnah at all). On the one side, there is no consideration or will or attitude of animals, for these are null. On the other side, will and attitude of angels, where these are represented in later documents, are totally subservient to God's wishes. Only the human being, in the person of the farmer, possesses and also exercises the power of intentionality. And it is the power that intentionality possesses that forms the central consideration. Because a human being forms an intention, consequences follow, whether or not given material expression in gesture or even in speech. An account of the Mishnah's sages' philosophical anthropology – theory of the structure of the human being – must begin with the extraordinary power imputed by the Mishnah's system to the will and intentionality of the human being. We begin with a simple definition of what is at hand.

The basic definition of intentionality as a taxic indicator is simple: it is possible to make a mental stipulation to affect the status of a material object, for example, by an act of intentionality retrospectively to classify something, as in the following case:

Mishnah-tractate Pesahim

8:2   A.   He who says to his slave, "Go and slaughter a Passover-offering in my behalf" –

       B.   [if] he slaughtered a kid, let him eat it.

       C.   [If] he slaughtered a lamb, let him eat it.

       D.   [If] he slaughtered both a kid and a lamb, let him eat from the former.

       E.   [If the slave] forgot what his master said to him, what should he do?

       F.   Let him slaughter both a kid and a lamb and say, "If my master told me to prepare a kid, the kid is his and the lamb is mine, and if my master told me to prepare a lamb, the lamb is his and the kid is mine."

       G.   [If the slave did as specified but] his master forgot what he had said to him, both of them [the animals killed by the slave] go out to the place of burning.

       H.   But they are exempt from the requirement of preparing the second Passover.

But an action bears consequence even though improper intentionality accompanies it; if someone designates as holy for a particular purpose an animal that cannot serve that purpose, the beast is still consecrated and must be treated as such. So an act may have some bearing upon the classification of something, even though it is not wholly effective. The point is, the action is effective so far as the intentionality can be effected:

Mishnah-tractate Pesahim

9:7   A.   He who designates a female animal for his Passover-offering [which must be male (Ex. 12:5)],

B.   or a male two years old [though it must be one year old] –
C.   [the animal so designated] is set out to pasture until it suffers a blemish, then it is sold, and the coins received for it fall for a freewill-offering.
D.   He who designates an animal for his Passover-offering and who died –
E.   his son should bring it in his stead not as a Passover-offering, but as peace-offerings.

For an action to be valid, the intentionality must correspond to the requirement of the rite. If one does a valid action but for other than the specified purpose, the act is null. If an action required for the slaughter of the Passover-offering is carried out properly, but is designated for some purpose other than the Passover rite, the action is null, and so if the action is done properly but with the intention of carrying out the obligations of persons other than those for whom it is validly carried out, the action is null. Improper intentionality therefore invalidates an otherwise valid action:

5:2   A.   A Passover sacrifice which one slaughtered under an improper designation ["not for its name," that is, for another purpose than as a Passover sacrifice],
       B.   or received the blood and tossed the blood of which under an improper designation,
       C.   or under its proper designation and under an improper designation,
       D.   or under an improper designation and under its proper designation,
       E.   is invalid.
       F.   How [is it done] both under its proper designation and not under its proper designation?
       G.   [If one slaughtered it] for the sake of a Passover-offering and for the sake of peace-offerings.
       H.   Under an improper designation and under a proper designation?
       I.   [If one slaughtered it] for the sake of peace-offerings and for the sake of a Passover-offering.

The range of issues may be set forth very simply. As tractate Makhshirin works matters out, what is the relationship between intention and action? Does intention to do something govern the decision in a case, even though one's action has produced a different effect? For example, if I intend to wet down only part of an object, or make use of only part of a body of water, but then wet down the whole or dispose of the whole, is the whole deemed susceptible? Does my consequent action revise the original effects of my intention? The positions on the interplay of action and intention exposed in Mishnah-tractate Makhshirin are these:

1.   Judah has the realistic notion that a person changes his mind, and therefore we adjudge a case solely by what he does and not by what

he says he will do, intends, or has intended, to do. If we turn Judah's statement around, we come up with the conception predominant throughout his rulings: *A case is judged in terms solely of what the person does.* If he puts on water, that water in particular that he has deliberately applied imparts susceptibility to uncleanness. If he removes water, only that water he actually removes imparts susceptibility to uncleanness, but water that he intends to remove but that is not actually removed is not deemed subject to the person's original intention. And, it is fair to add, we know it is not subject to the original intention, because the person's action has not accomplished the original intention or has placed limits upon the original intention. What is done is wholly determinative of what is originally intended.

2. Yosé at M. Makhshirin 1:5 expresses the contrary view. Water that has been wiped off is detached with approval. But water that has remained on the leek has not conformed to the man's intention, and that intention is shown by what the man has actually done. Accordingly, the water remaining on the leek is not subject to the law, if water be put. The upshot is to reject the view that what is done is wholly determinative of what is originally intended. We sort things out by appeal to nuances of effect. Once, in assessing blame, we invoke the consideration of intentionality, then matters become more complicated.

3. Simeon's point at M. Makhshirin 1:6 is that the liquid left on the palm of the hand is not wanted and not necessary to the accomplishment of one's purpose. Simeon's main point is that liquid not essential in accomplishing one's purpose is not taken into account and does not come under the law, if water be put. Why not? Because water is held to be applied with approval *only* when it serves a specific purpose. That water which is incidental has not been subjected to the man's wishes and therefore does not impart susceptibility to uncleanness. Only that water that is necessary to carry out the farmer's purpose imparts susceptibility to uncleanness.

The concrete expression of the principle that intentionality effects classification occurs throughout. One instance is that we distinguish among the effect of a sequence of actions by reference to the knowledge or intent of the one who does the actions. If all are done in a single spell of inadvertence, all are classified as a single action; it follows that attitude or intention forms a principal point of differentiation:

Keritot

3:2   A.   [If] he ate [forbidden] fat and [again ate] fat in a single spell of
             inadvertence, he is liable only for a single sin-offering,
       B.   [If] he ate forbidden fat and blood and remnant and refuse [of an
             offering] in a single spell of inadvertence, he is liable for each and
             every one of them.

C. The Nature of Mixtures

The disposition of mixtures of diverse matter forms a subdivision of
the inquiry into the hierarchical classification of all things. We wish to
know how to deal with a mixture of two things since we need to classify
that mixture and wish to know the indicators that dictate the correct
classification. We begin with a point that will recur in its own terms:

1.   When we deal with what is primary, what is secondary in the same
      circumstance is adequately covered as well; what is primary to a
      circumstance (a situation, a mixture) dictates the status of what is
      secondary or derivative (M. Ber. 6:7, 8):

      A.   [If] they placed before him a salted relish and with it, a loaf [of
            bread],
      B.   he recites the blessing over the salted relish and this exempts the
            loaf [from the requirement of a blessing],
      C.   for the loaf is secondary to it.
      D.   This is the general rule: Any primary [food] accompanied by a
            secondary [food] – one recites the blessing over the primary and
            [thereby] exempts the secondary.

2.   Identifying the principal, and the subordinate, component of a given
      composite is required if we are to find out the principle that governs
      the whole of the composite; it is, of course, the principle governing
      the principal part, in which case we have to compare and contrast the
      components to determine which predominates, and on what basis.
      This is expressed in an essay on the relationship between a trained
      vine and its supporting structure, for example, do we measure from
      the vines or from the fence on which they are trained, thus M. Kil.
      6:1:

M. Kilayim

6:1   A.   What is an espalier?
       B.   He who plants a row of five vines beside a fence which is ten
             handbreadths high, or beside a ditch which is ten handbreadths
             deep and four wide –
       C.   they allow it its area of tillage of four amot.
       D.   House of Shammai say, "They measure four amot from the base of
             the vines to the field."
       E.   House of Hillel say, "From the fence to the field."
       F.   Said R. Yohanan b. Nuri, "All err who say so.

    G.   "Rather, [the four amot are measured as follows:] If there are four amot from the base of the vines to the fence, they allow it its area of tillage and he sows the rest."

    H.   And how much is the area of tillage of a [single] vine?

    I.   Six handbreadths in all directions.

    J.   R. Aqiba says, "Three [handbreadths]."

At issue is which part of the espalier is considered primary to it, the base of the vines, since they not the fence are primary to the espalier, so the House of Shammai; or the fence, which is primary to the espalier (Mandelbaum, pp. 203-4).

The same consideration – identifying the greater part of a mixture for purposes of classification – is expressed in the following:

M. Kilayim

9:1   D.   Camel's hair and sheep's wool which one hackled [combed] together –

    E.   if the greater part is from the camels, it is permitted.

    F.   But if the greater part is from the sheep, it is prohibited [to mix the fibers with flax].

    G.   [If the quantity of camel's hair and sheep's wool is divided] half and half – it is prohibited [to mix the fibers with flax].

    H.   And so [is the rule for] flax and hemp which one hackled together [if at least half of the hackled fibers are of flax, it is prohibited to mix them with wool].

3.   We determine whether two separate species have combined to form a single entity by examining the flavor of the mixture. If the flavor of the forbidden part pervades the whole, then the whole is forbidden. If both batches are of the same species, of course, it is not possible to determine whether the forbidden part has taken over the mixture overall (Newman, p. 149):

M. Shebiit

7:7   A.   A fresh rose [of the Sabbatical Year] which has been preserved in old oil [of the Sixth Year] –

    B.   one removes the rose [from the oil, and the oil is then exempt from removal].

    C.   But an old [rose, of the Sabbatical Year which has been preserved] in new [oil, of the year following the Sabbatical] –

    D.   [the oil] is subject to removal.

    E.   Fresh carobs [of the Sabbatical Year] which have been preserved in old wine [of the Sixth Year],

    F.   and old [carobs of the Sabbatical Year which have been preserved] in new [wine, of the year following the Sabbatical Year] –

    G.   [in both cases, the wine together with the carobs] are subject to removal.

    H.   This is the general rule:

I.   [In the case of] any [produce which is subject to removal] which imparts its flavor [to produce with which it is mixed] –

J.   one must remove [the resulting mixture, even if it consists of] two separate species [only one of which is subject to removal].

K.   But [if all produce is] of the same species [and only one is subject to removal],

L.   [one must remove the resulting mixture] however [small the amount of produce, i.e., even if it is not enough to impart its flavor to the mixture as a whole].

M.   [Produce of the] Sabbatical Year renders forbidden [subject to the laws of the Sabbatical Year] all other [permitted produce] of the same species [with which it has been mixed].

N.   But [if the two lots of produce are] not of the same species,

O.   [only if the produce of the Sabbatical Year] imparts its flavor [does it render the other produce forbidden].

4.   The problem of mixtures is resolved in a variety of ways but within a few clearly articulated principles. When heave-offering is mixed with unconsecrated produce and constitutes only a minute proportion of the mixture (one percent), it loses its integrity and the mixture is permitted to the nonpriest (Peck, p. 131). The question of differentiation in mixtures is then raised: what traits allow us to know whether mixtures coalesce?

M. Terumot

4:7   A.   R. Eliezer says, "Heave-offering is neutralized [takes on the status of unconsecrated produce] [when one part of heave-offering is mixed] in [a total of] a hundred and one [parts of produce]."

B.   R. Joshua says, "[It is neutralized when there is one part of heave-offering] in a hundred [parts of produce] plus [a bit] more.

C.   "And this more has no [fixed] measure."

D.   R. Yosé b. Meshullam says, "[This more is] an additional qab per hundred seahs,

E.   "[which equals] one-sixth of [the quantity of] heave-offering in the mixture."

4:8   A.   R. Joshua says, "Black figs neutralize white ones, and white ones neutralize black ones.

B.   "[And in the case of] cakes of pressed figs – (1) "large ones neutralize small ones, and small ones neutralize large ones; (2) "round ones neutralize square ones, and square ones neutralize round ones."

C.   R. Eliezer deems [heave-offering mixed with such different types of its same genus of produce to remain] forbidden [for consumption as common produce].

D.   And R. Aqiba says, "When it is known which [type of produce in the status of heave-offering] fell [into the unconsecrated produce, the two different types] do not neutralize one another.

E.   "But when it is not known which [type of produce in the status of heave-offering] fell [into the unconsecrated produce, the two different types of produce] neutralize one another."

5. The prohibited part of a mixture imparts its status to the entire mixture, if it dominates the mixture, for example, by imparting its flavor to the mixture as a whole; then unconsecrated food takes on the status of heave-offering:

M. Terumot

10:1   G.   [An onion in the status of heave-offering] renders forbidden the unconsecrated food with which it is cooked if it imparts its flavor to that food.

      H.   R. Judah permits [for the consumption of a nonpriest] a pickled fish [which was cooked with an onion in the status of heave-offering],

      I.   for the purpose [of the onion] is only to absorb the stench [of the fish, and not to flavor the brine].

6. Where the mixture is made up of things that can be distinguished from one another and do not coalesce with one another, then we do separate the originally mixed items:

M. M.S.

2:6   A.   A sela which is second tithe and an unconsecrated [sela] which were confused [such that the consecrated coin could not be identified] –

      B.   he brings a sela's worth of [copper] coins and says,

      C.   "The sela which is second tithe, wherever it may be, is deconsecrated with these coins."

      D.   And [after consecrating the copper coins] he selects the finer [coin] between [the two selas]

      E.   and deconsecrates [the copper coins] with it.

      F.   For they ruled, "They deconsecrate silver with copper [only] out of necessity. But [if they do deconsecrate silver with copper] it may not remain so, but they must immediately deconsecrate [the copper coins] with silver [coins]."

7. Mixtures present problems for sorting out. First, a requisite volume is liable to the offering, so we have to know how to determine whether such a volume has been reached. The criterion is, perfect and complete fusion, and that takes place only with certain grains, but not others, as in the following:

M. Hallah

4:2   A.   [In considering whether or not batches of dough combine with each other to comprise the minimum volume liable to dough-offering,] what [grains] constitute a single species?

      B.   [Flour made from] wheat combines with nothing but [flour made from] spelt.

      C.   [Flour made from] barley combines with all [types of flour], except for [that made from] wheat.

      D.   R. Yohanan b. Nuri says, "The other species combine with each other."

A-C thus take for granted that complete fusion of dough takes place only with flour made from the specified grains.

8.   The case of mixtures of forbidden with permitted produce has to be worked out.   Where a mixture is not a complete fusion, we take account of the proportions of the forbidden and permitted parts. What happens when a piece of forbidden fruit is used in an item, and that item is mixed with permitted items? The answer is, an item that is separate, distinct, and in no way fused cannot be neutralized in a mixture. But after the fact, we do permit neutralization, C-F.

M. Orlah

1:6   A.   [As for] a sapling [subject to the restriction] of orlah, or [a sapling prohibited under the laws] of diverse kinds in a vineyard, which was mixed together with [permitted] saplings –

      B.   behold, this one may not pick [fruit from any of the trees].

      C.   If he picked,

      D.   [the forbidden produce] is neutralized in [a ratio of] one [part of forbidden fruit] to two hundred parts of permitted fruit].

      E.   And this is so provided that he does not purposely [pick the produce in order to have it neutralized].

      F.   R. Yosé says, "Even [if] he purposely picks [the produce], it is neutralized in two hundred and one."

9.   When dealing with mixtures, in the case of animals that were designated for various offerings, if, in the confusion, are included animals that were left to die even among ten thousand animals that are suitable for an offering, all have to be left to die; in cases in which lesser restrictions pertain, there are solutions that allow for the correct disposition of the value of the beasts. Where we have consecrated beasts but do not know to whom they belong, a stipulation covers all possibilities:

M. Zebahim

8:1   A.   All animal-offerings with which were mixed up (1) sin-offerings that were left to die [M. Tem. 2:2] or (2) an ox to be stoned –

      B.   even one [sin-offering left to die] in ten thousand [suitable animal-offerings] –

      C.   let all of them be left to die.

      D.   [If] they [animal-offerings] were mixed up with (1) an ox upon which a sin was committed, or (2) [an ox] which had been found guilty of killing a man on the evidence of a single witness or on the evidence of the owner,

      E.   (1) with an ox which had sexual relations with a human, or (2) with an ox with which a human had sexual relations, or (3) with an ox which had been set aside [for idolatry (M. Tem. 6:1)], or (4) with an ox which had been worshipped, or (5) with an ox which had served as a harlot's hire, or (6) with an ox which had served as the price of a dog, or (7) with an ox which was crossbred, or (8) with an ox which was terefah, or (9) with an ox born from the side –

F.   let them [all] pasture until they suffer a blemish [since one of them is a valid consecrated beast], and [then] be sold, and let [the owner] bring [another sacrifice, purchased] with the proceeds of the best of them of that kind [that had been mixed up with the invalid beasts].

G.   [If] they were mixed up with unblemished unconsecrated beasts, the unconsecrated beasts are to be sold to those who require that particular kind [of sacrifice].

8:2   A.   Consecrated beasts [belonging to several owners, which were mixed up] with [other] consecrated beasts of the same kind [of offering, so we do not know to whom the several beasts belong] – this one is offered for the sake of one [among the owners] and that one is offered for the sake of one [among the owners].

B.   Consecrated beasts [which were mixed up] with other consecrated beasts [for example, burnt-offerings and peace-offerings], not of the same kind [of offerings] [and which therefore are offered with different rites, for example, different numbers of acts of sprinkling blood, rules of consuming the flesh, and the like] –

C.   let them pasture until they suffer a blemish, and [then] be sold [separately], and let [the owner] bring with the proceeds of the best of them [a sacrifice] [for example , peace-offerings] of that kind, and let him lose [make up] the [added] difference from his own property.

D.   [If] they were mixed up with a firstling or with tithe [of cattle] –

E.   let them pasture until they suffer a blemish, and be eaten as a firstling [by priests] and as tithe [by ordinary folk] [but not slaughtered in the public market or sold by weight].

F.   All can be mixed up [without the possibility of discerning an animal for one sacrifice from that for another], except a sin-offering, [which is female or which is a male goat], with a guilt-offering, [which is a male sheep or ram].

10. In the case of the mixture of fluids, the fluid that imparts its character to the whole is deemed dominant and becomes the definitive indicator:

8:6   A.   Blood which was mixed with water,
      B.   if it [the mixture] has the appearance of blood, is valid.
      C.   [If] it was mixed in wine,
      D.   they regard it as if it were water [and if the mixture is blood color, it is valid].

11. If there is a mixture of liquids, the liquid that imparts its traits to the whole defines the character of the whole:

M. Hullin

6:5   A.   Blood which was mixed with water,
      B.   if it has the appearance of blood,
      C.   one is liable to cover it up.
      D.   [If] it was mixed with wine, they regard it as if it were water.

E. [If] it was mixed up with blood of a [domesticated] beast or with blood of a wild beast, they regard it as if it were water.

F. R. Judah says, "Blood does not annul blood."

In the case of solids, if the forbidden component of the mixture imparts its flavor to the whole brew, the whole is forbidden. If one can identify the forbidden component, one removes it; if not, the entire brew is prohibited:

M. Hullin

7:4   A.   A thigh with which the sinew of the hip [which was not removed] was cooked, if it [the sinew] is sufficient to impart a flavor [to the thigh], lo, this is prohibited.

      B.   How do they estimate the matter?

      C.   Like meat [cooked] with turnips.

7:5   A.   The sinew of the hip which was cooked with [other] sinews, and one recognizes it – [it must be removed, and the remainder is prohibited if there is enough] to impart a flavor.

      B.   And if [one does] not [recognize the presence of the sinew of the hip], all of them are prohibited [for any one might be the sciatic nerve].

      C.   As to the broth, it is prohibited if it imparts a flavor.

      D.   And so with a piece of carrion, and so with a piece of unclean fish which were cooked with [other] pieces:

      E.   When one recognizes their [presence], [they must be removed and the rest are forbidden if there is enough] to impart flavor.

      F.   And if [one does] not [recognize their presence] they are all forbidden.

      G.   As to the broth, [it is forbidden only if the carrion or unclean fish] imparts a flavor.

11. Where there is a mixture containing something that cannot be absorbed into the whole, being a solid, and that also cannot serve for a given purpose, then none of the things in the mixture can serve for that purpose:

M. Temurah

6:1   A.   All [animals] which are prohibited for the altar prohibit in any number at all [animals among which they are confused]: (1) the one which has sexual relations with a human being; (2) and the one with whom a human being has sexual relations; (3) and the one which is set aside [for idolatrous worship]; (4) and the one which is actually worshiped; (5) and the [harlot's] hire; (6) and the price of a dog [one given in payment for a dog]; (7) and the hybrid; (8) and the terefah; (9) and the one which is born from the side.

12. When there is a mixture of unclean and clean matter of the same species, then the classification of the greater part of the mixture dictates the status of the entire mixture:

M. Kelim

11:4 A. [As to] unclean iron which one smelted with clean iron –
 B. if the greater part [was] from the unclean [iron], it is unclean.
 C. And if the greater part [was] from the clean, it is clean.
 D. Half and half – it is unclean.
 E. And so [a utensil made] from cement and from cattle dung.

13. The dominant material in a mixture defines the classification of the mixture as to the rules of uncleanness:

M. Kelim

13:6 A. Wood that serves [as subsidiary to] the metal is unclean. And the metal which serves the wood is clean.
 B. How so?
 C. A lock [which is] of wood and its clutch of metal, even one [clutch], is unclean.
 D. A ring which is of metal and its seal of coral is unclean. A ring which is of coral and its seal of metal is clean.
 E. The tooth in the plate of the lock or in the key is unclean by itself.

Along these same lines, when there is a mixture of two distinct substances, the classification of the greater part defines that of the whole:

M. Negaim

11:2 A. Camel's hair and sheep's wool which one hackled together –
 B. if the larger part is from the camels, they are not susceptible to uncleanness through plagues.
 C. If the larger part is from the sheep, they are susceptible to uncleanness through plagues.
 D. Half and half – they are susceptible to uncleanness through plagues.
 E. And so the flax and the hemp which one hackled together.

14. A mixture of liquids is complete even though only a small portion of one body of liquid is joined to a small portion of the other:

M. Parah

6:3 A. He who mixes in the trough, and the flask is in it –
 B. even though its mouth is ever so narrow [in any amount at all]
 C. the water which is in it is mixed.

Along these same lines, the water must be drawn by the person's own power, not simply supplied by an action that fulfills his intention:

M. Parah

6:5 A. He who diverts the spring into the wine vat or into the cistern – it [the water] is unfit for Zabs [Lev, 15:13] and for lepers [Lev. 14:5] and to mix therein purification water,
 B. because they have not been filled up by means of a utensil.

15. Where there is a mixture of solid foods that are made unclean at diverse removes of uncleanness or by sources of uncleanness of diverse virulence, the two are deemed to join together to make up the prescribed volume, but convey the lesser remove of uncleanness of the two degrees that have been joined together:

M. Tohorot

1:5   A.   The food which is made unclean by a Father of Uncleanness and that which is made unclean by an Offspring of Uncleanness join together with one another to convey the lighter remove of uncleanness of the two. How so?

     B.   A half-egg's bulk of food which is unclean in the first remove and a half-egg's bulk of food which is unclean in the second remove which one mixed with one another – [the consequent mixture is unclean in the] second [remove of uncleanness].

     C.   A half-egg's bulk of food unclean in the second remove of uncleanness and a half-egg's bulk of food unclean in the third remove of uncleanness which one mixed together with one another – [it is unclean in the] first [remove of uncleanness].

16. What is connected at the point of contamination shares in the contamination of the whole; what is added thereafter to the mixture shares in the contamination of the whole thing so long as it is part of the whole, but, when separated, remains unclean only by virtue of its former condition:

M. Tohorot

1:7   A.   Pieces of dough stuck together,

     B.   and loaves stuck together –

     C.   [if] one of them is made unclean by a dead creeping thing,

     D.   they are all unclean in the first remove.

     E.   [If] they were separated, they are all unclean in the first remove.

     F.   [If they were made unclean by] liquid, they all are unclean in the second remove.

     G.   [If] they separated, they all are unclean in the second remove.

     H.   [If they were made unclean by] hands, they all are unclean in the third remove.

     I.   [If] they separated, they all are unclean in the third remove.

1:8   A.   A piece of dough, which was unclean in the first remove, and one stuck others to it, they all are unclean in the first remove.

     B.   [If] they separated, it is unclean in the first remove, but all [the rest] are unclean in the second remove.

     C.   [If] it was unclean in the second remove and one stuck others to it, they all are unclean in the second remove.

     D.   [If] they separated, it is unclean in the second remove, but all [the rest] are unclean in the third remove.

     E.   [If] it was unclean in the third remove, and one stuck others to it, it is unclean in the third remove, but all [the rest] are clean, whether they separated or whether they did not separate.

D. The Effect of Human Attitude and Action on the Making of Divisions and Distinctions

This category differs only in nuance from rubric B. Its basic propositions are complementary to those in the earlier set.

1. Divisions or boundaries in the natural world are established by the pattern of human action, for example, uninterrupted or interrupted. These same divisions or boundaries also are established by natural barriers, rivers or hills. Where a vast area of land obliterates physical features, natural landmarks will not do; a fence then has to establish a natural boundaries (Brooks, p. 53). A contrary view is that physical barriers, natural or man-made, are ignored; boundaries are established by the character of a species. A single species forms a single unit, without regard to landmarks or fences (Brooks, p. 53). But time and circumstance in either case are ignored; these are null when it comes to delineating the divisions of an area. Thus:

M. Peah

2:1   A.   And these [landmarks] establish [the boundaries of a field] for [purposes of designating] peah:

        B.   (1) a river, (2) pond, (3) private road, (4) public road, (5) public path, (6) private path that is in use in the hot season and in the rainy season, (7) uncultivated land, (8) newly broken land, (9) and [an area sown with] a different [type of] seed.

2. Is there an objective standard for classification, or do circumstantial and relative criteria pertain? If a whole field is made up of defective clusters, then do the poor have a claim on that crop? If they do, then the definition is objective, formal, and not relative and circumstantial, as in the following:

     A.   [As regards] a vineyard [the produce of which] is entirely defective clusters –

     B.   R. Eliezer says "[The produce] belongs to the householder."

     C.   R. Aqiba says, "[It] belongs to the poor."

     D.   Said R. Eliezer, "[Scripture states], 'When you harvest the grapes of your vineyard, you shall not strip it bare of defective clusters afterward' (Deut. 24:21).

     E.   "If there is no harvest [because the entire yield is defective clusters], how can there be defective clusters [left after the harvest]?"

     F.   Said to him R. Aqiba, "[Scripture states], 'And you shall not strip your vineyard bare of defective clusters' (Lev. 19:10).

     G.   "[This verse applies] even if [the produce of the vineyard is] entirely defective clusters, [such that there will be no harvest]."

     H.   [In Aqiba's view, then,] why does [Scripture] state, "When you gather the grapes of your vineyard, you shall not glean it of defective clusters afterward" (Deut. 24:21)?

I.   [This verse teaches that] the poor may not [claim] the defective clusters before the harvest.

E. The Resolution of Doubt

The matter of doubt concerns classification; most cases in the Mishnah that concern the resolution of doubt pertain to the classification of persons, places, or things. Here, too, therefore we deal with a subset of the matter of classification.

1.   Doubts are resolved in a simple way. What is subject to ambiguity is assigned its presumptive status, what is unambiguous in its status then goes to the poor (in this context); or we assign what is ambiguous to the poor. At stake is whether the farmer will take what God has assigned to the poor (M. Peah. 4:10-11).

M. Peah

4:11   A.   [As regards] anthills in the midst of a standing [crop] –
       B.   lo, [grain which falls into them] belongs to the householder, [for produce does not become subject to the law of gleanings until after the harvest] –
       C.   After the harvesters [have gone through the field],
       D.   the [grain at the] tops [of the anthills, which fell after the harvest, belongs] to the poor, while the [grain at the] bottoms [of the anthills, which probably fell before the harvest,] belongs to the householder.
       E.   R. Meir says, "All [grain which falls into anthills after the harvesters have gone through the field belongs] to the poor,
       F.   for produce which might be [subject to the law of] gleanings [produce which might have fallen after the harvest] is [deemed in fact to be subject to the law of] gleanings."

2.   In resolving a problem of doubt, we have to decide upon the governing metaphor, and the rule that pertains is that of the metaphor. To take the concrete case at hand, M. Peah 5:1-2, in the case of mixtures of food in the status of gleanings and ordinary produce, we assign the poor all produce in a doubtful status, which makes certain the householder does not take what does not belong to him; gleanings are like Holy Things. Or the poor have no claim on those particular stalks of grain that fall to the ground as gleanings; the farmer may give them food of equal value; gleanings are in the status of second tithe (Brooks, p. 87).

3.   As a rule of thumb, if someone is assumed to have an interest in a matter, he is not believed when subject to doubt; but when he has no reason to lie, he is believed:

M. Demai

4:6   A.   He who enters a city, and does not know anyone there,

- B. [and] he said, "Who here is trustworthy? Who here separates tithes?"
- C. [and] one said to him, "I do,"
- D. he is not believed.
- E. [If] he said, "So-and-so is trustworthy,"
- F. behold, this one is believed.
- G. [If] he went to purchase from him, and said to him, "Who here sells old [produce, viz., from the previous year, which may be eaten before the offering of the sheaf from the new year's crop; cf. Lev. 23:14 and M. Men. 10:5]?"
- H. [and] he [the one announced to be trustworthy] said to him, "The one who sent you to me,"
- I. even though they are like those who render service to each other [by mutual recommendations],
- J. behold, they are believed.

4. Where we face doubt, we resolve matters in favor of the status quo. If we assume leaven will not be present, we do not undertake a search for leaven that may or may not be present, as at M. Pesahim 1:1B: "Any location into which people do not ordinarily bring leaven does not require examination for leaven."

1:2
- A. They do not scruple that a weasel might have dragged [leaven] from house to house and place to place.
- B. For if so, [they will have to scruple that the weasel has dragged leaven] from courtyard to courtyard and from town to town,
- C. [so] there is no end to the matter.

The same conception – we follow the prevailing assumption or the established facts – animates the following as well:

3:2
- H. Dough which is "dumb" –
- I. if an equivalent amount has already fermented,
- J. lo, this is prohibited.

5. Another way of resolving a situation of doubt is to cover all possible exigencies, for example, through a statement bearing an intentionality that covers every conceivable situation as in the following:

9:10
- A. Two associations, the Passover-offerings of which were confused –
- B. these take [draw] possession of one of them for themselves, and those take possession of one of them for themselves.
- C. One [member] of these goes to the others, and one [member] of the others comes to these.
- D. And thus do they say, "If this Passover-offering is ours, withdraw from yours and register with ours. And if this Passover-offering is yours, we withdraw from ours and register with yours."

E.   And so, too, five associations, each with five or ten members – each one of the associations takes possession of [one of the confused Passover-offerings] and so do they declare.

9:11   A.   Two people whose Passover-offerings were confused –

B.   this one takes possession of one of the animals, and that one takes possession of one of the animals.

C.   This one registers with himself a third party, and that one registers with himself a third party.

D.   This one approaches that, and that one approaches this, and thus do they declare:

E.   "If this Passover-offering is mine, then you withdraw from yours and register with mine. And if this Passover-offering is yours, then I withdraw from mine and register with yours."

In the first case, the statement at E-F makes each association consist of four new members and one original member; in the second, 9:11C assures that there will be two registered parties on each animal, so neither is left ownerless.

6.   Where we have a case of doubt, we resolve it in favor of the more likely of two possibilities:

M. Sheqalim

7:1   A.   Money which is found between the chest for sheqels and that for freewill-offerings –

B.   [if it is] nearer to the chest for sheqels, it falls to that for sheqels.

C.   [If it is] nearer to that for freewill-offerings, it falls to that for freewill-offerings.

D.   [If it is] halfway in between, it falls to that for freewill-offerings.

E.   [If it is found] between the chest for wood and the chest for frankincense, [if it is] nearer to the chest for wood, it goes to the chest for wood.

F.   [If it is] nearer the chest for frankincense, it goes for the chest for frankincense.

G.   [If it is] halfway in between, it goes to the chest for frankincense.

H.   [If it is found] between the chest for bird-offerings and the chest for young birds for whole-offerings,

I.   [if it is] nearer the chest for bird-offerings, it goes to the chest for bird-offerings.

J.   [If it is] nearer the chest for young birds for whole-offerings, it goes to the chest for young birds for whole-offerings.

K.   [If it is] halfway in between, it goes to the chest for young birds.

L.   [If it is found] between unconsecrated coins and coins in the status of second tithe,

M.   [if it is] nearer the unconsecrated coins, it goes to the purposes of unconsecrated coins.

N.   [If it is] nearer to the coins in the status of second tithe, it falls for the purposes of money in the status of second tithe.

O.   [If it is] halfway in between, it goes to the purposes of money in the status of second tithe.

P. This is the governing principle: They follow the status of that which is nearer, [even if this produces] a lenient ruling.

Q. But if the money is found exactly halfway in between, they impose the more stringent ruling.

7. In a case of doubt, we make provision for all possible outcomes; in the following, we do not know whether or not the rite is required, so we do require its performance:

Mishnah-tractate Yebamot

7:4 A. The foetus, the levir, betrothal, a deaf-mute, a boy nine years and one day old

B. invalidate [a woman from eating heave-offering] but do not validate [her to do so].

C. [If] it is a matter of doubt whether or not the boy is nine years and one day old,

D. [or if] it is a matter of doubt whether or not he has produced two pubic hairs,

E. [If] a house collapsed on him and on the daughter of his brother [his wife] and it is not known which of them died first, her co-wife performs halisah and does not enter into levirate marriage.

In the following case, we do not know which mother has produced which son, each mother having one other son whose identity is known. When the five brothers in doubt on their mothers' identity die, the five whose identities are known treat all widows as if they are the widow of a brother, and that takes account of the various possibilities; so, too, in the second case, in a different way:

Mishnah-tractate Yebamot

11:3 A. Five women [each of whom already has a son and then produced another], whose [other] offspring became confused with one another –

B. they grew up in this state of confusion –

C. and married wives and died –

D. four [of the surviving brothers, whose mothers are known] perform the rite of halisah with one widow, and one of them [the fifth] enters levirate marriage with her.

E. He and three [of the brothers] enter into the rite of halisah with another, and one [other] enters into levirate marriage with her [and so on]. It turns out that there are four rites of halisah and one levirate marriage for each of the surviving widows.

8. When someone is subject to doubt as to what he has done, if he has the power to do such a deed, we take account of the possibility that he has done it; but if he does not have that power, we ignore the possibility altogether:

M. Qiddushin

3:8   J.   He who betroths his daughter without specification – the one past girlhood is not taken into account.

3:9   A.   He who has two groups of daughters by two wives [in succession], and who said,

           B.   "I have betrothed my oldest daughter, but I do not know whether it is the oldest of the older group or the oldest of the younger group, or the youngest of the older group, who is also older than the oldest of the younger group" –

           C.   "all of them are prohibited [to marry without a writ of divorce], except for the youngest of the younger group," the words of R. Meir.

           D.   R. Yosé says, "They are all permitted, except for the oldest of the older group."

           E.   "I betrothed my youngest daughter, but I do not know whether it was the youngest of the younger group, or the youngest of the older group, or the oldest of the younger group, who is younger than the youngest of the older group" –

           F.   "all of them are prohibited except for the oldest of the older group," the words of R. Meir.

           G.   R. Yosé says, "All of them are permitted, except for the youngest of the younger group."

9.   If we do not know for certain what circumstances prevailed at the time of damages, we split the difference, exacting half of the compensation that would otherwise have been required:

M. B.Q.

5:1   A.   An ox [deemed harmless] which gored a cow [which died] and her newly born calf was found [dead] beside her –

           B.   and it is not known whether, before it gored her, she gave birth, or after it gored her, she gave birth –

           C.   [the owner of the ox] pays half-damages for the cow, and quarter-damages for the offspring.

           D.   And so too, a cow [deemed harmless] which gored an ox, and her newly born young was found beside her,

           E.   and it is not known whether before she gored, she gave birth, or after she gored, she gave birth –

           F.   [the owner of the cow] pays half-damages from the corpus of the cow, and a quarter-damages from the corpus of the offspring.

10.   In a case of doubt, we resolve the doubt in a lenient manner if we can think of any extenuating circumstance that permits doing so:

M. Kelim

9:3   A.   [As to the case of] the insect which is found below the ground of the oven,

           B.   [the oven is] clean.

           C.   For I say, "It fell while alive and now has died."

           D.   A needle or ring which were found below the ground of the oven –

E. [the oven is] clean.
F. For I say, "They were there before the oven came."
G. [If] they [the ring or needle] were found in the wood ashes,
H. [the oven is] unclean.
I. For it has nothing on which to blame it.

11. When it comes to declaring something unclean, matters of doubt are resolved as clean wherever this is feasible; once a decision is reached, however, where there is a doubt, it is resolved as unclean:

M. Negaim

5:1
A. Every doubt [concerning] plagues is [regarded as] clean,
B. except for this one, and one other. And what is this?
C. He on whom was a bright spot the size of a split bean, and one shut it up –
D. at the end of one week –
E. and behold, it is about the size of a sela –
F. it is a doubt that this is it –
G. it is a doubt that another has come in its place –
H. he is unclean.

5:4
A. Every doubt concerning plagues in the first instance is clean
B. before it has been subjected to uncleanness.
C. Once it has been subjected to uncleanness, its [condition of] doubt is unclean.

5:5
A. Once it has been subjected to uncleanness, its [condition of] doubt is unclean.

12. A principle of the resolution of doubt is that where the doubt occurs is taken into account. If it is in private domain, it is resolved as unclean; in public, clean. If there is the possibility of interrogation as to the facts, matters of doubt are resolved in favor of cleanness. If a person of sound senses, who can be consulted, is in doubt as to whether he has touched uncleanness, and the doubt concerns private property, the resolution is in favor of uncleanness:

M. Tohorot

3:6
A. A deaf-mute, an imbecile, and a minor who are found in an alley in which is uncleanness, lo, these are assumed to be clean.
B. But any person of sound sense is assumed to be unclean.
C. And whoever lacks understanding to be interrogated –
D. a matter of doubt concerning him is resolved in favor of cleanness.

6:4
A. As much as you can multiply doubts and doubts about doubts –
B. in connection with private domain, it is unclean;
C. In connection with public domain, it is clean.
D. How so?
E. One entered an alley, and (1) the uncleanness is in the courtyard –
F. it is a matter of doubt whether he entered [the courtyard] or whether he did not enter –
G. (2) uncleanness is in the house –

H.   it is a matter of doubt whether he entered or whether he did not enter –
I.   (3) and even if he did enter –
J.   it is a matter of doubt whether it was there or whether it was not there –
K.   (4) and even if it was there –
L.   it is a matter of doubt whether it contains sufficient bulk or whether it does not contain sufficient bulk –
M.   (5) and even if it does contain a sufficient bulk to convey uncleanness –
N.   it is a matter of doubt whether it is uncleanness or whether it is cleanness –
O.   (6) and even if it is uncleanness –
P.   it is a matter of doubt whether he touched it or whether he did not touch –
Q.   his matter of doubt is deemed unclean.
R.   R. Eleazar says, "A matter of doubt concerning entry is deemed clean.
S.   "A matter of doubt concerning contact with that which is unclean is deemed unclean."

13. We assess the case involving doubt in terms of the facts that prevail at the moment of discovery:

M. Tohorot

3:5   A.   All unclean things [are adjudged] in accord with [their condition] at the moment that they are found.
B.   (1) If they are unclean, they are unclean; and (2) if they are clean, they are clean; (3) if they are covered up, they are covered up; and (4) if they are uncovered, they are uncovered.
C.   A needle which is found full of rust or broken is clean.
D.   For all unclean things [are adjudged] in accord with [their condition] at the moment that they are found.

If things are in motion, we resolve doubt in favor of cleanness:

M. Tohorot

4:1   A.   He who threw something unclean from place to place –
B.   a [clean] loaf of bread among [unclean] keys –
C.   an [unclean] key among the [clean] loaves of bread –
D.   it is clean.
6:1   A.   A place which was private domain and became public domain and once again was made private domain –
B.   when it is private domain, a matter of doubt concerning it is deemed unclean.
C.   When it is public domain, a matter of doubt concerning it is clean.
D.   He who was on the point of death in private domain and they brought him out to the public domain, and brought him back to private domain –
E.   when he is in the private domain, a matter of doubt concerning him is deemed unclean.

    F.   When he is in the public domain, a matter of doubt concerning him is clean.

    G.   R. Simeon says, "The public domain intervenes."

16. Where we have a compounding of matters of doubt, we resolve matters in favor of cleanness:

M. Tohorot

4:7   A.   These are [conditions of] doubt which sages have declared clean:

    B.   (1) A doubt concerning drawn water [that falls into] the immersion pool.

    C.   (2) A doubt concerning uncleanness floating on the surface of the water.

    D.   (3) A doubt concerning liquids, in respect to contracting uncleanness – it is unclean.

    E.   [A doubt concerning liquids, in respect to] conveying uncleanness – it is unclean.

    F.   (4) A doubt concerning hands,

    G.   either in respect to contracting uncleanness,

    H.   or in respect to conveying uncleanness,

    I.   or in respect to being made clean –

    J.   it is clean.

    K.   (5) A doubt concerning public domain.

    L.   (6) A doubt concerning rulings of the scribes.

    M.   (7) A doubt concerning the unconsecrated food.

    N.   (8) A doubt concerning creeping things.

    O.   (9) A doubt concerning plagues.

    P.   (10) A doubt concerning Naziriteship.

    Q.   (11) A doubt concerning firstlings.

    R.   (12) A doubt concerning sacrifices.

But if we know with certainty that uncleanness is present, matters of doubt are resolved as unclean:

M. Tohorot

5:8   A.   [If there is] one [female] idiot in the village –

    B.   or [one] gentile woman –

    C.   or one Samaritan woman –

    D.   all drops of spit which are in the village are unclean.

    E.   He on whose garments a woman has stepped,

    F.   or next to whom a woman sat down on a ship –

    G.   if she knows him, that he eats heave-offering –

    H.   his utensils are clean.

    I.   And if not, he will interrogate her.

17. Matters of doubt involving the policy toward uncleanness of those who do not observe themselves the laws of uncleanness are resolved in favor of cleanness. We assume that the unobservant person knows full well the affects of his touch and takes into consideration the situation of the one who observes the cleanness laws:

M. Tohorot

7:1   A.   The potter who left his pots and went down to drink –
      B.   the innermost ones are clean.
      C.   And the outermost ones are unclean.
      D.   Said R. Yosé, "Under what circumstances? When they are untied. But when they are tied up, the whole is clean."
      E.   He who gives over his key to an am haares – the house is clean,
      F.   for he gave him only [the charge of] guarding the key.
7:6   A.   The tax collectors who entered the house
      B.   the house is unclean.
      C.   If there is a gentile with them,
      D.   they are believed to state, "We did not enter."
      E.   But they are not believed to state, "We entered, but we did not touch [anything]."
      F.   The thieves who entered the house –
      G.   unclean is only the place [trodden by] the feet of the thieves.
      H.   And what do they render unclean?
      I.   The foods, and the liquids, and clay utensils which are open.
      J.   But the couches and the seats and clay utensils which are sealed with a tight seal are clean.
      K.   If there is a gentile with them, or a woman,
      L.   everything is unclean.

18. When we have a matter of certainty and one of doubt, we confirm what is certain. In this case we know the man is unclean, but do not know whether he has immersed properly. We resolve the doubt in favor of uncleanness:

M. Miqvaot

2:1   A.   The unclean person who went down to immerse –
      B.   it is a doubt whether he immersed or whether he did not immerse –
      C.   [and] even if he did immerse –
      D.   it is a doubt whether there are forty seahs in it, or whether there are not –
      E.   two immersion pools, in one of which there are forty seahs, and in one of which there are not forty seahs –
      F.   he immersed in one of them and does not know in which one of them he immersed –
      G.   his matter of doubt is deemed unclean.

But if the pool is assumed valid, we confirm the supposition that it is so:

M. Miqvaot

2:3   A.   A doubt about drawn waters which sages have declared clean –
      B.   it is a matter of doubt whether they [three logs of drawn water] fell or did not fall.
      C.   [And] even if they did fall, it is a matter of doubt whether there are forty seahs in it or whether there are not –
      D.   two immersion pools, in one of which there are forty seahs and in one of which there are not –

E. it fell into one of them, and one does not know into which one of them it fell –

F. its [the pool's] matter of doubt is deemed clean,

G. because it has something upon which to depend.

H. [If] both of them were less than forty seahs, and if [drawn water] fell into one of them and one does not know into which of them it fell –

I. its matter of doubt is deemed unclean,

J. for it has nothing upon which to depend.

F. Primary and Secondary Effects

The premise that we make such a distinction of course forms a subset of the basic exercise of natural history, since the purpose of the distinction at hand always is taxonomic.

1. We take account of the secondary effects of an action, for example, if an action's primary purpose is legitimate but it has a secondary effect that is not, the action may be prohibited. In this case, even though storing dung is permitted, storing it in the field may fertilize the crop of the Seventh Year:

M. Shebiit

3:1 A. From what time [during the Sabbatical Year] may they bring manure [out into the field to pile it up] in dung heaps [for use during the following year]?

B. "From the time [during other years of the Sabbatical cycle] when workers 'transgressors [of the laws of the Sabbatical Year]' cease [spreading manure in the fields]," the words of R. Meir.

C. R. Judah says, "From the time when the [ground] moisture [lit.: sweetness] dries up."

D. R. Yosé says, "From the time when [the ground hardens] forming clumps."

2. We recognize the difference between direct and indirect causation, for example, of heat. Because of the prohibition against cooking, one may not directly add heat to what is warm; but one may keep food warm if he does not add to the warmth present as of twilight at the advent of the Sabbath. If what one does directly causes heat to be added, that is forbidden; if what one does indirectly adds heat, not through direct action, that is permitted:

Mishnah-tractate Shabbat

3:1 A. A double stove which [people] have heated with stubble or straw –

B. they put cooked food on it.

C. [But if they heated it] with peat or with wood, one may not put [anything] on it until he has swept it out,

D. or until he has covered it with ashes.

Indirect consequences of an action are distinguished from direct, and not taken into account, in the following as well:

Mishnah-tractate Shabbat

16:3   A.   They save a basket full of loaves of bread,

         B.   even if it contains enough food for a hundred meals,

         C.   a wheel of pressed figs, and a jug of wine.

         D.   And one says to others, "Come and save [what you can] for yourselves [as well]."

         E.   Now if they were intelligent, they come to an agreement with him after the Sabbath.

16:4   B.   And he puts on all the clothing which he can put on, and he cloaks himself in all the cloaks he can put on.

         C.   R. Yosé says, "Eighteen items of clothing."

         D.   And he goes back, puts on clothing, and takes it out,

One may not carry the clothing, but it is permitted to wear it, and, wearing it, one saves it from a fire on the Sabbath. An Israelite may derive benefit from an action that he could not have carried out but which someone else has carried out, as in the following:

Mishnah-tractate Shabbat

16:8   A.   A gentile who lit a candle –

         B.   an Israelite may make use of its light.

         C.   But [if he did so] for an Israelite, it is prohibited [to do so on the Sabbath].

         D.   [If a gentile] drew water to give water to his beast, an Israelite gives water to his beast after him.

         E.   But [if he did so] for an Israelite, it is prohibited [to use it on the Sabbath].

         F.   [If] a gentile made a gangway by which to come down from a ship, an Israelite goes down after him.

         G.   But [if he did so] for an Israelite, it is prohibited [to use it on the Sabbath].

         H.   M^cSH B: Rabban Gamaliel and elders were traveling by boat, and a gentile made a gangway by which to come down off the ship, and Rabban Gamaliel and sages went down by it.

3.   We take account of causation of an action, for which a person may be culpable, only if one and the same person carried out a single coherent and complete action. Then the person will be liable. But if one parts starts a deed and another finishes it, then neither is fully responsible for the prohibited deed, neither one bearing full responsibility for causing it:

Mishnah-tractate Shabbat

13:6   A.   A deer which entered a house, and someone locked it in –

         B.   he [who locked it in] is liable.

         C.   [If] two people locked it in, they are exempt.

	D	[If] one person could not lock the door, and two people did so, they are liable.
	E.	And R. Simeon declares them exempt [M. 10:5].
13:7	A.	[If] one of them sat down at the doorway and did not completely fill it [so that the deer could yet escape], but a second person sat down and finished filling it,
	B.	the second person is liable.
	C.	[If] the first person sat down at the doorway and filled it up, and a second one came along and sat down at his side,
	D.	even though the first one got up and went along, the first remains liable, and the second exempt.
	E.	Lo, to what is this equivalent? To one who locks his house to shut it up [and protect it], and a deer turns out to be shut up [and trapped] inside.

4. We distinguish between direct and indirect causation. One covered by a vow not to derive benefit from another may not receive direct benefit from him, but he may receive indirect benefit from him:

Mishnah-tractate Nedarim

4:2	A.	He who is prohibited by vow from deriving benefit from his friend –
	B.	he [the friend] nonetheless (1) pays out his sheqel [half-sheqel tax to the Temple],
	C.	(2) pays back his debt,
	D.	and (3) returns to him something which he [the one who took the vow] has lost.
	E.	But in a place in which for this action a reward is paid out, the benefit [of the reward] should fall to the sanctuary.
4:3	A.	(1) And he takes up his heave-offering or his tithes with his permission.
	B.	(2) And he offers in his behalf bird-offerings for (1) Zab men or (2) Zab women, (3) bird-offerings for women who have just given birth, (4) sin-offerings, and (5) guilt-offerings.
	C.	(3) And he teaches him midrash, laws, and stories.
	D.	But he does not teach him Scripture.
	E.	But he teaches his sons and daughters Scripture.
	F.	(4) And he takes care of his wife and children, even though he [who vowed] is liable for their care.
	G.	(5) But he should not take care of his domesticated animal, whether unclean or clean.
	H.	R. Eliezer says, "He takes care of the unclean one, and he does not take care of the clean one."
	I.	They said to him, "What is the difference between the unclean one and the clean one?"
	J.	He said to them, "As to the clean one: Its soul belongs to Heaven, and its body belongs to him. But as to the unclean one, its soul and its body belong to Heaven [it is prohibited to him]."
	K.	They said to him, "Also the unclean one: Its soul belongs to Heaven, but its body belongs to him.
	L.	"For if he wants, lo, he can sell it to gentiles or feed it to dogs."

5. We distinguish between primary and secondary effects of an action, thus, direct and indirect causation:

Mishnah-tractate Makkot

2:1   M.   [If] the iron flew from the heft and killed someone,
      N.   Rabbi says, "He does not go into exile."
      O.   And sages say, "He goes into exile."
      P.   [If] it flew from the wood which is being split,
      Q.   Rabbi says, "He goes into exile."
      R.   And sages say, "He does not go into exile."

6. We distinguish what is primary to an action from what is incidental to it, and if what is primary is licit, then what is incidental does not affect our judgment of the action; if what is primary is illicit, then what is legitimate but incidental is null:

Mishnah-tractate Abodah Zarah

5:1   A.   [A gentile] who hires an [Israelite] worker to work with him in the preparation of libation wine –
      B.   [the Israelite's] salary is forbidden.
      C.   [If] he hired him to do some other kind of work,
      D.   even though he said to him, "Move a jar of libation wine from one place to another,"
      E.   his salary is permitted.
      F.   He who hires an ass to bring libation wine on it –
      G.   its fee is forbidden.
      H.   [If he hired it to ride on it, even though the gentile [also] put a flagon [of libation wine] on it, its fee is permitted.

This is a variation on the distinction between the genus and the species, or the principal and the subordinate.

7. We differentiate direct from indirect action. What must be done by direct action may not be validly accomplished by indirect or secondary action:

M. Parah

6:1   A.   He who mixes [ash and water in a trough],
      B.   and the ash fell on his hand,
      C.   or on the side [of the trough],
      D.   and afterward it fell on the trough,
      E.   it [the act of mixing] is unfit.

II. The Tosefta, Tractate Abot, and the Earlier Midrash Compilations: Sifra, Sifré to Numbers, and Sifré to Deuteronomy

A. The Method of Hierarchical Classification

1. The status of an object is determined by the character of its functionally effective component(s):

Tosefta Kelim Baba Mesia

1:3   E.   A spade which one made from the unclean [utensil], [with] [and] its adze [made] from the clean [utensil], is clean. [If] he made it from clean [material] and its adze from unclean, it is unclean.

     F.   Everything follows after [the status of the part of the object which actually] does the work.

     G.   [If] one made it from clean [material], even though it is covered [with metal] from the unclean, it is clean.

Tosefta Kelim Baba Mesia

1:13   A.   All ornaments of a beast, such as the chains and the nose-rings and the hooklets and the rings, are clean. Unclean is only the clapper which makes a sound for the man to hear.

     B.   One who makes bells for the mortar and for a cradle and for mantels for scrolls or for children's mantels – [lo,] they are clean. [If] one made for them a clapper, they are unclean. [If] their clapper is removed, they are clean.

     C.   The bell of the door is clean, and of the beast is unclean.

     D.   The bell or a door which one made for a beast is unclean, and of a beast which one made for a door, even if one affixed it to the ground and even if one nailed it with a nail, is unclean.

2. Taxonomic differences yield that similar categories do not follow the same rule, so if the same rule is to pertain to both classes, it must be made explicit by Scripture:

Sifra to Emor CCXI

I.10   A.   Why does Scripture refer to "his son" and why does Scripture refer to "his daughter"?

     B.   The reason is that there are indicative traits pertaining to the son and not the daughter, and there are indicative traits pertaining to the daughter and not the son.

     C.   As to the son, the father bears responsibility in his regard for various religious duties, to circumcise him, to redeem him if he is kidnapped, to teach him Torah, to teach him a trade, to marry him off, which is not the case in regard to the daughter.

     D.   As to the daughter, the father enjoys the right to keep things that she may find and the work of her hands, as well as to annul her vows, none of which rights he possesses in the case of the son.

     E.   Accordingly, [these taxonomic differences made it] necessary to refer explicitly both to the son and to the daughter.

B. The Message of the Taxonomic Power of Human Intentionality

I find nothing both relevant and new.

C. The Nature of Mixtures

I find nothing both relevant and new.

D. The Effect of Human Attitude and Action on the Making of Divisions and Distinctions

I find nothing both relevant and new.

E. The Resolution of Doubt

1. Matters of doubt about topics subject to stringent rules of cleanness are resolved negatively. Matters of doubt concerning what is already subject to doubt are resolved negatively:

Tosefta Kelim Baba Mesia

11:1	B.	Any matter of doubt which is clean for heave-offering is clean for the purification rite
	C.	except for the hands, since they are a matter of doubt which pertains to the body.
	D.	A matter of doubt concerning QWPSYN [?] is clean for heave-offering [and] unclean for the purification rite, since it is a matter of doubt about that which is unfit.

2. In cases of doubt, we resolve matters by assessing possibilities; where something is impossible, that resolves the doubt:

Tosefta Tohorot

4:1	A.	[If a person] was wrapped in his cloak,
	B.	with unclean things and clean things at his side,
	C.	and unclean things and clean things above –
	D.	there is doubt whether he touched or did not touch –
	E.	his matter of doubt is deemed clean.
	F.	And if it is not possible for him [not to come] into [contact]
	G.	his matter of doubt is deemed unclean.

3. When we have a case of doubt, we have to discover the governing analogy, and then resolve the doubt by appeal to the rule yielded by that analogy. In the following, the governing analogy is decided by the parallel in the source of invalidation, and that solves the problem:

Tosefta Miqvaot

1:16	A.	An immersion pool which was measured and found lacking – all the acts requiring cleanness which were carried out depending upon it
	B.	whether this immersion pool is in the private domain, or whether this immersion pool is in the public domain – [Supply: are unclean].

C. R. Simeon says, "In the private domain, it is unclean. In the public domain, it is clean."

1:17 A. Said R. Simeon, "There was the following precedent: The water reservoir of Disqus in Yavneh was measured and found lacking.

B. "And R. Tarfon did declare clean, and R. Aqiva unclean.

C. "Said R. Tarfon, 'Since this immersion pool is in the assumption of being clean, it remains perpetually in this presumption of cleanness until it will be known for sure that it is made unclean.'

D. "Said R. Aqiva, 'Since this immersion pool is in the assumption of being unclean, it perpetually remains in the presumption of uncleanness until it will be known for sure that it is clean.'

1:18 A. "Said R. Tarfon, 'To what is the matter to be likened? To one who was standing and offering [a sacrifice] at the altar, and it became known that he is a son of a divorcée or the son of a halusah – for his service is valid.'

B. "Said R. Aqiva, 'To what is the matter to be likened? To one who was standing and offering [a sacrifice] at the altar, and it became known that he is disqualified by reason of a blemish – for his service is invalid.'

1:19 A. "Said R. Tarfon to him, 'You draw an analogy to one who is blemished. I draw an analogy to the son of a divorcée or to the son of a halusah.

B. "'Let us now see to what the matter is appropriately likened.

C. "'If it is analogous to a blemished priest, let us learn the law from the case of the blemished priest. If it is analogous to the son of a divorcée or to the son of a halusah, let us learn the law from the case of the son of the divorcée or the son of a halusah.'

1:20 A. "R. Aqiva says, 'The unfitness affecting an immersion pool affects the immersion pool itself, and the unfit aspect of the blemished priest affects the blemished priest himself.

B. "'But let not the case of the son of a divorcée or the son of a halusah prove the matter, for his matter of unfitness depends upon others.

C. "'A ritual pool's unfitness [depends] on one only, and the unfitness of a blemished priest [depends] on an individual only, but let not the son of a divorcée or the son of a halusah prove the matter, for the unfitness of this one depends upon ancestry.'

D. "They took a vote concerning the case and declared it unclean.

E. "Said R. Tarfon to R. Aqiva, 'He who departs from you is like one who perishes.'"

F. Primary and Secondary Effects

I find nothing both relevant and new.

III. The Later Midrash Compilations: Genesis Rabbah, Leviticus Rabbah and Pesiqta deRab Kahana

We find in Genesis Rabbah numerous discussions about the mysteries of the creation of the natural world, but these do not bear comparison to philosophical discussions of the same matter, being framed in entirely mythic language and appealing to Scripture, for example, *creatio e nihilo* in the following:

I:IX

1. A.   A philosopher asked Rabban Gamaliel, saying to him, "Your God was indeed a great artist, but he had good materials to help him."
    B.   He said to him, "What are they?"
    C.   He said to him, "Unformed [space], void, darkness, water, wind, and the deep."
    D.   He said to him, "May the spirit of that man [you] burst! All of them are explicitly described as having been created by him [and not as pre-existent].
    E.   "Unformed space and void: 'I make peace and create evil' (Isa. 45:7).
    F.   "Darkness: 'I form light and create darkness' (Isa. 45:7).
    G.   "Water: 'Praise him, you heavens of heavens, and you waters that are above the heavens' (Ps. 148:4). Why? 'For he commanded and they were created' (Ps. 148:5).
    H.   "Wind: 'For lo, he who forms the mountains creates the wind' (Amos 4:13).
    I.   "The depths: 'When there were no depths, I was brought forth' (Prov. 8:24)."

A. The Method of Hierarchical Classification

In this corpus of material, I find nothing that bears upon the issue of this category of thought.

B. The Message of the Taxonomic Power of Human Intentionality

In this corpus of material, I find nothing that bears upon the issue of this category of thought.

C. The Nature of Mixtures

In this corpus of material, I find nothing that bears upon the issue of this category of thought.

D. The Effect of Human Attitude and Action on the Making of Divisions and Distinctions

In this corpus of material, I find nothing that bears upon the issue of this category of thought.

E. The Resolution of Doubt

In this corpus of material, I find nothing that bears upon the issue of this category of thought.

F. Primary and Secondary Effects

In this corpus of material, I find nothing that bears upon the issue of this category of thought.

IV. The Latest Midrash Compilations:
Song of Songs Rabbah, Ruth Rabbah, Esther Rabbah I, and Lamentations Rabbati, and The Fathers According to Rabbi Nathan

These compilations produce not a single line of philosophical interest.

V. General Observations

Only the Mishnah may be classified as a document that uses a philosophical method to demonstrate a philosophical proposition. We cannot, therefore, find surprising that only the Mishnah yields a rich harvest of premises. The rich corpus of cases, spread over diverse tractates, yield presuppositions that are both weighty and also of broad application and consequence. The contrast with the paltry and trivial premises yielded by legal writing shows the character of what is before us. The matter of classification proves paramount, since not only does the method and result of classification form the premise of a vast range of Mishnah discussions, but all the other philosophical presuppositions, for example, the taxonomic power of human intentionality, the nature of mixtures, the resolution of doubt, and the like, turn out to form subdivisions of the basic philosophical principle that, as I said at the outset, all things may be classified and ordered by classification. In the later compilations, by contrast, I find nothing of philosophical weight. The Mishnah's principal philosophical concern finds no counterparts, let alone continuators, in the successive writings, and, as we see in Genesis Rabbah, when questions of a philosophical character are raised, they are not treated in a philosophical manner.

5

Legal Premises

In this chapter I list those principles or premises that are not particular to a given topic or tractate (in the Mishnah the two are the same) but transcend a specific area of law. I want to know whether we can identify principles of a specifically legal character that come to the surface in diverse cases or areas of law. These would form premises not limited to the topic or the case at hand, comparable to the theological and philosophical premises that we have identified in abundance. What we find is remarkably trivial, banalities really; in fact, in the documents, whether or Mishnah or of Scripture exegesis, prior to the Talmud of Babylonia, we identify no legal premises at all. Premises that do surface in discussions of law prove either banal or not of a legal character at all. In the former category is the conception that the law takes account of practicalities, or that individual idiosyncrasy is not allowed to affect the shape of the law overall. In the latter are theological principles given expression in concrete laws, such as that the law must be extended beyond its narrow limits, so as to assure conformity overall, and that the law preserves the paradigmatic actions of God and the patriarchs and matriarchs.

Most laws can yield generalizations of one kind or another. But those that we examine in the writings exclusive of the Bavli turn out to generalize a single case or topic, so that we have in fact premises that prove only ad hoc and topical. These do not yield in legal form and expression that encompassing "Judaism" that we seek. Let me give some examples of legal premises, susceptible of generalization, that I do not catalogue here. The following, drawn from Mishnah-tractate Erubin, can yield a rich account of thinking about the interplay of time and space, for example, the enchantment of space at the advent of holy time. But all of these premises are particular to their tractate and therefore do not allow generalization of the kind that I seek:

1.   The premises of this tractate are these facts: [1] remaining in one's place on the Sabbath (Ex. 16:29-30) does not mean one may not leave his house,

2.   but it does mean one should remain in his own village, which consists of the settled area of a village as well as its natural environs.

3.   But one may establish residence, for the Sabbath, in some place other than his normal abode,

4.   by making provision for eating a meal at that other place. Where one eats is where one dwells. Where someone eats defines his and his family's residence.

5.   Doing so allows a person to measure his allotted area for travel from that other place.

6.   The measure is 2,000 cubits.

7.   To establish a symbolic place of residence, one must set out, prior to sundown on the Sabbath or festival, a symbolic meal,

8.   or through a verbal declaration accomplish the same end, making provision for a temporary Sabbath abode.

9.   One may not move something from private to public domain.

10.   There are areas the status of which is ambiguous, since they are neither wholly private nor completely public domain. These are the courtyard, on which private dwellings abut; or an alleyway, onto which a number of courtyards open up.

11.   But one may commingle individual rights of residence, through a fictive fusion meal, so that an area of shared ownership may form a single domain for the purpose of the Sabbath. By this fictive, common meal, the various owners mingle their rights of ownership to a courtyard. The symbolic gesture bears material consequences in the concrete rights of persons affected by the gesture. Let us glance at the source that bears this statement:

7:6   A.   How do they make a partnership [a shittuf] in an alleyway?

B.   One [of the residents] sets down a jar [of food or drink] and states, "Lo, this belongs to all the residents of the alleyway."

C.   And thus he effects possession for them through his adult son or daughter, his Hebrew slave boy or slave girl, or his wife.

D.   But he does not effect possession in their behalf by means of his minor son or daughter, or by means of his Canaanite slave boy or slave girl,

	E.	because their hand is as his hand.
7:7	A.	[If] the food diminished in volume [to less than the prescribed quantity], one adds to it and effects possession for the others.
	B.	And he need not inform them.
	C.	[But if] the number [of residents of the alleyway] became larger, one adds to the food and effects possession for them.
	D.	And he does need to inform them.

One may readily generalize into philosophy the notion of a fictive action, the notion that a symbolic gesture bears weight. But then we should look with little success in other tractates or topics of the law for expressions of the same premise, though the premise itself is of broad and general interest. Indeed, one may formulation generalizations of considerable breadth out of the premises of all of the foregoing statements. When we do, however, we generalize without consequence, there being in other tractates or topics of the law no further examples of the workings of the same premises. The purposes of this inquiry into the Judaism – the broad based, encompassing system – behind the documents requires generalizations that circulate over many topics of the law, such as we have seen in the case of philosophical and theological premises.

I. The Mishnah

A. Rules Govern Acts in Relationship to Heaven, for Example, Prayer

1. Rules govern the recitation of prayers, including the Shema and the Prayer (Eighteen Benedictions). These rules preclude reciting the obligatory prayers ad lib (the premise of M. Berakhot Chapters One through Six, Eight). Recitation of an improper formula in prayer is suppressed (M. Ber. 5:3). One who errs in reciting the Prayer in behalf of the community is replaced. Specific formulas, appropriate to diverse types of food, are to be recited for specific classes of food (M. Ber. 6:1-4). There has to be a suitable match between the prayer that is said and the substance to which it refers, so that the words accord with the classification of that which they concern. Other givens of religious practice are the recitation of the Prayer, posting a mezuzah, reciting the Grace after Meals (M. Ber. 3:4), saying blessings before eating various foods and on the occasion of noteworthy events.

B. The Law Legislates for the World as It Is

1. The given of Mishnah-tractate Demai is that some Israelites do not fully carry out the law, and those who do must so behave as to take account of the condition of what they receive from and what they hand over to, those who are neglectful of some details of the law. All

Israelites are responsible for one another, with the result that the more observant must accommodate the situation of the less observant, so far as they can. One who is scrupulous about the law will preserve the cleanness of foodstuffs, on the one side, and will avoid handing over to unscrupulous people what may be mishandled by them:

Mishnah-tractate Demai

2:2   A.   He who undertakes to be trustworthy [one who is assumed to tithe all of his produce]

B.   tithes (1) what he eats, and (2) what he sells, and (3) what he purchases,

C.   and (4) does not accept the hospitality of an am haares.

D.   R. Judah says, "Also one who accepts the hospitality of an am haares is trustworthy."

E.   They said to him, "[If he is not trustworthy concerning himself [viz., concerning food which he himself eats], how should he be trustworthy concerning that of others [viz., concerning food which he feeds or sells to others]?"

2:3   A.   He who undertakes to be a haber ["comrade," "fellow," "member," "associate"; member of a group which scrupulously observes the laws of Levitical cleanness]

B.   (1) does not sell to an am haares wet or dry [produce, either produce which has been rendered susceptible to uncleanness or produce which has not been rendered susceptible],

C.   and (2) does not purchase from him wet [produce, produce which has been rendered susceptible to uncleanness],

D.   and (3) does not accept the hospitality of an am haares,

E.   and (4) does not receive him [the am haares] as his guest while he [the am haares] is wearing his [the am haares'] own clothes.

F.   R. Judah says, "Also (1) he should not raise small cattle,

G.   and (2) he should not be profuse in [making] vows or in levity,

H.   and (3) he should not defile himself for the dead,

I.   and (4) he should minister in the study house."

J.   They said to him, "These [rules] do not enter the category [under discussion, viz., they do not deal with matters of cleanness]."

2.   We do take account of the possibility of deceit (M. Dem. 3:5-6). There are, moreover, extenuating circumstances, in which we may believe someone who is ordinarily not trustworthy (Demai 4:1, Sarason, p. 153). When instructions are general, we assume the worst; when they are specific and particular, we assume the agent does what he is told to do (M. Dem. 4:5-7).

3.   Man always bears responsibility for what he does, whether the deed is inadvertent or deliberately, whether the man is awake or asleep:

2:6   A.   Man is perpetually an attested danger [cf. M. 1:4G] –

B.   whether [what is done is done] inadvertently or deliberately,

C. whether man is awake or asleep.
D. [If] he blinded the eye of his fellow or broke his utensils, he pays the full value of the damage he has caused.

4. We assign responsibility for an action or event to the last person who can have prevented the event from taking place; we take account of what is ordinary and extraordinary and impute responsibility only for what can have been predicted or is ordinary:

Mishnah-tractate Baba Qamma

5:6
A. A pit belonging to two partners
B. one of them passed by it and did not cover it,
C. and the second one also did not cover it,
D. the second one is liable.
E. [If] the first one covered it up, and the second one came along and found it uncovered and did not cover it up,
F. the second one is liable.
G. [If] he covered it up in a proper way, and an ox or an ass fell into it and died, he is exempt.
H. [If] he did not cover it up in the proper way and an ox or an ass fell into it and died, he is liable.
I. [If] it fell forward [not into the pit] because of the sound of the digging, [the owner of the pit] is liable.
J. [If] it fell backward [not into the pit] because of the sound of the digging, [the owner of the pit] is exempt.
K. [If] an ox carrying its trappings fell into it and they were broken, an ass and its trappings and they were split,
L. [the owner of the pit] is liable for the beast but exempt for the trappings.
M. [If] an ox belonging to a deaf-mute, an idiot, or a minor fell into it, [the owner] is liable.
N. [If] a little boy or girl, a slave boy or a slave girl [fell into it], he is exempt [from paying a ransom].

5. Right of ownership ends when someone gives up hope of regaining the thing that has been lost. Hence ownership depends on the attitude of the owner; once the owner gives up the object, it is no longer his property:

Mishnah-tractate Baba Mesia

10:2
A. [If] excise collectors took one's ass and gave him another ass,
B. [if] thugs took his garment and gave him another garment,
C. lo, these are his,
D. because the original owners have given up hope of getting them back.
E. He who saves something from a river, from a raid, or from thugs,
F. if the owner has given up hope of getting them back, lo, these belong to him.
G. And so a swarm of bees:

H.   If the owner had given up hope of getting it back, lo, this belongs to him.

6.   One may not buy from someone who may be assumed to have stolen what he is selling:

Mishnah-tractate Baba Mesia

10:9   A.   They do not purchase from herdsmen wool, milk, or kids,
       B.   or from watchmen of an orchard wood or fruit.
       C.   But they purchase clothing of wool from women in Judah,
       D.   flax clothing in Galilee,
       E.   and calves in Sharon.
       F.   And in all cases in which [the sellers] say to hide them away,
       G.   it is prohibited [to make such a purchase].

7.   In assessing the culpability on account of lying, we take account of the intention of the lie. If it is to his own advantage, the man is liable; if it is to his detriment, he is exempt:

8:6   X.   This is the governing principle: Whoever [by lying] changes [his claim] from one sort of liability to another sort of liability, from one count of exemption to another count of exemption, or from a count of exemption to a reason for liability, is exempt.
      Y.   [If he changed his claim, by lying] from grounds for liability to a reason for exemption [from having to make restitution], he is liable.
      Z.   This is the governing principle: Whoever [falsely] takes an oath so as to lighten the burden on himself is liable.
      AA. Whoever takes an oath so as to make more weighty the burden on himself is exempt.

C. A Fence Must Be Erected around the Law

1.   The law is protected by a fence, secondary restrictions which prevent people from violating the law of the Torah. Thus we add to the spell of time in the Seventh Year in which it is forbidden to work the land (Newman, p. 18).

M. Shebiit

1:1   A.   Until what time do they plough an orchard during the year preceding the Sabbatical Year?
      B.   The House of Shammai say, "As long as [the ploughing] continues to benefit the produce [of the Sixth Year. Until that year's fruit ripens and is harvested]."
      C.   But the House of Hillel say, "Until Pentecost."
      D.   And the opinion of the one is close to the opinion of the other.

2.   What appears to look like work in violation of the law is forbidden, even though the work does not actually benefit the land. What appears to be clearing the land for planting is not permitted, even though removing the stones for use in construction has nothing to do

with clearing the land for planting. Here appearance overrides intentionality or purpose. Appearing to improve the land during the Seventh Year is a violation of the law. In the following, we so legislate that actions not only do not violate the law, but also do not appear to violate the law:

M. Shebiit

3:3   A.   A man constructs within his field three dung heaps per seah space.
    B.   "More than that [constructing more than three dung heaps per seah space, likewise is permitted]," the words of R. Simeon [cf. M. 3:2].
    C.   And sages forbid [the construction of more than three dung heaps per seah space] unless he either deepens [the ground where the manure is to be deposited by] three [handbreadths] or raises [the ground by] three [handbreadths].
    D.   A person places [all] the manure in his possession in [one large] pile.
    E.   R. Meir forbids [the farmer from doing this] unless he either deepens [the ground by] three [handbreadths] or raises [the ground by] three [handbreadths].
    F.   If one had a small amount [of manure already piled up in the field], he continually adds to it.
    G.   R. Eleazar b. Azariah forbids [the farmer from doing so] unless he either deepens [the ground by] three [handbreadths] or raises [the ground by] three [handbreadths].
    H.   or unless he places [the manure] on rocky ground.

By limiting the area that is covered, the farmer shows he is not using the dung for fertilizer (Newman, p. 77). So, too, as to removing stones from the field without appearing to prepare the field for planting:

M. Shebiit

3:5   A.   [During the Sabbatical Year] a man may not begin to open a stone quarry in his field,
    B.   unless it contains [enough stones to construct] three piles [of hewn blocks],
    C.   each [pile] three [cubits long] by three [cubits wide] by three [cubits] high,
    D.   [so that] their measure is [equivalent to] twenty-seven stones. [That is, each pile must contain no less than twenty-seven blocks, each measuring one cubic cubit].

The main point is that if the stones that are gathered are large enough to use in construction, so it is clear the farmer is not clearing the field for cultivation, he may remove them (Newman, p. 87).

3.   One must extend the law beyond its minimal requirements so as to erect a fence about the Torah, preventing violation of the law by adding to its restrictions:

Mishnah-tractate Shabbat

1:2   A.   A man should not sit down before the barber close to the afternoon [prayer],

       B.   unless he has already prayed.

       C.   Nor [at that time] should a man go into a bathhouse or into a tannery,

       D.   nor to eat, nor to enter into judgment.

       E.   But if they began, they do not break off [what they were doing].

       F.   They do break off [what they were doing] to pronounce the recitation of the Shema.

       G.   But they do not break off [what they were doing] to say the Prayer.

1:3   A.   A tailor should not go out carrying his needle near nightfall,

       B.   lest he forget and cross [a boundary];

       C.   nor a scribe with his pen.

4.   One must not perpetrate, or perpetuate, injustice, and one must take account of the possibility that out of doing good, evil will come about; one is responsible for his own place in a sequence of actions that he did not initiate:

Mishnah-tractate Baba Mesia

1:6   A.   [If] one found bonds of indebtedness,

       B.   "If they record a lien on [the debtor's] property, he should not return them.

       C.   "For a court will exact payment on the strength of them.

       D.   "[If] they do not record a lien on property, he should return them,

       E.   "for a court will not exact payment on the strength of them," the words of R. Meir.

       F.   And sages say, "One way or the other, he should not return them.

       G.   "For a court will exact payment on the strength of them."

1:7   A.   [If] he found (1) writs of divorce for women, (2) writs of emancipation for slaves, (3) wills, (4) deeds of gift, or (5) receipts for the payment of marriage settlements,

       B.   lo, he should not return them.

       C.   For I maintain that they were written out, but [then] the one [who is answerable] for them changed his mind and decided not to hand them over,

1:8   A.   [If] one found (1) documents of evaluation, (2) letters of alimony, (3) deeds of halisah rites or (4) of the exercise of the right of refusal, (5) deeds of arbitration, or any document which is prepared in a court,

       B.   lo, this one should return [them].

D. Individual Preference Is Not Taken into Account by the Law

1.   The law may not be decided by individual preference or perception, but must be given fixed rules, so that everyone will keep the law at the same time:

M. Shebiit

2:1   A.   Until what time do they plough in a field of grain (lit.: a white field) during the year preceding the Sabbatical Year?

B.   Until the moisture [in the ground] is gone.

C.   As long as people plough in order to plant chatemelons and gourds.

D.   Said R. Simeon, "You have put the law into the hands of each individual.

E.   "Rather, [one may plough] in a field of grain until Passover [when Israelites offer the first sheaf of new grain at the Temple; cf. Lev. 23:10] and [one may plough] in an orchard until Pentecost [when they present the first fruits; cf. Ex. 23:19 and M. 1:1C].

E. The Law Is Modeled after God's Actions, which Dictate what is Normative

I find nothing relevant to this category. But the later compilations provide statements of that proposition.

II. The Tosefta, Tractate Abot, and the Earlier Midrash Compilations: Sifra, Sifré to Numbers, and Sifré to Deuteronomy

Since these documents cover numerous legal topics, we may reasonably have anticipated fresh ideas on law in general. I find none; the principles we were able to extract from the Mishnah, moreover, prove particular to that document.

A. Rules Govern Acts in Relationship to Heaven, for Example, Prayer

I find nothing that pertains to this rubric.

B. The Law Legislates for the World as It Is

I find nothing that pertains to this rubric.

C. A Fence Must Be Erected around the Law

I find nothing that pertains to this rubric.

D. Individual Preference Is Not Taken into Account by the Law

I find nothing that pertains to this rubric.

E. The Law Is Modeled after God's Actions, which Dictate what is Normative

I find nothing relevant to this category.

III. The Later Midrash Compilations: Genesis Rabbah, Leviticus Rabbah and Pesiqta deRab Kahana

These are exegetical compilations, and we have no reason to anticipate a rich corpus of legal premises or the inquiry into legal presuppositions. We find nothing of consequence, other than the theology of the law at rubric E.

A. Rules Govern Acts in Relationship to Heaven, for Example, Prayer

I find nothing relevant to this category.

B. The Law Legislates for the World as It Is

I find nothing relevant to this category.

C. A Fence Must Be Erected around the Law

1. Scripture supports changes in the law when these are called for:

Leviticus Rabbah XXIX

XII.1 A. R. Yohanan and R. Simeon b. Laqish were in session, raising a question about traditions. Kahana came by. They said, "Lo, here comes the authority for the tradition. Let us arise and raise our question for him."

B. They arose and asked him as follows: "We have learned [at M.R.H. 4:1], 'In the case of the festival day of the New Year that coincided with the Sabbath, in the sanctuary they would sound the shofar horn, but not in the countryside. When the house of the sanctuary was destroyed, Rabban Yohanan ben Zakkai made the ordinance that they should sound the shofar horn wherever a court was located.'

C. "Now if it is a matter of Torah law [that the shofar is sounded], then it should override [the considerations of Sabbath rest even] in the provinces. And if it is not [a matter of Torah law], then even in the sanctuary, [sounding the shofar horn] should not override [the considerations of Sabbath rest]."

D. He said to them, "One verse of Scripture states, 'You will have a day for sounding the horn' [Num. 29:1]. Another verse of Scripture says, 'A Sabbath of remembrance of the sounding of the horn, a holy convocation' [Lev. 23:24].

E. "Now how [may the two verses be harmonized]? On an occasion on which [the holiday] coincides with an ordinary day [not a Sabbath], 'You will have a day for sounding the horn' [Num. 29:1]. On an occasion on which [the holiday] coincides with the Sabbath, 'A Sabbath of remembrance of the sounding of the horn, a holy convocation,' [Lev. 23:24], meaning that they make mention [of the sounding of the horn] but they do not sound [the horn]."

D. Individual Preference Is Not Taken into Account by the Law

I find nothing relevant to this category.

E. The Law Is Modeled after God's Actions, which Dictate what is Normative

Here we have an important category, in which the premise is that the details of the law derive from God, either through God's own actions, or through the exemplary actions of those whom God has instructed, the patriarchs and matriarchs, prophet Moses, or sages of the Mishnah themselves.

1.   The rites imitate God's actions on comparable occasions:

Genesis Rabbah I

III.2   A.   "And God saw the light" (Gen. 1:3):
        B.   R. Zeira son of R. Abbahu gave an exposition in Caesarea: "How do we know that **people may not say a blessing [for the rite of Habdalah, separating the Sabbath from the ordinary week] making use of a light, unless they have actually made use of its light** [M. Ber. 8:5]?
        C.   "From the following statement: 'And God saw... then God divided...' [as in saying a blessing to divide the Sabbath from the ordinary weekday. So God first made use of the light by looking at it and only then divided it.]"

2.   The law derives from the acts of the patriarchs and matriarchs:

Genesis Rabbah XLV

III.2   A.   "So after Abram had dwelt ten years in the land of Canaan" (Gen. 16:3):
        B.   R. Ammi in the name of R. Simeon b. Laqish: "How on the basis of Scripture do we know that rule that we have learned in the Mishnah: **If one has married a woman and lived with her for ten years and not produced a child, he is not allowed to remain sterile [but must marry someone else]** [M. Yeb. 15:6]? Proof derives from this verse: 'So after Abram had dwelt ten years.' The statement, '...in the land of Canaan...' further proves that the years of marriage spent outside of the Land of Israel do not count."

The same point occurs in the following, which maintains that the laws express in prescribed gestures what the Torah tells of the actions of the patriarchs and matriarchs:

XLIX

XI.2   A.   We have learned in the Mishnah: **What is the rite for the conduct of a fast? People bring the ark out into the public square and put burned ashes on the ark** [M. Ta. 2:1].
        B.   R. Yudan bar Menasseh and R. Samuel bar Nahman:
        C.   One of them said, "It is on account of the merit attained by Abraham, as it is said, 'I who am but dust and ashes' (Gen. 18:27)."
        D.   The other said, "It is on account of the merit attained by Isaac." But the latter memorized the statement of the Mishnah so that it referred only to ashes and not dust.
        E.   A ruling of R. Yudan b. Pazzi stands at issue with this formulation [of C].
        F.   For R. Yudan b. Pazzi would announce in the community, saying, "Whoever has not been reached by the leader of the congregation for the pouring of ashes on his head should take ashes and pour

them on his head on his own." [Hence he did not require both dust and ashes, but only ashes.]

G.   The ruling of R. Yudan b. Pazzi treats dust and ashes as the same thing [so it does not prove that he differs from C's position].

Here again, the law realizes the practices of the patriarch:

Genesis Rabbah LVIII

VI.2   A.   Said R. Yohanan, "From whence do we derive scriptural support for that which we have learned in the Mishnah: **He who has yet to bury his deceased is exempt from the requirement of reciting the Shema [M. Ber. 3:1]?**

B.   "It is from this passage: 'And Abraham rose up from upon the face of his dead and [without reciting his prayers, he turned directly to the business of the burial, for] he said...' (Gen. 23:3)."

3.   The laws of the Mishnah correspond to the narratives of Scripture:

Genesis Rabbah LXV

XX.6   A.   "The voice is Jacob's voice": In the incident of the concubine of Gibeah.

B.   "Cursed is he who gives a wife to Benjamin" (Judg. 21:18).

C.   "The voice is Jacob's voice":

D.   In the days of Jeroboam: "Neither did Jeroboam recover strength again in the days of Abijah, and the Lord smote him and he died" (2 Chr. 13:20).

E.   Said R. Samuel bar Nahman, "Do you think that Jeroboam was smitten? But in fact Abijah was smitten."

F.   Why was Abijah smitten?

G.   Said R. Abba b. Kahana, "Because he removed the identifying marks of the faces of the Israelites, as it is written, 'The show of their countenance does witness for them' (Isa. 3:9)."

H.   Said R. Assi, "Because he set up guards over them for three days until the features of their faces were disfigured."

I.   "For so we have learned in the Mishnah: **People give testimony to the identity of a corpse only through the features of the face together with the nose, and that is the case even if there are other marks of identification on the body and the garments; and one may give testimony only within three days of death [beyond which point the face is disfigured] [M. Yeb. 16:3]."**

4.   The law realizes in general rules the precepts of the patriarchs and matriarchs, expressed through their deeds:

Genesis Rabbah LXXII

IV.1   A.   "[Rachel said, 'Then he may lie with you tonight for your son's mandrakes.'] When Jacob came from the field in the evening, [Leah went out to meet him and said, 'You must come in to me, for I have hired you with my son's mandrakes.' So he lay with her that night]" (Gen. 30:15-17):

B. We have learned in the Mishnah: **He who hires workers and made an agreement with them to get up for work earlier than is the norm or to work later in the evening than is the norm – in a place in which it is not customary to get up early or to stay late, he cannot force them to do so [M. B.M. 7:1].**

C. Said R. Mana, "In a place in which there is no customary practice, the rule is covered by the generally applicable stipulation of the court. This requires that going forth to work is on the householder's time, and coming home from work is on the worker's time, as it is said, 'The sun rises, they [animals] slink away and couch in their dens,' and then: 'Man goes forth to his work, and to his labor until the evening' (Ps. 104:22-23)."

D. Said R. Ammi in the name of R. Simeon b. Laqish, "If it is a Friday afternoon, they have placed on the householder the burden, so that the return from work is on his time.

E. "To what extent [must the householder allow the workers on Friday to come home early]? To such an extent that each one has the time to fill a jug of water and to roast a fish for himself and to light a candle."

5. The patriarchs founded certain legal institutions:

Genesis Rabbah LXXXV

V.1 A. "Then Judah said to Onan, 'Go in to your brother's wife and perform the duty of a brother-in-law to her, and raise up offspring for your brother'" (Gen. 38:9):

B. Judah began the practice of levirate marriage.

C. It has been taught on Tannaite authority: Any matter which had been in the category of what was permitted and then was forbidden and still later was permitted again, when permitted the second time does not revert to the status of what was permitted the first time around, but only to its status as it was ultimately permitted.

D. Thus a deceased childless brother's widow was once permitted [before she was married to the brother], then she was prohibited [while she was married to the brother] and now she is permitted again [as the deceased childless brother's widow, but, as we shall see, the way in which she is permitted at the end is not the same as the way in which she was permitted at the outset].

E. Might one suppose that she reverts to the original status of availability?

F. Scripture states, "Her husband's brother shall go in to her" (Deut. 25:5), as a matter of carrying out a religious duty. [The marriage is not one of choice or love, but only to carry out a religious duty.]

IV. The Latest Midrash Compilations: Song of Songs Rabbah, Ruth Rabbah, Esther Rabbah I, and Lamentations Rabbati, and The Fathers According to Rabbi Nathan

As before, we cannot expect in the exegetical compilations to find premises of a legal character.

A. Rules Govern Acts in Relationship to Heaven, for Example, Prayer

I find nothing relevant to this rubric.

B. The Law Legislates for the World as It Is

I find nothing relevant to this rubric.

C. A Fence Must Be Erected around the Law

1. Making a fence around the Torah requires extending the law to areas that, by strict rule, are permitted; by doing so, one makes certain of not violating those rules' main point:

The Fathers According to Rabbi Nathan II

I.1   A.   What sort of fence did [3] the Torah make around its words?

      B.   Lo, Scripture says, *To a woman during the unclean time of her menstrual period you shall not draw near* (Lev. 18:17).

      C.   Is it possible to suppose that one may nonetheless hug and kiss her and exchange billydoos with her?

      D.   Scripture says, *you shall not draw near.*

      E.   Is it nonetheless possible to suppose that if she is fully clothed, one may sleep with her in the same bed?

      F.   Scripture says, *you shall not draw near.*

      G.   Is it possible to suppose that a woman my pretty her face and put on eye makeup?

      H.   Scripture says, *And of her that is sick with her impurity* (Lev. 15:33), meaning, all the days of her menstrual period she shall be put away.

      I.   On this basis they have said: Whoever neglects herself during her menstrual period enjoys the approbation of sages, and whoever pretties herself during her menstrual period does not enjoy the approbation of sages.

D. Individual Preference Is Not Taken into Account by the Law

I find nothing relevant to this rubric.

E. The Law Is Modeled after God's Actions, which Dictate what is Normative

1. The laws are to be inferred from the actions of sages, as much as from the Mishnah's or Scripture's explicit formulations:

CXX

I.1   A.   "The breath of our nostrils, the Lord's anointed, was taken in their pits, he of whom we said, 'Under his shadow we shall live among the nations'":

      B.   Rabbi [Judah the Patriarch] and R. Ishmael b. R. Yosé were explaining passages of the scroll of Lamentations on the eve of the ninth of Ab that coincided with a Saturday. They omitted one go-around of the alphabet [that is, a chapter], saying, "Tomorrow we'll come back and finish it."

C. When Rabbi went home, he had an accident that injured his finger, and recited in his own regard the following verse of Scripture: "Many are the sorrows of the wicked" (Ps. 32:10).

D. Said to him R. Ishmael b. R. Yosé, "Were we not engaged in the matter and such a thing had happened to you, I all the more so would have said what I shall now say: The breath of our nostrils, the Lord's anointed, was taken in their pits, he of whom we said, 'Under his shadow we shall live among the nations.'"

E. When they went into his house, he put on it a dry sponge and tied it around the outside with reed grass.

F. R. Ishmael b. R. Yosé said, "From that action of his we have derived three things [concerning conduct on the Sabbath day]: [1] a dry sponge may be used on the Sabbath not because it can heal the wound but because it guards the wound; [2] reed grass inside the house is deemed made ready in advance of the Sabbath for use on the Sabbath [and hence permissible; by contrast, objects not designated in advance of the holy day for use on that day may not be used]; [3] people may recite Scripture [on the Sabbath] only after the afternoon prayer, but they may study and expound them."

V. General Observations

These results are paltry and trivial, and they call into question whether we may speak of presuppositions or premises that infuse the law throughout, let alone any that move from document to document and form a substrate of conviction beneath all concrete formulations. When we seek legal, as distinct from theological, premises that animate a variety of documents, we find a remarkably thin corpus. The conception that the laws speak in behalf of law, that rules yield jurisprudence, and jurisprudence, philosophy or theology, may find ample justification in the pages of the Talmud of Babylonia; so I have argued at some length in *The Bavli's Unique Voice*. But the laws themselves, abstracted from certain recurring issues of theology, such as the matter of intentionality, and philosophy, such as issues of classification or resolution of doubt, even in the Mishnah yield very little that transcends the topic that realizes the abstract principle. Not only so, but the kind of presuppositions we are able to identify, for example, the practicality of the legislation, the law makers' capacity to deal with the social facts of the world they knew, hardly presents stands for more than the banality that practical law is practical. Not accommodating individual cases but insisting on objective criteria of judgment, building a fence around the law, and the like – these hardly represent premises that generate laws about diverse topics; rather they present us with rather unremarkable observations of broad application but shallow consequence.

The one important point we do observe is the claim that, on the one side, rules govern acts in which Heaven takes a keen interest, and on, the other, the law is modeled after God's or the patriarchs' and the matriarchs' actions. These in fact form theological points, expressed in discussions about the laws in general; they do not present us with premises of a legal character that surface in numerous concrete topics and come to expression in details of a practical order. We may therefore say that the search for legal premises or presuppositions, even in the context of the legal literature, turns up nothing. Now we appreciate the formidable weight of the task taken for themselves by the authors of the compositions of the Talmuds, particularly the Talmud of Babylonia. They asked for generalizations, premises, presuppositions, of a prior literature that contained none of a legal character.

6

When We "press behind the contents of the Mishnah and attempt to discover what the contents of the Mishnah presuppose," Do We Find Judaism?

I. Do the Premises of the Canonical Documents of Judaism Transcend their Documentary Setting?

When we press behind the contents of the Mishnah, we find the premises and presuppositions of the Mishnah. We cannot show that these form generative conceptions for other documents. We can demonstrate that most of them do not. We may dismiss as particular to its task the entire corpus of legal premises and presuppositions. Those of the Mishnah prove tied to the context of law, and the other documents have none of consequence that are comparable.

The same is true of the Midrash compilations, with their rich heritage of theological premises. The two densest conceptions, concerning Israel and the nations and the meaning of history, do not lie at the foundations or form the presuppositions of the Mishnah or Tosefta. When it comes to the law, a single proposition strikes me as important, that the law preserves the example of the patriarchs and matriarchs or embodies what God did and does. That broadly circulated proposition then maintains that, in conforming to the law, holy Israel imitates God. As to the Mishnah's philosophical and theological premises, the most important philosophical givens functions only in the Mishnah. The paramount matter – hierarchical classification serves only there. More to the point, no other document works out its ideas along the lines of philosophical thought. And that leaves theology. So, in the aggregate, premises appear bound to the documents that rest upon them, and those that circulate through the canonical writings examined here are vastly outweighed in volume and impart by those that do not. True, as we noted at the outset, certain premises "surely" or "obviously" are everywhere taken for granted, for example, the unity of God, the importance of the Torah, and the like. But these remain inert, or, when they generate thought, accommodate themselves to context, for example, the Mishnah's use of monotheism is distinctive to the Mishnah's interest in hierarchical classification.

True, the picture is somewhat more complicated, since, as we have seen, all documents rest upon theological convictions of one sort of another. And we have no basis on which to suppose that the convictions important in one document and absent in another will have elicited objections among the authors of the writings in which they play no role. Nonetheless, when we raise the question of whether important theological conceptions unify all of the documents, providing the substrate of conceptions or attitudes for each one, the results prove somewhat puzzling. An idea that takes priority in one set of writings attracts slight attention elsewhere; premises that prove pressing here scarcely appear elsewhere. Two absolutely critical premises show what is at stake. The emotions, sentiments, and attitudes of God and humanity correspond. With the centrality of intentionality throughout the Mishnah – along with the method of hierarchical classification the generative premise of that document – simply does not prepare us for the fact that, beyond the Mishnah, intentionality does not define an area of exploration, not at all. The rabbis not only take the centrality of intentionality for granted, they build upon it. Then if they take it for granted throughout but neglect that same idea, we have to wonder whether that enormous premise of thought makes much impact where it is not urgent for a given document's larger program; then the premise follows the documentary program and gains entry only where the document requires it.

The upshot is that we cannot show many ideas that run from document to document, or group to group, and that enter into the definition of how a document finds its place in the canon. Then, it would appear, no traits tell us why one book would gain its place in the canon of the Judaism of the Dual Torah examined here, and another would not. That is not to suggest the identification of writings for the canon is arbitrary, only that on the basis of what documents appear to have taken for granted, we do not know what the criteria for admission might have been. To repeat my observation in Chapter Three, I find myself unable to point to a setting in the exegetical compilations, early, middle, and late, in which intentionality plays a part in the formation of a concrete idea, on the one side, or itself presents a critical consideration, on the other.

The other set of ideas that take a prominent place in a variety of writings concern the meaning and structure of history, on the one side, and theories that concern Israel and the nations, on the other. Richly expounded in some writings, the matter of history never appears as a premise in others; the later Midrash compilations represent the one, the Mishnah and the Tosefta the other. That fact is shown by the one passage in the Mishnah in which specific propositions concerning history, and therefore by implication, Israel and the nations, are laid out, which is Mishnah-tractate Sotah 9:15. That passage formally is anomalous, and its entire topical program – one cannot speak of a problematic – falls outside of its context, on the one side, and far beyond the program of the Mishnah in general, on the other. Where history and the Messiah emerge as major players, in some of the Midrash compilations, by contrast, the form of the compositions in which they occur is native to those collections, and the issues of history and Messiah occur throughout and define those documents' primary concern. So to allege that what we find, for example, in Genesis and Leviticus Rabbah but not in the Mishnah, or in the Mishnah but not in Pesiqta deRab Kahana or Song of Songs Rabbah, is nonetheless taken for granted in the documents in which these absent premises play no role defies the traits, both formal and programmatic, of the very writings in which they occur. Only if we imagine for ourselves that all documents are just random collections of this and that can we introduce such an argument, and that defies the evidences collected here.

What is presupposed and also generative in one set of writings plays no role in others, with the one important exception of the general themes of covenant, commandment, Torah, and God's dominion; but these, we now realize, are topical: subjects that form premises quite particular to documents where they play a role, no more than that. Contrast the remarkable cogency of the presentation of premises particular to documents, for example, history in the later Midrash compilations, intentionality and hierarchical classification in the earlier legal ones, with the diffuse character of presuppositions with respect to covenant, commandment, Torah, and God's dominion. Our results point to a different conclusion from the one I had anticipated. Specifically, these represent themes that move from one document to another, rather than propositional premises that form the intellectual foundations of any one of them. Indeed, a closer look at my formulation of matters shows that I have joined as a single rubric matters that may well be differentiated, and, when differentiated, prove as particular to documents as hierarchical classification, intentionality or the meaning and structure of history.

Take covenant, commandment, and kingdom of God, for example. While assuredly at the foundation of every Judaic writing that appeals to Scripture, the notion that Israel is covenanted with God, and that the Torah defines the terms of the covenant, is surely more critical in the Midrash compilations than in the Mishnah and the Tosefta. There, when we speak of God's kingdom, we formulate matters not in mythic terms but in the definition of the realm of the sacred. But I was the one to identify the realm of the sacred – space and time in the interplay on Sabbath and festival, Israel's space in God's time in their interpenetration – with the kingdom of God. My assigning to M. Meg. 3:1 the premise that the kingdom of God is continuous with this world again accomplishes the purpose of treating the conception of sanctification as pretty much the same as the idea of God's dominion; but these surely are to be differentiated; they relate to a single theme, but the theme is worked out in strikingly different ways as we move into the later writings. The notion of God's rule expressed through the space and time continuum does not surface in later writings, where the kingdom of God bears quite a different set of meanings.

That specific case returns us to my earlier observation and now yields a general rule: the presuppositions or premises that form the foundations of a document's exegesis of its propositions prove particular to the document even when themes or topics or symbols or ideas appear to be shared with other writings or to have moved from document to document. For at stake are not merely opaque symbols, for example, the Torah, the covenant, the kingdom of heaven, but the shaping of these topics for some propositional or at least provocative purpose. And, more to the point, when we take a closer look at those premises that do appear to circulate beyond the narrow limits of a single compilation or set of compilations (for example, Genesis Rabbah, Leviticus Rabbah, and Pesiqta de Rab Kahana, or the late Rabbah compilations), we observe that what we define as premises in all their concreteness prove specific to the document, or set of documents, in which the ubiquitous idea is treated. A second glance at the treatment of the topic of the Torah leaves no doubt about that fact.

Some themes or ideas or images or symbols recur here and there. But when they do, they reach the level of premise and presupposition of concrete compositions in formulations that prove specific to the document that uses them. It follows that the premises of the canonical documents of Judaism do not transcend their documentary setting. That result calls into question the conception that a corpus of ideas at the deepest structure of the canonical writings hold those writings together and form of them all a single coherent statement. The opposite is the fact. In substance, we are unable to find ideas that are both active, not inert, and ubiquitous, not specific to a kind of writing (for example, law or exegesis) or a set of closely related writings (for example, the Mishnah and the Tosefta, or some of the subsets of the Midrash compilations). If, therefore, we had to explain what accounts for the inclusion, in a single coherent canon, of both the Mishnah and, for example, Song of Songs Rabbah or the Tosefta and Leviticus Rabbah, on the strength of matters of substance – premises that circulate throughout, givens of conviction or conception, attitude or sentiment – we should be unable to answer that question.

When we "press behind the contents of the Mishnah and attempt to discover what the contents of the Mishnah presuppose," we do not find "Judaism," in the sense that by "Judaism" we mean a coherent body of ideas that form the structure of a variety of authoritative documents. That is to say, we cannot show that a canon of writings – all of which, all together, comprise "Judaism" – takes shape around a coherent body of premises. The answer to the question that inspired this inquiry, is simple. when we "press behind the contents of the Mishnah and attempt to discover what the contents of the Mishnah presuppose," we find the presuppositions of the Mishnah. And those presuppositions form the basis for the very particular conceptions of the Mishnah. On what basis, then, we link the Mishnah to Leviticus Rabbah and allege that at their foundations, both documents lay out the same -ism, that is, the same systematic and cogent set of ideas and attitudes that form a coherent and entire account of the social order of holy Israel – way of life, worldview, theory of the social entity – I cannot say. There is no substantive basis at the level of premises and presuppositions that run from here to there and play a provocative role throughout for the conception of the canon of the Dual Torah.

II. Forms the Rabbis Take for Granted

If I can identify no substantive grounds for linking into a single intellectually coherent canon the principal documents of the Judaism of the Dual Torah, then can I not at least find formal reason to do so? The answer is ambiguous, but once we take up a single fundamental formal trait of all the writings, it proves one sided. We cannot. It is true that nearly all of the canonical documents link to two principal ones, Scripture and the Mishnah, so that in their basic structure, the Midrash compilations are organized around books of Scripture (except for Pesiqta deRab Kahana), and the Tosefta and two Talmuds around the Mishnah. But to regard more closely the way in which the documents organize themselves around the one or the other is to recognize that the very point in common proves a point of radical differentiation. Leviticus Rabbah and Sifra are both organized around Leviticus. But the latter works its way from verse to verse, which is precisely what the former does not do. And the same may be said for Tosefta and either of the two Talmuds. Both sets of writings are organized as exegesis of the Mishnah. But while the Tosefta's framers doggedly worked their way through nearly the entirety of the Mishnah, the Talmuds' did not even pretend to do so, and theirs are exegeses not of the Mishnah, but of this and that in the Mishnah, no different, in their way of dealing with the Mishnah, from Leviticus Rabbah's selectivity in dealing with the book of Leviticus.

Yet there is a single formal trait that characterizes every document, without exception – and every composition of every document, with few exceptions. It is the formal trait that supplies the name of this Judaism and its literature: the ubiquitous presence of named sages called rabbis. That is the appearance of the names of rabbis themselves, the attributions of sayings to named sages. Surely here we have a formal basis on which to regard all documents as sharing a single premise, which is, it is critical to assign sayings to sages. We may then say, a document bearing attributions of sayings to rabbis joins the canon, one that excludes them does not, and the premise is clear: what is so is certified by assigning a rabbi's authority to a statement. So if the documents' substantive premises prove insufficient to the task, their formal one serves.

That proposition surely defines a form that the rabbis take for granted, the formality of placing their names on sayings here, there, and everywhere. And, even the most superficial glance reveals, what every canonical writing has in common, but no noncanonical writing exhibits at all, is the extensive citation of rabbis themselves. But a closer look shows us that that formal given – the stated premise, that named rabbis belong in the documents of the rabbis – by no means yields uniform results, not at all. When we examine the uses of attributions in various documents, what we discover is that no common premise as to the meaning of assigning sayings to named authorities – the consequences, the implications, the purpose – characterizes all the documents. Rather, in a given piece of writing, an attribution signals one thing, in another, a different thing. And that bears the implication that even as to premises of formalities – and nothing is more of a matter of form than "Rabbi X says," it is the document that forms the outer limit of the premise of discourse. The presupposition introduced by "Rabbi X says" in the Mishnah and that contained in the same form in tractate Abot and in the Tosefta, we shall now see, simply are not the same. And it follows that even the simplest formal premise of the writings proves particular to the documents, so that the canon's deepest layers of premise turn out here again to be superficially extensive but in fact truncated, limited to this writing or that one.

Let us begin from the beginning. Where, when, and why, then, do the names of authorities play a consequential role in the unfolding of discourse? What role is assigned to them, and what premises seem to underpin the constant citation of sayings in the names of particular masters? Our task is to turn to the documents themselves and to ask the broad question, what role do named sages play in these compilations, and on what account do specific names joined with particular statements come under discussion? That question, of course, forms a particular detail of a broader issue, which is, how come specific sages play so critical a role in the Rabbinic literature?

A. THE PREMISE OF ATTRIBUTING A SAYING IN THE MISHNAH: SCHISMATIC AND NORMATIVE RULES. The first document, of course, is the Mishnah. There we find a principal and constitutive form, the dispute, built around the name of opposing authorities, for example, the Houses of Shammai and Hillel, or Aqiba and Tarfon, or Meir and Judah, and the like. We also find in some few passages clear evidence of the collection of statements on a given, cogent problem in the name of a specific authority, for example, Mishnah-tractate Kelim Chapter Twenty-Four is a statement of Judah's views. But, over all, the Mishnah must be described as an entirely anonymous document, which at the same time contains extensive citations of named figures. The same names occur throughout; we cannot demonstrate that a given authority was viewed as particularly knowledgeable in a specific area of law, most of the sages being treated as generalists. At the same time that names predominate everywhere, sixty-two of the sixty-three tractates are organized around not named figures but topics, and, as indicated, perhaps 98 percent of the chapters of which those tractates are made up likewise focus on subjects, not named authorities. Only tractate Eduyyot as a whole is set up around names.

If we turn to that tractate devoted to not a particular subject or problem but rather the collection of attributed sayings and stories told about authorities, what do we find? The answer is, collections of rules on diverse topics, united by the names of authorities cited therein, either disputes, for example, between Shammai and Hillel and their Houses, or sets of rulings representative of a single authority. A single representative passage shows how the document does its work:

1:2   A.   Shammai says, "[Dough which is made] from a qab [of flour is liable] to a dough-offering [Num. 15:20]."
      B.   And Hillel says, "[Dough made] from two qabs."
      C.   And sages say, "It is not in accord with the opinion of this party nor in accord with the opinion of that party,
      D.   "But: [Dough made] from a qab and a half of flour is liable to the dough-offering."

Now what is interesting here – and not characteristic of the document throughout – is the inclusion of a final ruling on the dispute, which is different from the rulings of the Houses' founders. That pattern being repeated and so shown to be definitive of the redactor's subtext, the question is raised: Why record not only the official rule, but the opinion of a named, therefore schismatic figure as well? And that of course forms the heart of the matter and tells us the document's answer to our question. First let us consider the source, then draw the conclusion it makes possible:

1:5   A.   And why do they record the opinion of an individual along with that of the majority, since the law follows the opinion of the majority?

      B.   So that, if a court should prefer the opinion of the individual, it may decide to rely upon it.

      C.   For a court has not got the power to nullify the opinion of another court unless it is greater than it in wisdom and in numbers.

      D.   [If] it was greater than the other in wisdom but not in numbers,

      E.   in numbers but not in wisdom,

      F.   it has not got the power to nullify its opinion –

      G.   unless it is greater than it in both wisdom and numbers.

1:6   A.   Said R. Judah, "If so, why do they record the opinion of an individual against that of a majority to no purpose?

      B.   "So that if a person should say, 'Thus have I received the tradition,' one may say to him, 'You have heard the tradition in accord with the opinion of Mr. So-and-so [against that of the majority].'"

The premise of this passage is simple. The law follows the position of the anonymously formulated rule. Then why attribute a rule to a named figure? It is to identify the opinion that is not authoritative, but, nonetheless, subject to consideration. Then it follows, the purpose of citing sayings in the names of authorities is to mark those positions as schismatic and not authoritative – not to validate, but to invalidate.

To test this surmise, we turn to the Tosefta's commentary on the passage of Mishnah-tractate Eduyyot that is before us. Here we find explicitly articulated the premise I identified:

1:4   A.   Under all circumstances the law follows the majority, and the opinion of the individual is recorded along with that of the majority only so as to nullify it.

      B.   R. Judah says, "The opinion of an individual is recorded along with that of the majority only so that, if the times necessitate it, they may rely upon [the opinion of the individual]" [cf. M. Ed. 1:5B].

      C.   And sages say, "The opinion of the individual is recorded along with that of the majority only so that, if later on, this one says, 'Unclean,' and that one says, 'Clean,' one may respond that the one who says it is unclean is in accord with the opinion of R. Eliezer [and the law must follow the majority, which opposed his opinion], so they say to him, 'You have heard this opinion in accord with the ruling of R. Eliezer.'"

Judah's theory of matters – that of the minority – is that the minority opinion registers, so that, under duress, it may serve as precedent; sages take the view that the very opposite consideration pertains; once an opinion is given to an individual, that opinion is to be dismissed as schismatic wherever it occurs – even when not in the name of the individual. So we find here confirmation of the surmise that at stake in assigning opinions to names is the formulation of the legal process in such a way as to permit reliable decisions to be made.

But there is a second consideration important to the Mishnah, and that emerges in another passage in the same tractate:

5:6   A.   Aqabia b. Mahalalel gave testimony in four matters.
       B.   They said to him, "Aqabia, retract the four rulings which you laid down, and we shall make you patriarch of the court of Israel."
       C.   He said to them, "It is better for me to be called a fool my whole life but not be deemed a wicked person before the Omnipresent for even one minute,
       D.   "so that people should not say, 'Because he craved after high office, he retracted.'"

The passage proceeds to specify the disputes, and then the narrative continues, reporting that because he refused to retract, sages excommunicated him:

       M.   They excommunicated him, and he died while he was subject to the excommunication, so the court stoned his bier....
5:7   A.   When he was dying, he said to his son, "My son, retract in the four rulings which I had laid down."
       B.   He said to him, "And why do you retract now?"
       C.   He said to him, "I heard the rulings in the name of the majority, and they heard them in the name of the majority, so I stood my ground on the tradition which I had heard, and they stood their ground on the tradition they had heard.
       D.   "But you have heard the matter both in the name of an individual and in the name of the majority.
       E.   "It is better to abandon the opinion of the individual and to hold with the opinion of the majority."
       F.   He said to him, "Father, give instructions concerning me to your colleagues."
       G.   He said to him, "I will give no instructions."
       H.   He said to him, "Is it possible that you have found some fault with me?"
       I.   He said to him, "No. It is your deeds which will bring you near, or your deeds which will put you off [from the others]."

The crux of the matter then comes at 5:7C: Aqabia has received rulings in the name of the majority and therefore regards them as valid. So the purpose of assigning names to sayings once more is to label the unreliable ones: those in the names of individuals. And at stake, underneath, is of course the shape and structure of the tradition, which is once more stated explicitly: "I stood my ground on the tradition that I had heard...." What comes down anonymously is tradition – from Sinai, obviously – and what bears a name is other than tradition. But matters we see also prove subject to negotiation. Sages bear the obligation to remember what they heard in the name of the majority but also in the name of individuals. So the inclusion of names forms part of a larger theory of tradition and how to be guided by tradition, and the Mishnah's account of itself makes that point in so many words.

B. THE PREMISE OF ATTRIBUTIONS IN TRACTATE ABOT: THE TRADITION OF SAGES AND DISCIPLES OF MOSES: We hardly need to find that fact surprising, since the Mishnah's first apologetic, Pirqé Abot, the sayings of the fathers, points to Sinai as the origin of the Mishnah's tradition when it formulates its opening chapter. Tractate Abot in its opening chapter responds to the question: What is the Mishnah? Why should we obey its rules? How does it relate to the Torah, which, we all know, God gave to Israel through Moses at Sinai? The answer is contained in the opening sentence:

The Sayings of the Fathers Chapter One

1:1 Moses received the Torah a Sinai and handed it on to Joshua, Joshua to elders, and elders to prophets. And prophets handed it on to the men of the great assembly. They said three things: Be prudent in judgment. Raise up many disciples. Make a fence for the Torah.

What is important here is three facts. First, the verbs, receive...hand on..., in Hebrew yield the words *qabbalah*, tradition, and *masoret*, also tradition. There is no more lucid or powerful way of making the statement than that: the Torah is a matter of tradition. Second, the tradition goes from master to disciple, Moses to Joshua. So the tradition is not something written down, it is something that lives. Third, we know that the tradition is distinct from the Written Torah, because what is attributed to "the men of the great assembly" (and we have no interest in who these might be assumed to have been) are three statements that do not occur in Scripture. In fact, among all of the sayings in the entire tractate, only very rarely is there attributed to a sage who stands in this chain of tradition a verse of Scripture. So the essence of "the tradition" is not what is said, for example, citing a verse of Scripture and expanding on it, but that a saying is said and who does the saying: a master to a disciple, forward through all time, backward to Sinai. Torah – revelation – stands for a process of transmitting God's will. That process is open-ended but it also is highly disciplined.

How is the question of the origin and authority of the Mishnah answered? The chain of tradition from Sinai ends up with names that are prominent in the Mishnah itself, for example, Shammai and Hillel, and their disciples, the House of Shammai and the House of Hillel. So the message is blatant: major authorities of the Mishnah stand in a chain of tradition to Sinai; hence, the Mishnah contains the Torah of Sinai. It is that straightforward: through discipleship, we reach backward; through the teaching of the sage, we reach forward; the great tradition endures in the learning of the ages. It follows that when sayings are assigned to sages, a quite separate issue is in play. I cite only a small sample of the opening chapter of Abot, which suffices to make my point:

1:2   Simeon the Righteous was one of the last survivors of the great assembly. He would say: On three things does the world stand: On the Torah, and on the Temple service, and on deeds of loving kindness.

1:3   Antigonus of Sokho received [the Torah] from Simeon the Righteous. He would say: Do not be like servants who serve the master on condition of receiving a reward, but [be] like servants who serve the master not on condition of receiving a reward. And let the fear of heaven be upon you.

1:4   Yosé ben Yoezer of Zeredah and Yosé ben Yohanan of Jerusalem received [the Torah] from them. Yosé ben Yoezer says: Let your house be a gathering place for sages. And wallow in the dust of their feet, and drink in their words with gusto.

1:5   Yosé ben Yohanan of Jerusalem says: Let your house be open wide. And seat the poor at your table ["make the poor members of your household"]. And don't talk too much with women. [He referred to a man's wife, all the more so is the rule to be applied to the wife of one's fellow. In this regard did sages say: So long as a man talks too much with a woman, he brings trouble on himself, wastes time better spent on studying the Torah, and ends up an heir of Gehenna.]...

1:12 Hillel and Shammai received [the Torah] from them. Hillel says: Be disciples of Aaron, loving peace and pursuing grace, loving people and drawing them near to the Torah.

1:15 Shammai says: Make your learning of the Torah a fixed obligation. Say little and do much. Greet everybody cheerfully.

1:16 Rabban Gamaliel says: Set up a master for yourself. Avoid doubt. Don't tithe by too much guesswork.

1:17 Simeon his son says: All my life I grew up among the sages, and I found nothing better for a person [the body] than silence. And not the learning is the thing, but the doing. And whoever talks too much causes sin.

1:18 Rabban Simeon ben Gamaliel says: On three things does the world stand: on justice, on truth, and on peace. As it is said, "Execute the judgment of truth and peace in your gates" (Zech. 8:16).

Now the key point comes with the beginning of the Mishnah sages
themselves, and that is with the pairs, five sets. What is important in this
list is the pairs of names and how they are arranged:

Moses
Joshua
Elders
Prophets
Men of the Great Assembly
Simeon the Righteous
Antigonus of Sokho

1.	Yosé ben Yoezer	Yosé b. Yohanan
2.	Joshua b. Perahyah	Nittai the Arbelite
3.	Judah b. Tabbai	Simeon b. Shetah
4.	Shemaiah	Abtalyon
5.	Hillel	Shammai

Gamaliel
Simeon his son
Rabban Simeon b. Gamaliel

The numbered list carries us deep into the pages of the Mishnah itself.
But there is another point not to be missed. Once the pairs end, whom
do we find? Gamaliel, who is (later on) represented as the son of Hillel,
and then Gamaliel and Simeon, his son, Hillel's grandson. The names
Gamaliel, then Simeon, continued through this same family, of primary
authorities, through Gamaliel II, ruler of the Jewish community after the
destruction of the second Temple in 70 and into the second century, then
his son, Simeon b. Gamaliel, ruler of the Jewish community after the
defeat of Bar Kokhba in 135 – and also, as it happens, the father of Judah
the Patriarch, this same Judah the Patriarch who sponsored the Mishnah.
So Judah the Patriarch stands in the chain of tradition to Sinai. Not only
the teachings of the sages of the Mishnah, but also the political sponsor of
the document, who also was numbered among the sages, formed part of
this same tradition. What the sages say in these sayings in no way
contradicts anything we find in Scripture. But most of what is before us
also does not intersect with much that we find in Scripture.

The point for our inquiry is not to be missed. In tractate Abot,
attributions bear the premise of a continuous tradition to Sinai, and that
is their principal polemical task. In some ways then we deal with the
reverse of what is presupposed about attributions by the Mishnah. What
in the Mishnah bears the name of an authority is marked as schismatic,
while what in Abot bears the same name is classified as authoritative.
The meaning is completely different, and the formal point in common

obscures the substantive premise concerning what is intended, what is taken for granted.

C. THE USES OF ATTRIBUTIONS IN THE TOSEFTA: FIXED DIFFERENCES ON AN AGENDUM OF VARIABLE ISSUES: We see, then, two distinct but closely related considerations that operate in the persistent interest in assigning sayings to named authorities. Identifying an authority serves as a taxic indicator of the standing of a saying – classified as not authoritative; but identifying an authority bears the – both correlative and also contradictory – indication that the authority had a tradition. Enough has been said even in these simple observations to point to a broader conclusion. If we wish to ask why names are included, we have to examine the various writings that contain assigned sayings, looking for the importance accorded to attributions by the authors of the compositions and redactors of the composites of each such compilation.

It suffices to note that in the later documents, a variety of positions emerges. One of the most weighty is also most surprising. In the Tosefta, we find that what is attributed in the Mishnah to a given authority will be rewritten, so that the cited sage will say something different from what he is supposed in the Mishnah to have said. Nothing in the Mishnah's statements' theory of matters prepares us for the way in which the Tosefta's authorities treat attributions. So far as they are concerned, I shall now show, while attributions set forth fixed positions on a disputed point, precisely what was subject to dispute was itself a contentious matter. The use of attributions signaled, then, that the point of dispute concerned not only the ruling on a contended issue, but the definition of that issue itself, with fixed differences responding to a changing program of controversy.

Attributions in the Tosefta bear a quite distinct task from those in the Mishnah. A set of names signifies two persistent positions, principles guiding the solution to any given problem. We find in the Tosefta two or more positions assigned to the same named authority, and these positions contradict one another. It follows that attributions bear a quite distinct sense. What they stand for, as we shall see now, is a fixed difference. Party A and Party B will differ in the same way on a variety of issues, and if we know the issues, we also know the positions to be taken by the two parties. Then all consideration of tradition is set aside; all we have in the attribution is the signification of a fixed difference, a predictable position on an unpredictable agenda of issues. A fair analogy, I think, will be the fixed difference between political conservatives and political liberals; whatever the issue, the positions are predictable. Then in place of the House of Shammai and the House of Hillel, X and Y or black and white or pigeon and turtledove would serve equally well. Neither history, nor tradition, nor designation of the accepted and the schismatic position, comes into play, when all that is at stake is the matter of invoking fixed and conventional positions. Then the attributive serves as a formal protocol, nothing more.

What we shall see in the following is that the Mishnah presents a picture of a dispute and the opinions of cited authorities, and the Tosefta provides a quite different account of what was said. The Tosefta has opinions attributed to Judah and Yosé and "others say," and at stake is three distinct positions on the law. So the framers of the Tosefta's composition exhibit access to no single tradition at all; and subject to dispute is not the outcome of a case, but the formulation of the case itself.

Mishnah-tractate Besah Chapter One

1:6   A.   The House of Shammai say, "They do not bring dough-offering and priestly gifts to the priest on the festival day,

       B.   "whether they were raised up the preceding day or on that same day."

       C.   And the House of Hillel permit.

       D.   The House of Shammai said to them, "It is an argument by way of analogy.

       E.   "The dough-offering and the priestly gifts [Deut. 18:3] are a gift to the priest, and heave-offering is a gift to the priest.

       F.   "Just as [on the festival day] they do not bring heave-offering [to a priest], so they do not bring these other gifts [to a priest]."

       G.   Said to them the House of Hillel, "No. If you have stated that rule in the case of heave-offering, which one [on the festival] may not designate to begin with, will you apply that same rule concerning the priestly gifts, which [on the festival] one may designate to begin with?"

The Hillelites allow designating and delivering the priestly gifts owing to the priests from animals slaughtered on the festival day. They House of Shammai do not allow doing so, since the restrictions of the festival day come to bear. We shall now see a completely different picture of matters; I underline the points at which the dispute is reformulated:

       A.   Said R. Judah, "The House of Shammai and the House of Hillel concur that they bring [to the priest] gifts <u>which were taken up on the day before the festival along with gifts which were taken on the festival</u> [vs. M. 1:5A-C].

       B.   "Concerning what did they differ?

       C.   "Concerning [bringing to the priest on the festival] gifts <u>which were taken up on the day before the festival by themselves.</u>

       D.   "For the House of Shammai prohibit.

       E.   "And the House of Hillel permit.

       F.   *"The House of Shammai said, 'It is an argument by way of analogy. The dough-offering and the priestly gifts are a gift to the priest, and heave-offering is a gift to the priest. Just as they do not bring heave-offering [to a priest on the festival day], so they do not bring these other gifts [to a priest on the festival day]'* [M. 1:6D-F].

G.   *"Said to them the House of Hillel, 'No. If you have said that rule in the case of heave-offering, which one may not designate to begin with, will you say that same rule concerning the priestly gifts, which one may designate to begin with?'"* [M. 1:6G].

H.   R. Yosé says, "The House of Shammai and the House of Hillel concur <u>that they do bring the priestly gifts to the priest on the festival day.</u>

I.   "Concerning what do they differ?

J.   <u>"Concerning heave-offering.</u>

K.   "For the House of Shammai prohibit [bringing heave-offering to the priest on the festival day].

L.   "And the House of Hillel permit."

T. 1:12, ed. Lieberman, p. 283, lines 46-54

A.   *"Said the House of Hillel, 'It is an argument by way of analogy. Dough-offering and priestly gifts are a gift to the priest, and heave-offering is a gift to the priest. Just as they do bring the priestly gifts to the priest on the festival day, so they should bring heave-offering to the priest on the festival day.'*

B.   "Said the House of Shammai to them, 'No. If you have stated the rule in the case of the priestly gifts, which is permitted to be designated [on the festival], will you state that rule concerning heave-offering, which may not be designated [on the festival day]?'"

C.   Others say, "The House of Shammai and the House of Hillel concur <u>that they do not bring heave-offering on a festival.</u>

D.   "Concerning what did they differ?

E.   <u>"Concerning priestly gifts.</u>

F.   "For the House of Shammai prohibit [bringing them to the priest on the festival].

G.   "And the House of Hillel permit" [= M. 1:6A-C]

T. 1:13, ed. Lieberman, pp. 283-284, lines 54-60

What we see is three distinct positions on what is at stake in the dispute of the Houses of Shammai and Hillel, and, a bit of study would show us, these positions express three distinct principles concerning what is at stake. The second century authorities are alleged to have three distinct "traditions" on what is at issue between the Houses; each then assigns to the Houses the same language in the same words, along with the same secondary arguments for its distinctive viewpoint. All that varies is the definition of that about which the Houses to begin with are conducting their dispute – no small thing!

Attributions serve, even in the Mishnah and the Tosefta, to carry out three quite distinct functions – distinguishing regnant from schismatic opinion, identifying the traditionality of a saying, and marking off fixed points of difference concerning a variable agendum of issues. Certainly a survey of the two Talmuds, with their intense interest in the consistency of positions assigned to principal authorities, alongside their quite facile practice of following the dictates of logic, not tradition at all, in switching about among various names the opinions assigned to one or authorities, will yield a fourth, and perhaps a fifth and a sixth, premise as to the meaning of attributions. The materials before us suffice to make the main point, which is that no single premise as to the implication of the formality of assigning sayings to named authorities governs throughout the documents, even though all of them ordinarily assign sayings to specific sages.

III. Do the Presuppositions of the Documents of the Dual Torah Comprise (a) Judaism?

A Judaism sets forth a coherent account of the social order of holy (or supernatural) Israel, comprising a theory of the way of life, worldview, and definition of the social entity, "Israel." By reference to such a cogent theory of the social order, spelling out the ethics, ethos, and ethnos, that all together form "Judaism," we should be able to spell out in an authoritative way who the group is, what it does, and why it is what it is and does what it does, that is, again, the ethnos, ethics, and ethos. A complete Judaism ("the one whole Torah of Moses, our rabbi") then will answer the generative questions of a religious system for the social order. By that schematic definition, the premises of the Rabbinic literature prove necessary but insufficient. If we add up all of the various premises that the documents have given us and view them all together, what we find is necessary to a Judaism, but not sufficient for one. At the layers of presupposition of the documents we have examined, what we find is partial and not proportionate to the task.

The way of life is defined as accepting the yoke of the kingdom of heaven and the commandments, accepting that rules govern the relationship with heaven, that the rules are set forth in the model of God and the patriarchs' and matriarchs' actions, forming a fence around the law. The worldview consists of two fundamental convictions, first, that intentionality is the key to most things, because God responds to matters in the way that we do; and that all things must be kept in their proper place and order. The social entity, this Israel, is holy, so, too, its land, and it is holy because it is governed by the Torah; its history, among the nations, forms an indicator of the level of the observance of the Torah among both Israel and the nations. These premises of various documents do coalesce into a coherent statement, which is that God has called Israel into being to form of the group a holy people, living in a holy land, so reconstituting that Eden that was lost by Adam. In that statement, explicitly referring to commandment, on the one side, and implicitly alluding to attitude (obedience, rebellion), on the other, does serve to frame a Judaism. But if we compare that picture of matters to the actualities of documents, we find only a sketch, and one that leaves many open spaces at that.

What troubles me in the end is not that we cannot hold together the components of the various documents, framing them into a coherent statement. We assuredly can do just that. What I find troublesome is a different result of our survey. Let me first show how a single statement can encompass many of the premises scattered through our documents, giving a complete and mythic statement to the Judaic system just now adumbrated. Here is an explicit comparison of Adam and Israel, Eden and the Land of Israel, Adam's tragic history and Israel's tragic history – but Israel's power to bring to resolution of the tension between God and humanity precipitated by Adam's rebellion:

Genesis Rabbah XIX

IX.2 A. R. Abbahu in the name of R. Yosé bar Haninah: "It is written, 'But they are like a man [Adam], they have transgressed the covenant' (Hos. 6:7).

  B. "'They are like a man,' specifically, like the first man. [We shall now compare the story of the first man in Eden with the story of Israel in its land.]

  C. "'In the case of the first man, I brought him into the Garden of Eden, I commanded him, he violated my commandment, I judged him to be sent away and driven out, but I mourned for him, saying, "How..."' [which begins the book of Lamentations, hence stands for a lament, but which also is written with the consonants that also yield, 'Where are you'].

  D. "'I brought him into the Garden of Eden,' as it is written, 'And the Lord God took the man and put him into the Garden of Eden' (Gen. 2:15).

  E. "'I commanded him,' as it is written, 'And the Lord God commanded...' (Gen. 2:16).

  F. "'And he violated my commandment,' as it is written, 'Did you eat from the tree concerning which I commanded you' (Gen. 3:11).

  G. "'I judged him to be sent away,' as it is written, 'And the Lord God sent him from the Garden of Eden' (Gen. 3:23).

  H. "'And I judged him to be driven out.' 'And he drove out the man' (Gen. 3:24).

  I. "'But I mourned for him, saying, "How...."' 'And he said to him, "Where are you"' (Gen. 3:9), and the word for 'where are you' is written, 'How....'

  J. "'So, too, in the case of his descendants, [God continues to speak,] I brought them into the Land of Israel, I commanded them, they violated my commandment, I judged them to be sent out and driven away but I mourned for them, saying, "How...."'

K.   "'I brought them into the Land of Israel.' 'And I brought you into the land of Carmel' (Jer. 2:7).

L.   "'I commanded them.' 'And you, command the children of Israel' (Ex. 27:20). 'Command the children of Israel' (Lev. 24:2).

M.   "'They violated my commandment.' 'And all Israel have violated your Torah' (Dan. 9:11).

N.   "'I judged them to be sent out.' 'Send them away, out of my sight and let them go forth' (Jer 15:1).

O.   "'...And driven away.' 'From my house I shall drive them' (Hos. 9:15).

P.   "'But I mourned for them, saying, "How...."' 'How has the city sat solitary, that was full of people' (Lam. 1:1)."

Lamentations Rabbati IV

I.1   A.   R. Abbahu in the name of R. Yosé bar Haninah commenced [discourse by citing this verse]: *"'But they are like a man, they have transgressed the covenant. There they dealt treacherously against me'* (Hos. 6:7).

B.   *"They are like a man,* specifically, this refers to the first man [Adam]. [We shall now compare the story of the first man in Eden with the story of Israel in its land.]

C.   "Said the Holy One, blessed be He, 'In the case of the first man, I brought him into the Garden of Eden, I commanded him, he violated my commandment, I judged him to be sent away and driven out, but I mourned for him, saying "How..."' [which begins the book of Lamentations, hence stands for a lament, but which also is written with the consonants that also yield, *Where are you*].

D.   "'I brought him into the Garden of Eden,' as it is written, *And the Lord God took the man and put him into the Garden of Eden* (Gen. 2:15).

E.   "'I commanded him,' as it is written, *And the Lord God commanded...* (Gen. 2:16).

F.   "'And he violated my commandment,' as it is written, *Did you eat from the tree concerning which I commanded you* (Gen. 3:11).

G.   "'I judged him to be sent away,' as it is written, *And the Lord God sent him from the Garden of Eden* (Gen. 3:23).

H.   "'And I judged him to be driven out.' *And he drove out the man* (Gen. 3:24).

I.   "'But I mourned for him, saying, How....' *And He said to him, Where are you* (Gen. 3:9), and the word for 'where are you' is written, *How....*

J.   "'So, too, in the case of his descendants, [God continues to speak,] I brought them into the Land of Israel, I commanded them, they violated my commandment, I judged them to be sent out and driven away but I mourned for them, saying, *How....'*

K.   "'I brought them into the Land of Israel': 'And I brought you into the land of Carmel' (Jer. 2:7).

L.   "'I commanded them': 'And you, command the children of Israel' (Ex. 27:20). 'Command the children of Israel' (Lev. 24:2).

M.   "'They violated my commandment': 'And all Israel have violated your Torah' (Dan. 9:11).

N.   "'I judged them to be sent out': 'Send them away, out of my sight and let them go forth' (Jer. 15:1).

O.   *"'...And driven away': 'From my house I shall drive them'* (Hos. 9:15).
P.   *"'But I mourned for them, saying, How...': How lonely sits the city [that was full of people! How like a widow has she become, she that was great among the nations! She that was a princess among the cities has become a vassal. She weeps bitterly in the night, tears on her cheeks, among all her lovers she has none to comfort her; all her friends have dealt treacherously with her, they have become her enemies]* (Lam. 1:1-2)."

The account before us leaves ample space for most, though not all of the premises we identified. So the answer to the question at hand is, that the presuppositions of our documents do comprise a Judaism.

But that answer misleads. It ignores the striking finding with which we began, that premises important here pay no role somewhere else; the powerful role accorded to history and Israel's relationships to the gentiles in the later documents and its absence in the earlier ones, the primary position assigned to hierarchical classification, on the one side, and intentionality, on the other, in the initial compilations, and its near-absence later on – these facts about the documentary premises call into question the result just now proposed, that out of the premises we can indeed compose a Judaism. That the Mishnah and Tosefta contain no doctrine of history, or that we find in the Midrash compilations no doctrine of intentionality or of human divine consubstantiality in the matter of intentionality, points to discontinuities from the one to the next set of writings. That fact calls into question the notion of not only an exegetical foundation for the canon, but a comprehensive theory of the social order for the Judaism that the canon sets forth, in one detail here, in another detail there. The reason I suggest so derives from not an argument from silence (they don't say it, so they don't think it) but a consideration of an altogether different order.

It is that the conceptions I identify as forming important, deep layers of premise and preconceptions at the foundations of the Mishnah and its associated writings and those I deem absolutely fundamental to the middle and later Midrash compilations strike me as incompatible; the sets of documents that use the one group find the other useless or improbable. I contrast, therefore, the Mishnah's deepest conceptual and methodological premises, hierarchical classification and intentionality, with the later Midrash compilations' most profound presuppositions, first, the notion that Israel and the nations form a continuum, and, second, that Israel's participates in the same history as do the nations, and that what happens to Israel has any bearing on the meaning of what happens to the nations at all.

These two sets of doctrines strike me as incompatible because for the Mishnah, Israel stands for an ontological and philosophical category, entire unto itself, upon which the nations have no bearing. For the later

Midrash compilations, Israel stands for a historical and theological category, into which the nations find admission as well. The Mishnah describes the life of Israel in terms wholly internal to Israel, and that is why at issue are the matters of intentionality – how Israel thinks, how the Israelite intends matters to be, with God's response to Israel's attitudes, feelings, sentiments and emotions. The later Midrash compilations encounter Israel in the context of world history and deal in the data of not individual Israelites' intentionality but collective Israel's actions. I contrast, then, the Mishnah's Israelite's deliberations and deeds and the later Midrash compilations' Israel's actions in time. To the latter, intentionality is irrelevant; the national attitude takes its place. What the farmer conceives to be the status of a beast or of a portion of the crop makes a difference in nature, but does not register in the continuum of time. And the attitude of all Israel toward its situation among the nations, so critical to the Midrash compilations, in no way intersects with how a given farmer conceives the condition of his crop or his herd. Intentionality in the context of the Mishnah excludes the holy nation's attitude toward the world of politics and public policy, and that is why the one set of documents concerns itself with the former, the other with the later. The two generative premises that we found pervasive, each in its setting, prove incompatible and mutually exclusive.

The same is so of the other two enormous conceptions, hierarchical classification on the one side, the classification of human history into a beginning, middle, and end, on the other. The method of the Mishnah requires no further exposition here; readers know full well how classification covers the data of the natural world and orders all things from lowest to highest, yielding a complete account of the structure of being: nature and humanity alike. But why the notion of history with a beginning, middle, and end, history made up of Adam and Eden, Israel and the land of Israel, as one dimension of matters, the rule of the four kingdoms ending with Israel at the end, as the second dimension of matters, proves equally clear. The Midrash compilations' conception of history, with the patriarchs at the start forming the counterpart of Adam in Eden, with Israel at Sinai beginning the return of God from the firmament back to earth to meet humanity at Sinai through the Torah, with the entry of Israel into, then its exile from, the Land, with the notion that through the Torah, Israel will find its way back to the Land, that when Israel does return to the Land it will lead all of humanity back to Eden – that coherent set of conceptions not only does not intersect with the premise of the ordered ontology rising to heaven. It competes with the philosophical ontology that organizes and explains being in so profoundly different a manner.

The contrast is to be drawn between natural history and myth, between an abstract inspection of objective indicative traits of things, and a concrete consideration of how different times turn out to recapitulate the same paradigms, between not details but the very definition of what is at issue and what is at stake in the life of Israel. If one set of ideas and modes of thought defines the premises of one group of writings, and a different set of ideas, of another group of writings, we are required to ask why that should be so. And a clear perspective on the issues addressed by the one set of presuppositions, their generative problematic, yields a simple observation. One group of documents asks its questions and sets forth at its deepest structure of thought the foundations of its response, and the other group of writings pursues its quite different questions and lays out its most fundamental premises. And it is at the level of the questions that the writings part company; the premises of thought give expression to the questions at that point at which answers are contemplated. What one set of writing wishes to investigate concerns the nature of being and Israel's place therein; the other, the nature of becoming, of history and its direction and goal, and Israel's place therein.

IV. Where and How Shall We Find the Judaism that is Taken for Granted, and of What Does It Consist?

In the rabbinic writings we have examined, the rabbis take for granted no single Judaism because the documents the rabbis set forth form divisions, demarcated at layers of contemplation still deeper than the level of premise and presupposition that we have explored in these pages. When we take up the entirely fair and legitimate challenge formulated as "what else," that is, "if we know this, what else do we know," or set forth in the language of "pressing behind the contents," we find ourselves with partial results alone, something on the order of a score of active, generative (not inert, not banal) premises or presuppositions. And these neither characterize all documents and therefore tell us how a document gains entry into the canon, nor on their own fully define an ample Judaism. So the results answer the question we asked at the outset in such a way as to indicate we have asked the wrong question. For we are left with only a partial answer to our question: What is the Judaism that the rabbis take for granted? We have answered the question in an obviously awry way. The answer does not derive from surveys of the canonical writings, because, in the end, the canon of the Judaism of the Dual Torah does not yield a coherent and adequate statement, being necessary to, but not sufficient for, the formulation of that statement. Then where shall we find the Judaism that is taken for granted? And of what does that Judaism consist? If not in these writings, then where? If not of the intellectual substance of deeply-buried active premises, then of what?

The answer, obviously, is the Talmud of Babylonia, on the one side, and its rationality, on the other. In that writing, which stands at the end and absorbs and recasts whatever of the prior heritage the Talmud's framers – the authors of its compositions, the compilers of its composites, but particularly the later – deemed consequential, we may expect to find that answer. For that is the final document of the Judaism of the Dual Torah in its formative age, the piece of writing that, from its closure to this very morning, has been identified by Judaism as authoritative, normative, and ultimately, compendious and comprehensive. To state the matter somewhat loosely, the tradition is its own best historian, and all that this analytical project can do is reach the conclusion that the participants in the tradition know through common consent and tacit concurrence.

But then the second part of the question presses: What is the character of that heritage of premises and presuppositions that comprise "Judaism"? What, precisely, the rabbis take for granted and bring to concrete expression here, there, and everywhere – that is what we need to find out. The negative results before us tell us something we cannot have anticipated. The "Judaism" the rabbis take for granted, that is, what else they know when they know anything at all – that itself requires specification. For, clearly, that "Judaism" consists of something other than premises and presuppositions of a propositional character. The score of proposed propositions we have found in this protracted exercise being necessary but insufficient, we are left to wonder what suffices. Beyond what people think, before the processes of thought take material form, lies the rationality that dictates the character of intellection. The "Judaism" that the rabbis take for granted reaches the first stage at the layer of rationality: what is self-evident, makes obvious sense, requires no demonstration at all, everyone knows, no one doubts. And, in simple terms, that rationality must be the answer to the question, one do one and one add up to two, or, more really, add up to anything at all?

The answer to that question awaits us in the only document out of the formative age of the Judaism of late antiquity that enjoys the standing of ultimate authority, on the one side, and also the character of pure intellection, on the other. My instincts told me, nearly forty years ago, when I first met a page of the Talmud of Babylonia, the answer to that question. And I propose now to discover the details of the answer: since that "Judaism" surpasses premises and presuppositions of a propositional character, the Judaism of our sages of blessed memory, the modes of thought and expression (not merely "method," for example, of argument) that defined the entirety of world order, must find its definition in what is prior to proposition and takes precedence over premises of thought. Our sages' "Judaism" must commence in the ways in which we make connections and draw conclusions. That is where all thought begins, and that is the point at which the social order dictates the wherewithal of rationality. If we know how people connect one thing to something else, making connections that yield a "therefore," we can follow onward and upward to the surface of the social order the processes that yield premises and define presuppositions, and so onward into the here and now of cows that gore and empires that reign for a moment.

Index

South Florida Studies in the History of Judaism